'What about the Children?'

'What about the Children?'

Sons and Daughters of Lesbian and Gay Parents Talk about Their Lives

Lisa Saffron

CASSELL

For a catalogue of related titles
in our Sexual Politics/Global Issues list
please write to us at the address below:

Cassell
Wellington House
125 Strand
London WC2R 0BB

127 West 24th Street
New York, NY 10011

First published 1996

British Library Cataloguing-in-Publication Data
A catalogue record for this book is available from the British Library.

ISBN 0-304-33522-3 (hardback)
     0-304-33523-1 (paperback)

Typeset by Ben Cracknell Studios

Printed and bound in Great Britain by Biddles Ltd, Guildford and
King's Lynn

Contents

Part II. The Issues and the Evidence

Appendices

Acknowledgements

Writing this book has been a labour of love. It kept me happy while I was employed in a stressful and undermining job as a health writer for a consumer magazine. It restored my sanity when I became sensible enough to leave the job and devote myself to the book full time.

Special thanks must go to the following people. To the twenty-two people I interviewed, for their willingness to share their insights and tell the stories of their lives, for their time and for their faith in the power of personal revelation to challenge prejudice and ignorance.

To my partner, Maria Kennedy, who supported me with her love and sense of humour, who has suffered my ups and downs with patience and steadfastness and who will probably throw the computer out the window if I don't turn it off as soon as this book is done. To my daughter, Dena Saffron, aged eleven, who has grown up with three lesbian mothers and a gay father and who finds the subject so ordinary and boring that she can't understand what there is to write about. Thanks for reading and commenting on the books for children, particularly the Pride Pack series. Thanks also for graciously relinquishing her chance to get on the computer and play games.

To the people who commented on the draft chapters and gave me relevant information and ideas: Ann Blackburn of the London Lesbian Parenting Group, Catherine Donovan and Brian Heaphy of the Families of Choice Project at South Bank University, Nikki Freeling, Professor Susan Golombok of City University, Paula Hajnal, Maria Kennedy, Sophie Laws, Kim Roberts, Judy Sherwood and Professor Fiona Tasker of Birkbeck College.

To Roz Hopkins of Cassell who suggested that I write this book. To Crown Publishers for permission to reprint copyright material from Laura Benkov's book, *Reinventing the Family*, published by Crown Publishers in 1994. To Suzanne Gilbakian and Susan Proctor for transcribing the tapes of the interviews.

And finally, to my great-aunt Rose Saffron, whose generosity came at just the right moment.

Introduction

'All the time I was growing up, the fact that my Dad was gay was a normal part of my life. I never thought about it as a phenomenon. I wasn't aware that there might be other children with gay dads or that people would want to write books about it or interview me on TV.'
(Mary, twenty)

As long as people have identified themselves as lesbian or gay, there have been lesbian and gay parents. Since the late 1970s in Britain lesbian mothers have become increasingly open about their sexuality, while lesbians who want children have come to see parenthood as a realistic option for them. The visibility of lesbian mothers challenges conventional attitudes towards homosexuality, the definition of families, sexual diversity and child development. In an ideal society where diversity in family structure and sexuality were accepted as the norm, perhaps no one would focus attention on the parents' sexuality. But we are living in the midst of a society that is trying to make sense of the diversity of values, sexualities, types of families and cultures which are part of it. Much has been written by and about lesbian and gay parents in an effort to explain what meanings these developments have for them (see Appendix A). This book takes another perspective and provides the opportunity for the sons and daughters of lesbians and gay men to give their views. But before I introduce the people I interviewed, I will say something about my own background and my reasons for writing this book.

In 1980, I left my husband of seven years and said goodbye to heterosexuality. I was thankful that we'd never had children in that marriage. I could imagine only too well the gender-based inequalities that would result from raising children in a heterosexual relationship sanctified by a patriarchal society. I was relieved there were no children to suffer from the divorce and to tie me to a man I no longer wanted a relationship with.

Several years later, living in a lesbian community in London, I met mothers who were out as lesbians when they conceived their children. They got pregnant by a method they called self-insemination. This is simply a non-medical way of bypassing heterosexual sex, effectively reducing the male contribution to that of a sperm donor. It means that lesbians and, for that matter, single heterosexual women, can have children without emotional or financial dependence on men. It was an exciting development in the evolution of the lesbian community, opening up new possibilities for self-determination and independence.

I decided to become a mother by self-insemination and was fortunate to find a gay man willing to be a donor. Unlike many other life decisions I have made, this was one of the easiest and one which I have never doubted or regretted. In 1985 I gave birth to my daughter, Dena. I now have eleven years of experience in a lesbian family of my own making. The structure of my family has changed over the years. Our relationship with the donor began with no contact, ripened to a close friendship without parental responsibility on his part and ended painfully with his illness and death. My family changed from that of a single lesbian mother to a lesbian step-family when my partner joined us. For me, mothering in a lesbian family supported by a lesbian community has been a wonderful, empowering experience, one that has brought me love and happiness and has challenged me to grow and mature in my personal relationships.

I was in no way unique but was part of a veritable baby boom that took place in the lesbian community in the mid- to late 1980s. In response to widespread interest and need for information, I wrote my first book, *Challenging Conceptions: Planning a Family by Self-insemination* (Cassell, 1994). This is a guide to donor insemination for lesbians and single women, and describes the issues women need to consider: whether to have an anonymous or known donor; the advantages and disadvantages of going to a clinic or doing it yourself; how to find donors; the different challenges of single and joint parenting; coming out as a lesbian mother; the legal position of all involved and the possibility of not conceiving. One chapter is devoted to telling the children about their families and how they were conceived. Except for interviews with two twelve-year-olds and four donors, the perspective throughout the book is that of the mothers and women planning to be mothers.

2

After the book was published, I received a letter saying: 'What a selfish woman you are, having a daughter and no father for her to turn to. No doubt you sponge on normal families with no thought of how you are undermining this country's structure. All you've thought about is your needs, no one else's as far as I can see. Grow up!' Although I wouldn't have expressed it as 'undermining the country's structure', I was pleased that our challenge was at least recognized, if not accepted. I wrote in *Challenging Conceptions* that

> The existence of lesbian and single mothers is a threat to traditional family values. Consciously or not, we are challenging the need for fathers, the institution of marriage and the male-female couple as the model of the ideal parents. We are saying that families can be made up of different people with a variety of relationships to each other and still be healthy places in which children can grow up and in which women can be mothers. We are changing the basic definition of a family. No longer is it limited to a group of people related by blood, marriage or divorce. We are expanding it to include a group of people who love and care for each other. It doesn't even have to include children. Our families are not lacking in anything. There is no need to compensate for the absence of a father or to apologize for not conforming to the expected family norm.

Several years more of lesbian parenting have not changed those views.

But what mother likes to be accused of selfishness, of thinking only of her needs and not of her children's? The letter arrived after my five years of single parenthood, covering the birth and early childhood of my daughter. After all those sleepless nights, endless nappy changes, days off work with a sick child, preparing food only kids eat, staying in because I couldn't get a babysitter, etc., etc., I wondered what exactly a mother has to do not to be accused of selfishness! However, the real issue is not the adequacy of the caring but the incompatibility between the archetypal good mother-woman and the lesbian-woman. (See Laura Benkov's book, *Reinventing the Family*, for a good discussion of this.) A good mother is expected to be selfless and to act in the interests of others before her own. She is supposed to socialize her daughters to be self-sacrificing and to teach her sons to look to women for emotional and physical servicing. But a lesbian is a woman who has claimed her own sexual identity in opposition to the norm. She has defined her own needs. How can she model selflessness to her children when she acts from her own strong sense of self?

Some lesbian mothers and gay fathers do sacrifice themselves for their children and are not open about their sexuality. But there are increasing numbers who are not prepared to deny such a fundamental aspect of their sense of self. Even though coming out makes them the target of hostile reactions, they are generally happier and more integrated when living a life true to their deepest selves. Their lives would be that much easier if other people accepted their families and their right to parent. Whether they are activists in the public eye or trying to lead a quiet life, their sexuality is an important part of their lives.

The issues for lesbian and gay parents are obvious, but it may not be so obvious what the issues are for their sons and daughters. Unlike their parents, they are not creating new kinds of families and positively asserting their own identity. They are in a situation they have not consciously chosen. Their perspective is bound to be different. Children are separate individuals with their own thoughts and experiences. Their views may be radically different from those of their parents. This book is devoted exclusively to the perspective of the sons and daughters of lesbians and gay men.

The interviews

During 1995, I interviewed twenty people who have lesbian mothers or gay fathers, or both. In their own words, they tell their stories and speak about the issues that are important for them. The interviews do not present the full story of their lives but rather highlight those aspects which relate in one way or another to having a lesbian or gay parent and which they identified as the main influences on their lives.

The sexuality of their parents is the only thing they have in common, and it is not a strong basis for solidarity. While lesbians and gay men have a sexual identity which loosely unites them, at least in spirit, the people I interviewed did not claim an identity as a daughter or son of a lesbian or of a gay man. They labelled themselves, if at all, by their own sexuality or their race, nationality, class background, occupation or by any number of characteristics intrinsic to them. This is not to say that their parents' sexuality was unimportant or had no effect on them. It merely means that it did not define them and did not form the basis for their self-identity. It is one characteristic among many about their parents.

These twenty people were chosen to illustrate the diversity of people with lesbian and gay parents and the range of family structures created by lesbians and gay men. They are not a representative sample but a disparate group of individuals articulating views based on their own unique experiences. It is extremely difficult to get a representative sample, as they are not an easily identifiable group. This feature of their lives is hidden, especially for adults who are no longer living with their parents. For this reason, I would not use these interviews to make a generalization about all people with lesbian and gay parents, even though the people I interviewed shared many views in common.

The sample was biased towards people who have fairly good relationships with their parents. I recruited people through lesbian and gay contacts, by advertising in the national gay media, by sending leaflets to all the lesbian and gay centres in Britain and by asking lesbian and gay parents I knew of personally or was told about. Parents asked their children if they were willing to be interviewed. Presumably they would not have done this if they thought it would embarrass their child. Nor would anyone volunteer to expose themselves in a book if the subject was deeply offensive or painful. Some sons and daughters, especially those who were lesbian and gay themselves, were eager to share their stories and make their case for lesbian and gay rights. Others needed to be convinced that their stories were worth hearing. Many believed that their experiences were unexceptional and couldn't understand how such ordinary lives might provoke such interest.

Everyone had the option of using a pseudonym or their real name. Seven chose pseudonyms and three wanted to be referred to by their first names, with pseudonyms for everyone else they mentioned. The motivation was to protect people they alluded to from potential embarrassment and a public outing not of their choosing.

The youngest person I interviewed was eleven, the oldest sixty-six. Most were between the ages of nineteen and thirty-five. I decided to focus on adults who were old enough to analyse their family of origin from an adult perspective – people who had left home, experienced adult sexual relationships and, in some cases, had children of their own. They can look back on their lives and assess the impact of their parents' sexuality more fully than those still living at home. I wanted to hear about their experiences of adolescence, the time purported to be most stressful for people who are different for any reason. In order to include the experiences of people from planned lesbian families, I interviewed several children under the age of fourteen.

Of the twenty, thirteen are female and seven are male. Although I aimed for half and half, I was not surprised that I ended up with more women and girls than men and boys. This reflects a gender difference in ease of talking about family and personal issues. I didn't find this to be true for gay men, however.

I interviewed six people with gay fathers and seventeen with lesbian mothers. It was easier for me as a lesbian mother to find other lesbian mothers; finding gay fathers was more of a challenge. But the preponderance of lesbian mothers also indicates a gender difference in primary parenting. Although 'parent' is a gender-neutral word, there is a world of difference between being a mother and being a father. They are not equivalent activities or identities. In our culture, mothers are the primary carers and fathers tend to have a less nurturing role. The consequence for lesbians and gay men is that there are many more lesbian mothers with custody of their children than there are gay fathers. This partly reflects the situation of divorce, where mothers are more likely to win custody than fathers, especially gay fathers. But the movement for gay fathers in Britain has lagged behind that of lesbian mothers. It is still easier for lesbians to integrate their identity as a mother and a lesbian than it is for gay fathers. Men are not oriented around children, and gay men are no exception.

Of the six with gay fathers, only one of the fathers was the primary carer for his daughter throughout her life. One man was a donor for a lesbian who conceived her son by self-insemination, but this gay father had very little involvement with the son; a gay couple acted as primary parents to a gay teenager for several years after he was sixteen in an informal fostering arrangement; one young woman went to live with her father when she was a teenager several years after her parents divorced; and two had lesbian mothers and gay fathers, but in both cases the father left and the mother was the primary carer after the parents divorced.

I also aimed to illustrate the diversity of the family situations in which the participants grew up. As emphasized in Chapter 23, there is no such thing as a typical gay or lesbian family, just as there is no single structure which fits the families heterosexual people make. Most had parents who were once married and then divorced. The parents of a smaller number were openly lesbian when they had their children. Some parents had live-in partners who became step-parents. Others had partners who did not become parents. One family situation involved fostering. I did not interview anyone who was adopted.

I asked the people I interviewed how they defined their own sexuality and in what ways they felt that their lesbian or gay parent's sexuality had influenced them. I wanted to reflect a range of experiences, so I selected people to interview who were at various points on the continuum of sexuality from exclusively homosexual to bisexual to exclusively heterosexual, plus a few who were too young to know or still unsure. It is not valid to draw any conclusions from this sample about the proportion of daughters and sons who are gay or lesbian.

I interviewed British people who grew up in Britain. Half were from London, where there are twice as many lesbians and gay men as anywhere else in the country (Wellings, 1994). The rest were from Birmingham, Brighton, Edinburgh, Gloucestershire and the north of England, Lancaster, Leicester, Shropshire and Sussex.

Most of the people I interviewed were white. Two had black mothers but identified as mixed race, and one was black.

Summary of chapters

I drew out five main issues from the interviews and related what people had told me to the research that has been carried out on sons and daughters of lesbians and gay men.

In Chapter 19, I explore the nature of prejudice against homosexuality as it relates to children in families where there is a lesbian or gay parent. I show some of the ways prejudice is experienced by daughters and sons, what strategies they use to deal with it and how they feel they can best be supported.

Chapter 20 asks what children need from their parents in order to grow up psychologically healthy and socially responsible. There is a sizeable body of research on lesbian and gay parents and their children. Though limited in scope and methods used, the research does challenge fundamental assumptions about childhood development. I have picked five main lessons about psychological development which say as much about parenting as they do about the abilities of lesbian and gay people to raise children.

Chapter 21 addresses questions about the influences of parents on their children's sexuality. Are the children of lesbian and gay parents more likely to be gay or lesbian than the children of heterosexual parents? Does having a lesbian or gay parent influence attitudes towards sexuality? Does having a lesbian or gay parent influence attitudes towards homosexuality? What attitudes do lesbian or gay parents take towards their heterosexual children's sexuality and sexual partners?

The particular concerns of lesbian, gay and bisexual sons and daughters are the focus of Chapter 22. Adolescence can be a difficult time for lesbian, gay and bisexual teenagers, more so than for homosexual adults, and much more so than for heterosexual teenagers. The problems are not only persecution but the denial of their emerging sexuality and the lack of support from their family and peers. Taken together, these problems can have a major effect on their mental health. Is it any easier for such teenagers when they have a lesbian or gay parent?

Chapter 23 is about the concept of family and the kinds of family lesbians and gay men create. Many lesbians and gay men have embraced the idea of family to describe the circle of meaningful people in their lives. It is done partly as a defiant gesture to a society which refuses to recognize the value of lesbian and gay relationships. But it is also a positive reclaiming of an institution from which lesbians and gay men have traditionally been excluded. While this is a significant political and psychological step for lesbians and gay men, the perspectives of their children may well be different. I asked the people I interviewed who they counted as family, what family meant to them and what the circumstances were of their particular families.

Words used

Throughout the book I have used separate words for lesbians and gay men. Even though it is long-winded, there is no appropriate inclusive word which satisfied me. The terms 'homosexual' and 'gay' are usually associated with men, contributing to the assumption that what is true for gay men is also the case for lesbians. However, and especially in the area of parenting, the experiences of gay men and lesbians are not the same.

How many sons and daughters of lesbians and gay men are there?

I am often asked by journalists to provide figures for the number of people with lesbian or gay parents in Britain. I always wonder whether to give them an answer in millions or thousands. Would the larger number mean that the existence of lesbian and gay families will be acknowledged and their challenge to traditional families be taken seriously? Or would the smaller number reassure society that lesbian and gay families are no threat and that their challenge can be ignored? I suspect it does not matter what the true answer is. Those who are threatened by the existence of openly lesbian and gay parents will be alarmed as much by a hundred as by a million. And whether there are a few or many, those children with lesbian or gay parents still have to confront anti-gay prejudice as it affects them.

Because of the prejudice against homosexuality, it is impossible to present accurate statistics about the number of people with lesbian and gay parents. To start with, the number of lesbians and gay men is not known. Partly this is a matter of definition. Is a woman a lesbian if she is sexually attracted to women but does not have any lesbian sexual experience? Is she a lesbian if she does not identify herself as a lesbian, even though she has sex with women? The most inclusive definition is that a lesbian is a woman who is sexually attracted to women regardless of how she identifies herself and of what her sexual experience is, but such a definition does not make it any easier to count lesbians. Where there is stigma, as there is against same-sex sexual attraction, there is reluctance to expose oneself, even anonymously. Not all people answer surveys honestly. The best attempts to encourage honesty still lead to under-reporting. The latest large-scale survey in Britain (Wellings, 1994) did not use the labels 'homosexual' or 'heterosexual', but asked people about their sexual experiences. The survey was conducted by questionnaires that were completed anonymously at home. It found that few men (6.1 per cent) and even fewer women (3.4 per cent) admitted to having ever had any same-sex experience. Only 3.5 per cent of men and 1.7 per cent of women reported ever having had even one same-sex partner. The authors believe this does not represent the full figure, as many lesbians and gay men congregate in large cities and can be missed in nationwide surveys.

No survey has been carried out of the numbers of lesbian and gay men who are biological parents, who have adopted or fostered children or who are step-parents. The British national survey did not ask whether any of the people who reported same-sex experiences were parents. But American researchers have made some reasonable (or perhaps wild) guesses of the numbers in the USA (Bozett, 1987; Patterson, 1992, 1995; Flaks *et al.*, 1995). Based on uncertain assumptions about the percentage of the total adult population who are lesbian or gay, about the percentage of the lesbian and gay population who are parents and about the number of children parents have, they came up with estimates of 6 to 14 million people with lesbian or gay parents. They estimate that 5,000 to 10,000 American lesbians have had children since coming out. The population of Britain is 58 million, compared to 258 million in the USA. Extrapolating to Britain may or may not be valid, but if it is, there could be between 1.4 and 3.2 million people with lesbian or gay parents in the UK. This is a respectable number but could be much too high. Would it matter if the assumptions were wrong and there were only one-tenth that number? Hopefully the research will encourage those people with lesbian or gay parents to realize that their situation is not all that unusual.

References

Benkov, L. (1994) *Reinventing the Family: The Emerging Story of Lesbian and Gay Parents*. New York: Crown Publishers.

Bozett, F.W. (1987) 'Gay fathers', in F.W. Bozett (ed.), *Gay and Lesbian Parents*. London: Praeger.

Flaks, D., Ficher, I. Masterpasqua, F. and Joseph, G. (1995) 'Lesbians choosing motherhood: a comparative study of lesbian and heterosexual parents and their children', *Developmental Psychology*, **31** (1), 105–14.

Patterson, C.J. (1992) 'Children of lesbian and gay parents', *Child Development*, **63**, 1025–42.

Patterson, C.J. (1995) 'Sexual orientation and human development: an overview', *Developmental Psychology*, **31** (1), special issue 3–11.

Wellings, K. (1994) 'Sexual diversity and homosexual behaviour', in K. Wellings, J. Field, A.M. Johnson and J. Wadsworth, *Sexual Behaviour in Britain: The National Survey of Sexual Attitudes and Lifestyles*. Harmondsworth: Penguin.

PART I

Life Stories

ONE

Alice and Lawrence

Alice, aged fifteen, and Lawrence, aged fourteen, are good friends who go to the same secondary school in London. They both have lesbian mothers. Alice has three lesbian mothers – Jane and Ruth are a lesbian couple she lives with for half the week in one house; during the other half of the week she stays with Francesca, whose girlfriend does not live with her. Lawrence lives with his mother. Her partner, Hannah, who lived with them for nine years has recently left. Lawrence still sees her son, Jonathan, conceived by donor insemination, every week.

Alice's story

My biological mother, Sarah, got pregnant by accident when she was on holiday in Australia. When she came home, she realized that she didn't want to be heterosexual any more. She lived in a communal household in Bristol, and all the women living there agreed to help with my birth and to bring me up in the household. Over the years, the number of women in the household dwindled away and we moved into our own house.

Eventually I ended up living with my aunt Jane, who is Sarah's sister, with Jane's girlfriend, Ruth, and with Francesca, who was a friend of Sarah's. When Jane, Ruth and Francesca moved to London, I moved up with them. Sarah stayed in Bristol. At first I saw Sarah on weekends. But the situation became more difficult and she came up to see me less and less often.

One day when I was four, Sarah came and took me away. She said, 'You're coming to live with me in Bristol. And you're not going to see Jane and Francesca and Ruth again.' I wasn't very happy. Three weeks later, strange people wearing wigs burst into the flat and carried me out. At first I was scared because I didn't know who they were. They'd

13

followed us to the flat in a blue van, burst in and snatched me back to London. The only person who didn't have a wig on was Ruth, because she was driving. I said to her, 'Ruth, who are all these funny people?' She said, 'My dance group.' They started taking their wigs off, and then I recognized them. I don't think they thought they could get me back any other way.

We had to go to court because it became a legal battle for custody. Jane and Sarah had a really big row about it. Sarah got cross with the rest of the family, who took Jane's side because they thought Sarah was unable to look after me properly at that time. I don't know the full story. In the end the court decided that I should stay living in London with Jane and Ruth. The fact that they were a lesbian couple was only brought up at the last minute. At one point they thought that I might be taken into care, because the court was freaked about me living with a lesbian couple. I was five at the time. It went on for about a year. Jane got legal custody of me and has had ever since.

I'm a ward of the court, which means I have to write to the court for permission every time I leave the country, and they have to know everything I do. It makes my life really complicated. We're going back to court to try and get the wardship abolished, which would give me more freedom. What I want is for Jane, Ruth and Francesca to get a joint residency order. It would be a precedent-setting case, because not only is it women sharing the wardship, it would be three women. What we really want is to get recognition for all three being my parents, and there is no history of anything like that. So whatever we get, a precedent will be set. That's why we feel it's so important to do it. All of us agree.

My family is great! I love it. My parents are particularly easy to talk to about nearly anything. I get on brilliantly with all of them. We hardly ever row. They each have their little irritating points. I'm sure I have mine. But on the whole, the four of us get on fantastically. I'm quite good about not playing one against the other. I have quite a lot of opportunity, but I don't take advantage.

The fact that we live in two separate houses is a plus. As soon as I get sick of one, it's time to go to the other house. That's how it's been since I was six, so I'm used to it. I don't find it at all disruptive. The only problem I have is that I'm always leaving my tapes at the other house, and that annoys me. Apart from that, I have my stuff at both houses and my own room in each house. Both of the houses are equally mine.

I have complaints, but not about my parents being lesbians. The only thing that really irritates me is when they get together and talk about me, when they start going, 'Alice never does do her homework at my house. She always spend hours on the phone.' Or, 'Alice goes to bed really early at my house. Alice is always tidy at my house.' And then they come back to me and say, 'Francesca says that you're always going to bed early at her house.' I have to come up with good excuses. I try and keep them apart. But it's nice to have family get-togethers and catch up on things. We do that very rarely, usually when I've been with one set of them and not seen the others for a while.

They all get on really well and trust each other, which helps. Francesca never knew whether Jane would honour Francesca's role as parent through the years, because they've got no kind of personal relationship to each other. With Jane and Ruth, it's easier because they're a couple.

Lawrence's story

My Mum wanted a child by herself. Instead of having artificial insemination, she had sex with a man she'd once had a relationship with. Their relationship was over, so she was using him as a donor. When I was one until I was five, we lived in a communal household with my uncle and other people. During that time my Mum met Hannah and she lived there with us for two years. But then everybody started leaving and we moved to where we are now. I lived with my Mum and Hannah since I was about four until last year. My Mum recently split up with Hannah.

Hannah has a son named Jonathan from artificial insemination who is eight years younger than me. I definitely consider him my brother. Jonathan made things a bit better in our family in some ways, worse in others. It's nice having a brother, even though he does annoying things like jumping on me. We see a lot of Jonathan – nearly every day. He stays with us one night a week and he comes after school three nights and on his free weekends. But I don't see that much of Hannah. I'm meant to see her at weekends, but it never happens because I'm always doing something else.

I'm not sure if it's made much difference not having been around a father or a man much. I think I missed having a relationship with a man when I was growing up. My father lives in Oxford, and I don't see him every month. I see my uncle – my mother's brother – once a week. I feel happy as it is. Sometimes when I've just had an argument with my Mum, then I do wish I had my Dad around more. I've never had anyone else to turn to really, even when Hannah was living with us. She was too much like my mother in the same way. But it wasn't that bad.

How would you describe yourselves?
Lawrence: I feel different. I don't trust anybody unless I know them. I think that's just how I am. But once I get to know somebody, I will trust them as much as I trust anybody else, which isn't much.
Alice: Whereas I'm very trusting. I'll trust anybody.
Lawrence: I'm not like most other people. I don't mind being different from them. I don't know whether that's logical. My friends and I have the same interests basically. That's part of the reason we're friends. My close friends are all boys, and they're pretty typical boys. I'm also friends with the girls from the crèche that my Mum and her friends organized when we were little. We're all together in the same secondary school. Their mums aren't lesbians. I'm quite closed to everybody. I don't tell anyone much.
Alice: Can't get anything out of him, ever.
Lawrence: It's what I want, what I need.
Alice: I've been trying for the last – I don't know how long – to fit in. But I'm just fed up with all of them. They can go their way. I'm very happy now being me. Now I say, 'This is me and if you don't like it, well that's tough. This is who I am.'
Lawrence: That happened to me when I started feeling a bit left out. I tried to adapt, and it didn't work. I got bored. I'm more closed now than I was before. I didn't tell them that much, but they know who I am, and if they don't like it, then they can just go away.
Alice: If they don't like you how you are, then they're not worth it. I get lonely because I'm an only child.
Lawrence: I never get lonely. I like being by myself.
Alice: I never used to be lonely. I like being by myself too. You're not a 'mess-around' kind of teenager really, are you?!
Lawrence: More than my mother was.

What's school been like for you?

Alice: Our school's lovely. I'm trying to work out if my English teacher is a dyke. She must be, she can't be straight.

Lawrence: You're very lucky. You have a really nice tutor. I have this horrible old man who is completely straight and normal and annoying.

Alice: My parents have decided that my tutor will be my foster mum if anything happens to them. And she's agreed. They say that her cats would be quite happy with me. It's all very jokey.

Lawrence: My class is quite different from Alice's. My form tutor is patronizing. My class is full of white skinheads.

Alice: There are a lot of very right-wing people at the school.

Lawrence: It's next to an estate which is full of BNP [British National Party] supporters. You just have to be careful who you talk to.

Alice: Considering the violent area the school's in, we have very few fights.

Lawrence: It's such a mixture. There are middle-class kids from the next borough who think our school is better than theirs. And all the kids who live on the estate come, because the school is right next to it.

Alice: There's a girl in my class whose father is in the BNP. She lives on the estate, is in a gang, and has got an eighteen-year-old boyfriend. She's as working class as they get. She's absolutely great. I explain about lesbians to her, and she goes, 'Well you know, my Dad would kick me out of the house, and kick me down the street, if he found out I was a lesbian. But you're an all right person. I don't care.' Some of the other kids are horrible.

Lawrence: That's why I'm careful who I talk to.

Alice: I'm not, because I'm not scared of being battered.

Lawrence: They wouldn't beat you up, because you're a girl.

Alice: They would.

Lawrence: They wouldn't. Boys get hit more often. I have to be more cautious.

Alice: If anybody ever tried anything, they would not get away with it. The school is very good actually in dealing with things if they know about them. They'd suspend the people involved and if it was very serious, they'd think about exclusion.

Lawrence: They take all bullying very seriously. The school already knows which people get into fights.

Alice: There hasn't actually been any gay-bashing.

Lawrence: Not in school.

Alice: There was a threat to beat up one boy because he got off with another boy. He was scared. He told his tutor and they dealt with it really seriously. They phoned his parents and sent him home. He didn't come to school for a few days. I spent a whole day with him, outside of lessons. But he has to be careful, really. He's quite camp and I feel protective of him.

Lawrence: Yeah, that kind of person sticks out. Still, the bullies wouldn't remember a month later that they had wanted to beat him up. That's the way their minds work.

Alice: A boy did beat me up in my primary school, but I fought him back. He got in trouble. My primary school took it very seriously. That was my last major fight.

Lawrence: In my primary school one kid started teasing me about my mother. I beat him up. He never did it again. But I got in serious trouble. My primary school never knew what the fight was about. I didn't explain, because that head teacher was just too straight. My Mum knew the parents of the kid and she rang them up and sorted it out outside of school, which helped.

Alice: I've had some bad reactions at secondary school. I get people judging me on my parents, saying, 'Your parents are gay, so you must be as well.' And I say to them, 'So what if I am? I can do what I want.'

Lawrence: I don't tell most people. You have to work out who you can trust.

Alice: I'm much more open.

Lawrence: Yeah, you are.

Alice: All my friends know. My class knows. All my teachers know. My form tutor's really supportive about it.

Lawrence: My friends know. Some of my friends weren't exactly encouraging at first. No one else knows though.

How do you deal with people who are prejudiced against lesbians?

Alice: I like people who just come up and say, 'So what's it like? Is it a bit odd?' One kid at school said to me, 'But your mum's a lesbian.' And I said, 'Yes', and he never spoke to me again. I can't say I was too upset!

Lawrence: There's a lot of people like that in our school.

Alice: Yeah, they use the word gay as an insult. I feel sorry for them that they're so ignorant about it. I don't get cross when people say anything homophobic. I just laugh at them.

Lawrence: What makes me angry is when people actually know but are still stupid about it. I get in big arguments with people like that. But I don't get in arguments with people who are stupid because they've never met a lesbian before. That's their problem.

Alice: When I see those talk shows about lesbian mothers, I sit there and laugh at them. I can't believe the people who go on them have ever met a lesbian.

Lawrence: I don't get angry at them. They're very funny. Those people just want money. They just want to get noticed.

Alice: I'd say the downside of having lesbian parents is other people's attitudes towards lesbians. In my religious education class they didn't know anything about lesbian mothers until about three months ago, when I said, 'You're speaking complete garbage because you've never met any lesbian mothers. And actually, why shouldn't lesbians be mothers? I have three who are my mothers.'

Lawrence: We always have to be training people. It's no worse than anything else people are prejudiced about.

Alice: I feel very strongly about gay rights. It makes me furious when anybody says anything against gays. I'm trying to set a legal precedent so that other lesbian families can establish themselves legally as families. And I always go to Gay Pride every year with my parents. I had a big banner last year that said, 'Gays make great parents'. I carried it the whole way. It was very heavy. I handed out leaflets for gay action.

Lawrence: I missed the last Gay Pride, but I usually go.

Is it important to you to know other children of lesbians?

Lawrence: It's not the reason that we're friends, is it?

Alice: I don't know. Well, I always knew you existed. But only that your mum was a lesbian. You were just some person around. I don't know any other children with lesbian mothers at the school. Just Lawrence.

Lawrence: My mother tried to get me together with another child who had a lesbian mother, but I punched the child. And that was it. Never saw him again.

Alice: All my friends have always been very supportive. The lesbian friends of my mothers don't have children. That's because my mothers are different. They've always seemed so much younger and not so typically middle class as some of the other lesbians that I've known. They're Australian, they're odd, they were punks, and they were in strange dance groups and bands. They're different.

Do you talk about who you fancy with your mothers?

Alice: Jane's a bit unreasonable about boyfriends. She keeps thinking I should be careful. She's the over-protective one of the three. Jane says, 'No, you can't spend the night with a boy. You might get pregnant. And you never know about date rape. Have you ever met him?' Pathetic. But Francesca goes, 'Oh yeah, it's fine as long as you're happy.' When I tell them about someone I fancy, all my parents are incredibly curious. They say, 'Oh no, not her!' or 'She's great'. Francesca tries to fix me up with people who are rich. She always says I should go out with N, because she's got lots of money. My Mums don't say, 'Yes it's all right if you go out with a friend of the same sex.' I know I'm allowed to – they don't even care what sex my friends are. Either one is absolutely fine with them. They're perfectly happy as long as they think the person is nice. I'm interested in boys or girls, depending on my current mood. My mothers don't like my taste in girls, actually.

Lawrence: I certainly can't talk to my mother about going out with girls. Oh God, no. I don't think she expects it this early. Because she never did it. She was very restrained. She actually didn't meet a boy until she was eighteen. Then she got married at nineteen. She was never a 'mess around and do what you want' kind of teenager.

Alice: She's suspicious.

Lawrence: Yeah. I don't know why I wouldn't feel comfortable talking to her about it. I just wouldn't. Your parents weren't brought up the way mine were. Her family is very strict. My grandparents are not the sort of people who go in for girlfriends and boyfriends. With them it's about getting engaged, getting married, and that's it.

Alice: My grandparents are so nosy. All of them. They try to fix me up with boys.

How do you define family? Who is your family?

Lawrence: Family is the people I live with. When Hannah lived with us, I didn't think of her as a stepmother exactly, but as another mother. Calling her a stepmother implies it's in place of my mother, and it wasn't. Hannah's not my family now that she's moved out. But I still think of her son Jonathan as family. My grandmother is family, even though she doesn't live with me, because she is my biological family.

I don't call my father Dad, but I consider him my father. He's got a daughter from another relationship. I think of her as my sister. I didn't see her for a while, but she's often there when I go to Oxford to see him. His parents are my grandparents naturally. They don't have many family gatherings, but when I go there, I go and visit them. I see his sister quite often. They're definitely my family.

Alice: I have a BIG, BIG family. I don't lose people from my family when they move out of the house. And I count close friends as family too. I have three mothers – Ruth, Jane and Francesca – and I've got all their extended families – their brothers, sisters, parents and children. I started with three mothers, but I've got four now that I've met up with my biological mother, Sarah, again. I didn't see Sarah for nearly ten years. We're very good friends now and get on really well. I just met my Dad for the first time, so I'm kind of gathering all my family back.

They're all really nice about counting me as family. Francesca's mum is the most straight and conservative out of all the immediate family I have. But she definitely counts me as her granddaughter, which I feel really happy about.

I've claimed Francesca's girlfriend as well. She's not a mother. She's like a partner. But she's definitely family. She'd hate me to think that she was another mother. She's not into all this family business. She's her own person.

I met my Dad in passing about two weeks ago in Bristol. He knew that I was his daughter. He and his new partner had arranged a birthday party for my Mum, and I was invited, not knowing that he was going to be there. Francesca suddenly came up to me and goes, 'Oh that's your dad.' I was shocked. He was actually too scared to say anything to me, and I was too scared to say anything to him. So I just went, 'Hello. Bye.' I wanted to see him, but now that I've seen him, that's enough. I don't need to collect any more family. I'm satisfied with my three immediate families.

Has living with lesbian mothers affected your views of men?
Alice: We're all very sarcastic and cynical about men. We think they serve their purpose. They have their up sides.
Lawrence: That's crap.
Alice: But we all know that it's crap. I get on brilliantly with boys. I think I get on much better with boys than I do with girls. I probably shouldn't say this, because of Lawrence, but I always end up fancying pathetic boys and wild, tearaway girls.

Lawrence: I think my Mum tried hard not to be anti-men.
Alice: I think it's quite funny. I don't take anything they say particularly seriously.
Lawrence: Neither do I.
Alice: They're not anti-men. They just rant. I don't even know any men who aren't family.
Lawrence: You know men at school.
Alice: Yes at school, and a boyfriend of a good friend of mine, who is great. That's it.

Are there any advantages or disadvantages to having lesbian parents?
Alice: I don't know. It doesn't make any difference.
Lawrence: I think it's better for a girl to have lesbian parents – to be around women.
Alice: I really don't know about that.
Lawrence: I'm not sure about boys in gay male families.
Alice: I think that would be fun.
Lawrence: I think having a lesbian mother has some disadvantages for boys. I think it's more a problem for boys growing up without a man in the house to explain things. My Mum never could. She bought me books and tried to show me. I guess you can always find someone else to talk to. I talked to my Dad and my uncle about growing up. But I was never that open with them. I kept quiet, which was fine with me.
Alice: One advantage of living with lesbians is that, in general, women are not that violent towards each other. We're safe. A disadvantage is that I'm actually quite scared of some men. I don't feel shy, but I don't feel very safe. I'm not scared of boys or people my own age, but I'm not sure I trust grown men.
Lawrence: I suppose it means that I can't be that open about my family to people I don't know. I didn't feel bad about it initially, because I didn't notice it. I think from about the ages of ten to twelve, I began to realize that I was odd because of having a lesbian mother. At secondary school, it was a problem. But I'm different because I want to be different. I don't want to be like other people.
Alice: I see myself as different, and it's kind of because my mothers are lesbian. My friends all have straight parents, but they think my family is fine. I don't feel uncomfortable about it.
Lawrence: It makes you different. You can try and be normal.

Alice: You can try and ignore it. I know a boy whose mum used to be a lesbian but she has now got married, and he's the most straight boy of anyone. He didn't want to be the child of a lesbian. He wanted to be like everyone else. I think boys do it more than girls.

Lawrence: I've never been that bothered.

Alice: It does give you a bit of a different outlook.

TWO

Josh

Josh is twelve and at secondary school. His mother, Maree, got pregnant with Josh by self-insemination using a gay friend, Steve, as a donor. Josh lives with Maree and her partner, Hazel, who have been together since Josh was six. From London, they moved to Leicester and lived there for two years. When Hazel's mother was unwell, the family moved to Brighton so Hazel could be near her family. At the time of the interview, they had lived in Brighton for a year.

Mum's partners

Maree is my Mum. She's a lesbian and has had several girlfriends in my lifetime. I like all the women that my Mum has been a partner with, apart from a horrible one Maree was seeing when I was four and five. Luckily she didn't live with us. Maree was with a nice woman when she got pregnant with me, but I was pretty young so I don't remember her much. Between the nice and the horrible one, there was a woman I liked a lot who I haven't seen for years now. That hurts. She was supposed to take me on holiday, then she said that she couldn't. She hasn't contacted me for about three years. I've written two letters to her and I've tried ringing her. But she's got a new partner with another little boy. Her phone number has changed. She hasn't been in touch.

Hazel came when I was six. Hazel's the best. She looks after me, so I'd say she's my mother. But when people ask me, I say that she's my aunt. I don't go around saying that I've got two mums. I say she's my aunt and that because my Mum works in London, Hazel lives with us so we can look after each other. Hazel doesn't mind me saying that. When I was younger I used to say that I just live with her.

Self-insemination

My Mum got sperm off my Dad. She did self-insemination. My Mum explained it to me when I was quite young, before I went to school, because she doesn't like keeping things from me. That's all I know about it. [**Maree:** Steve was a close friend of mine. We grew up together, and I asked him if he would sleep with me as I wanted to get pregnant. I was desperate to have a child. He said he couldn't even get a hard on and we'd need to find another way. I had a friend who was having donor insemination and she lent me the kit. Steve had to go to bed with his boyfriend to get the sperm. Then Steve gave me the sperm in a syringe and I inseminated and got pregnant first time, just like that. I never named Steve on Josh's birth certificate and I didn't intend him to be his father.]

Gay donor

I used to see Steve occasionally when I went to my Nan's, his mum, when I was very little. I asked my Mum a few questions about him, but at that age I didn't really want to see him. When I was about six, I took an interest and then I did want to see him. The kids at school were asking me whether I'd got a dad. I wanted Steve to come into the playground so that they could see that I did.

I started seeing Steve every Wednesday and used to go out with him and his boyfriend. I used to go round to his house after school and stay over. My Mum was having childcare problems after work, so I went with him once a week. Gradually I stayed longer, and then I started staying overnight and he would drop me off in the morning.

Eventually Steve split up with his boyfriend and got a new boyfriend, who I didn't like at all. Steve wasn't paying enough attention to me, so I didn't want to see him any more. I stopped seeing him when we moved away from London, and I haven't seen him for about four years. Sometimes I wouldn't mind seeing him again. I would say Steve's my father. I don't really see Steve's family as part of my family. I don't know them that much any more, so if they asked I would say that they are like my half relatives. [**Maree:** Steve is very close to his mum, and I used to work with her when I was a teenager. When I got pregnant, Steve told his mum that he was going to have a child. I used to take Josh on birthdays and Christmas over to their house when he was a very young child, but not at other times. They would always ring up with presents for Josh, wanting to bring them round. As far as they are concerned, he is their grandchild. When Josh goes round, he's got aunties and uncles.]

Family

Maree's sister is a lesbian as well. She has been trying to get pregnant. When she came down to look after me, she had to go up to London to be inseminated. But it didn't work. My grandmother doesn't really mind. Or if she does, she hasn't said anything.

I call Hazel's sister my auntie and her brother my uncle. Hazel's sister has a son and he's my cousin. Apart from them, I don't think Hazel's family really like her being lesbian, but they don't say anything. Her sister's got a horrible husband who is racist and sexist. I don't really know what to say to him when I speak to him, because I never know what nasty thing he's going to say. I don't think of him as my uncle.

Knowing men

I know quite a few men; some I see a lot and others occasionally. I see Hazel's brother and her sister's husband, Maree's brother and Hazel's nephew. I don't see my father any more or his boyfriend.

Sex education

Maree wants me to know things so that I'm not stupid. Other parents don't teach their kids about sex education, but Maree does all the time. If we are sitting in a restaurant eating, she'll say, 'I want you to know about all these sex things.' And she'll go on about everything, just shouting it out. Hazel says, 'Shut up Maree. We're eating.' But Maree says, 'I don't care if people know.' We were in Eastbourne one day in a pub and Maree was going on about sex education as usual. I was quite happy listening. Maree was asking me what I think about her and Hazel sleeping together. Hazel came over and sat down just as Maree said, 'Well, I'm a lesbian.' Hazel jumped up and walked over to the slot machine and started putting money in it. Hazel is not really open the way Maree is, though she is sometimes. At times she doesn't care if people hear, but sometimes she does care. It depends on the person she's with. Hazel goes all red when she talks about it. I don't feel embarrassed, not really. When we go somewhere public, I don't mind, because I know that I'm never going to see those people again.

I talk about a lot of things with Maree. I don't tell her everything. But I feel OK talking with her about things like growing pubic hairs. I've been learning about it in school as well. We're studying biology and growing up at school. Some of it's new and some of it I've already heard before. I don't wish I had a dad or a man to talk to about these things with, not really. But sometimes when Maree embarrasses me, I think, 'Oh God I wish I had a dad.'

Life at home

I spend time on my own with Hazel, and time on my own with Maree – Mondays with Maree and Thursdays with Hazel. Now my Mum's got a job somewhere else, so it's going to be different. Hazel and Maree have decided not to live in the same house for a while. They weren't getting on too well. Maree thought Hazel was having a breakdown after she lost both her parents last November and December. They were arguing a bit. I just close my door when they argue.

Maree makes me do jobs. I have to wash the bathroom, hoover the front room, hoover all the house, wash up every day [**Maree**: He's only on the rota twice a week.], iron my own uniform and feed the hamster. I normally do my chores on a Sunday. Maree is strict about it but Hazel isn't. When I ask my friends at school, they say they don't have to do chores. I've noticed that in families with lesbian mothers, the mothers make their kids do chores. The kids have to help. In a heterosexual family, the mum does everything. The kids only occasionally have to do one or two chores. Hazel's sister does everything for her husband and son. My cousin says to his mum, 'Come on Mum, I want my tea.'

During the week, we don't really get time to go anywhere because we are all pretty tired. I get up at quarter to seven. School starts at half eight. I've got a half-hour bus journey in the morning and the evening. Maree gets up at quarter past six. She has to commute and she's tired when she gets the bus. Hazel gets up at half seven. We are all pretty grumpy in the evening, so we just sit in and watch *EastEnders* and see Sharon cheat on Grant. Hazel likes *Brookside* and *Neighbours*. On weekends, I go roller skating with my cousin, we all go shopping together or we go swimming.

When we lived in London, we used to go ice skating every Saturday morning with Michael, a friend of mine who has a lesbian mother. I wanted to do something different when we moved to Leicester, instead of being bored at home all the time. I completed my skating course and then started karate. Now I do karate on Wednesdays and Fridays. I've been doing that for three years. My Mum wanted me to be able to defend myself, but that's not really why I do it. It's just a good sport. I also have piano lessons.

Dealing with prejudice at school

At my school in London everyone knew that I had lesbian parents and they didn't say anything about it. [**Maree:** When I used to collect him at his primary school in London, his friends would ask him, 'Your mum's a lesbian, isn't she, Josh?' And they would come and ask me.] In Leicester, they were saying horrible things about lesbians round the playground, so I didn't tell anyone in Leicester.

Maree doesn't keep it quiet. She doesn't mind what people think. She says they can think what they like, but I mind because it affects me at school. As far as I know, the teachers don't say anything, but they probably do when I'm not around.

When we moved to Brighton we visited five schools and I asked them questions about their policies on drugs and how many children at the school had lesbian parents. At the school I chose, the head knew of five or six – that was the highest. At the others, they only knew of two and at one school, they didn't know of any. I haven't met any of them yet. They could all be in my class, I don't really know. I feel I made the right choice. I feel OK where I am.

I've finished my first year at secondary school in Brighton. I haven't told any of my friends at secondary school about having lesbian mothers. I came close, but the person I was going to tell is a bit of a blabber and when I stopped and thought about it, I thought no. The kids say things like 'You're gay', and they say horrible things about it. They use the word 'queer'. I looked it up in the dictionary last week and it says peculiar, odd person. They don't even know what it means at school.

When they give out homework, they say get your mum or dad to help you. Once Maree told them that she wanted letters sent home to be addressed to her and to Hazel not just to her, because Hazel is my mum as well. Ever since then, they've been putting both Hazel's and Maree's names on letters home.

Lesbian parents group

I know a lot of children of lesbians. Some are my age and a few are little babies. Michael is the same age as me. He lives in London and I keep in touch with him.

Every month we go to a lesbian parents' group. It's a bit boring. The adults just go and talk and I sit downstairs playing darts. I don't know what they talk about. There are lots of other children, but I'm the oldest. I would like a group for kids my age who have lesbian mothers. I don't know what kind of things we'd talk about – the same things we talk about anyway – but at least I would feel safe. In case of a slip of the tongue – saying something about lesbians – it wouldn't matter.

Gay Pride

I've been on every Gay Pride march since I was born except two. I like Gay Pride. It's exciting meeting old friends. This year, we were a bit late. We got lost, because Maree went on the wrong motorway and missed the turning on the M25.

Last year I had a bad experience. I was with a friend and we went up to a field to play football, when two men came up to us. One of them started touching me. We just ran. I didn't want to go this year because of that. But I went anyway and I enjoyed it. I went to the fair. I was disappointed not to see Jimmy Sommerville. He didn't show up, he hurt his back I think.

We saw one man dressed as a woman standing on a windowsill with everyone watching him. He was there for about two hours, because we went into McDonalds and when we came out he was still standing there. It was funny. I think it's a bit strange the way people act so different when they are on a Gay Pride march. They dress differently. It seems like they're not being themselves really. It's not every day they dress up in what they dress up in, or walk around naked. I remember on one march, several men got some paint from a building site we were passing and climbed the scaffolding right up to the top. They painted the word 'GAY' in red on a plank of wood and everyone shouted 'Yeah!' That was good.

The other day in Brighton, I was standing at the bus stop when someone walked past wearing a T-shirt that said Gay Pride Victoria Park. He walked straight past and looked as if he didn't really care if anyone was looking. In Brighton I've noticed a lot more lesbians and gays on the street. We used to see three or four every day. Maree and I kind of spot gays. We say, 'There's a dyke then.' That's what we do. We spot them.

Lesbians as mothers

It's stupid the way some people go on about lesbians being mothers. It's up to the lesbian if she wants to be a mother, that's what I think. She's a woman, isn't she. She's a mother. I think two women looking after a child is exactly the same, really, as a man and woman looking after a kid. I don't think there is any difference. If it's two women, or a man and a woman, the child is still getting looked after.

THREE

Gretel Taylor

Gretel is eleven years old and in the top year of junior school. She lives in Leicester with her family, which consists of her mother, her mother's lesbian partner, Amanda, and Amanda's infant daughter, Brodie. Brodie was conceived by donor insemination. Gretel's mother and father separated when she was three and a half, but she still visits her father regularly.

How old were you when your Dad and Mum split up?
I'm not sure, but I was quite young. I can't remember living with my Mum and Dad at all. The saddest part I remember is waving goodbye to him and not understanding what was going on.

So you were living just with your mum for a while?
Yeah. We were living in Nottingham.

How did you come to be living with Amanda and Brodie?
I was about six or seven and we were still living in Nottingham when Mum met Amanda. I remember meeting her. We went somewhere with her and a few other friends. It was snowing and we had a big snowball fight and my Mum lost her car keys, so we had to go tracing back for them. I've known Amanda since then.

Where were you living?
We shared a flat with Amanda, and it was really squashed there. It was only one room, a bathroom and then a small kitchen. But we managed, because Amanda was away for ages. When Amanda came back, we bought a house and Amanda got a bigger flat. It was miles off and you had to walk up loads of stairs. It was horrible. I used to stay there sometimes. And then we all moved in together to another house in

Leicester. We had much more room. I have my own room, and Brodie has her own room, though it's smaller than mine. For at least three years now, we've lived in Leicester.

How did you feel about Amanda when you moved in together?
I liked her, but I'm usually like this when I first meet someone. And as I got to know her more, I liked her even more. But I didn't really understand what was happening. After a while I realized.

Did they tell you?
No, but after all the things that people have said at school, I realized that they were lesbians. But I didn't say anything. When I was nine, my Mum eventually said, 'You do know that we're lesbians?' And I said, 'Yeah, I do.' Mum, Amanda and me had been living together for a few years by then.

Tell me about Brodie.
After Christmas, Amanda and my Mum told me that Amanda was pregnant. I was really excited. I didn't know she was trying to get pregnant. They didn't tell me because if it didn't work out, I'd have been all excited for nothing.

Had she been trying for a long time?
No, I think it was the first time.

How did she get pregnant?
She went to the doctor and had it done. [Ed.: She had donor insemination at a clinic .]

Do you know how they did it?
Yeah. I don't know what it's called, but I know how they do it, but I don't know most of it. Anyway, she had a baby – that's Brodie – who is now six months old.

Did you go with them when Brodie was born?
I wasn't there straight away. My Mum phoned up a friend who I was staying with, and then I went straight to the hospital. It was really nice. She was a few hours old. Her contractions had started in the morning,

and then Brodie was born at five in the afternoon. It was funny, because at the time Amanda was giving birth, I was off playing crazy golf at the park. I thought that was really weird.

Do you call Amanda mum?
I just call her Amanda. On Valentine's Day I made them both cards and I said, 'To Mummy, be my Mum number one', and that was to my Mum, and then on the other one to Amanda I said, 'To Amanda, be my Mum number two'. So I was being silly.

Do you see her as a second mummy?
Yeah.

What do you think about the way Brodie came about?
I think it is all right, because quite a lot of women who are lesbian, or not lesbian but just not going out with anybody, go to the doctor's, don't they?

Do you worry that you've got a daddy and Brodie hasn't?
Not really. But my Mum and Amanda are a bit worried that she'll be wondering, 'Why haven't I got a dad and Gretel has?' I think I'm lucky that I've got two mummies and a dad and a sister. I've always wanted a sister or a brother, because I've always been the only child. I kept asking, 'Why haven't I got a sister?' I'm pleased I've got a sister.

Do you like to play with Brodie?
In the morning I play with her. Sometimes I make myself a bit late for school because I don't want to go to school. I'd rather play with Brodie. In the morning she's in a good mood. She just started giggling. I've got this slate and I rolled a pencil down it and she thought it was hysterical. My Mum was on the phone. It was the first time Brodie ever laughed. She's trying to sit up, but not getting very far, because when she sits up, she leans. She's sort of crawling, but she just kicks her legs on the floor hoping to get somewhere. By the time she gets moving, she starts screaming because she's bored. She likes to suck fingers and she's always sucking her hand. Amanda knows a baby who's always got her feet in her mouth. I can get my foot up there, but I can't put it in.

Is your mum a mother to Brodie as well?
Yeah.

Does Brodie wake you in the night?
On the first night when she came home from hospital, I heard her. And when they moved her back down to her little room from my Mum's and Amanda's room, she woke me up the first night. I thought, 'Oh no. I can't cope with this.' But since then I've only heard her scream at night about twice. So I'm very pleased about that. Brodie slept through one night, but that was quite recently. I thought that we're all going to be happy and she's going to go through the rest of the nights. But that was the only time that she's actually slept through the whole night.

Do you help look after her?
Amanda's still breastfeeding, but not as much because Brodie is eating solid foods now like mashed banana and apple. I tried to feed her, but she wasn't in a good mood and she didn't want to eat it, so I gave up and handed her back over.

Are Amanda and your mum strict?
No, I don't think they are.

Do they make you do a lot of chores?
No. When they ask me to wash up I'm not keen. But someone has to. I do it, but I don't like to. But I suppose nobody does.

What kind of things do they ask you to do?
Washing up and polishing the fireplace. I like that, because it's a really nice fireplace and I love polishing. I always used to ask Mum if I could do the polishing of tables and mirrors. My Mum has got a full-length mirror upstairs, so I spend ages on that. I like cleaning the sink and bath, but I'm not too keen on the toilet. Amanda usually does that.

Do you think you do more than your friends?
About the same really. Some of their mums have to stay at home and do all the work while the dads go out to work. So they're always doing it. I don't think that's right. It's not so fair.

What year are you in at school?

I'm in the fourth year, the top year at our school. I'm about to go into secondary school this summer. I might go to a girls' school. I don't really mind going to a girls' school. Anyway I'm not in the catchment area of the mixed school, and it's quite far away. I'd have to go there by a school bus. So I think I'm going to go to the girls' school, if we don't move that is.

Do you like school?

It depends. Some days I'm in a really happy mood, but sometimes I've got to do all this homework. But it isn't bad, everyone has to go to school I suppose.

What do you say to your friends at school about your family? What do you call Amanda and Brodie?

I say that Amanda's living with us, just sharing a house with us. I call Brodie my sister, except at school. At school I just call her a sort of sister, because people there don't understand. The only one I've told at school is my best friend, Clare. She doesn't mind. She really likes Brodie. Most of the kids are the sort of people who make jokes about all of this.

What kind of jokes do they make?

We sometimes get letters about things and the kids change all the words to gay, and they think it's really funny. They're so stupid. They say things like, 'Don't you think lesbians are funny?' One girl is racist and really hurtful. She kept making up silly rhymes about gays. I wondered why she was doing it. There's no point.

How does it make you feel when they do that?

I feel a bit uncomfortable when they're saying it, because sometimes I'm scared that my friend Clare might actually say something to one of them about my family. But she promised not to. That was in the first year when I was about eight, and she's kept her promise since then.

Is Clare the only one you've told?

Yeah, at school. I have another best friend, but she doesn't know about this either.

Why did you feel able to tell Clare?
Because I know her quite well and her mum is really nice, and she sort of understands more than anybody else. So I told her one day and she was fine about it. She thought it was all right.

Why do you think kids go on so much about lesbians?
My Mum said that maybe they're curious or maybe it's their parents.

What do the teachers say about your kind of family?
I used to talk to my teacher last year, because my Mum's dad wasn't very pleased when she told him she was lesbian. So I talked to my teacher and she knows a lot, and she thought it was all right. I really liked that teacher. She recently retired, but she still comes into school, and she was really happy that Amanda had had a baby. I showed her some photos.

What about your teacher this year?
Well, he doesn't know about it. But I've shown him pictures of Brodie, because I had a day off school when she was born and he thought she was really cute. I can't quite remember exactly what I said about her. I think I said Brodie lives with us and I call her a sister. He was all right.

Did you explain to him about Amanda and your mum?
No, because it was during class and though I like him, I'm not too keen on him. He's not the sort of person I would go up to and say, 'My Mum's a lesbian.' He never seems to have any time, because he's the deputy head as well and he is quite strict sometimes. But he's really funny as well.

What do they teach you at school about families?
They don't do much about families.

Did they talk about families in the infant school?
No, I don't think so.

Do they teach about how babies are made?
No.

Does your mum teach you about that?
Yes, she told me, and I also knew from all the gossip in the playground.

How often do you see your dad? What do you do when you see him?
I see him every three or four weeks. My Dad lives in a village near London, just down the road from my Nana and Granddad. He lives very much in the country in a tiny village. It's really nice there. I go and stay at my Nana's house, because my Dad has to get up really early in the morning to go to work. He has to work when I go over because he's a builder. He's got a girlfriend whose dad's got a farm with stables and she goes horse jumping in shows. I like going down with my bike and my two other friends, and maybe sometimes my Dad, to go and see the horses. I love it at my Dad's house, because you can go on really long bicycle rides. We can go on short ones as well, where you go past some horses if they're out.

What about your grandparents? How do they feel about your mum being a lesbian?
I don't talk to them much about it. I don't talk to my Dad about it either.

Did your mother ask you not to talk to him?
No, it's just that it's never the right time. They're not the sort of people I think I would like to talk to about it.

What do you think their reaction would be?
I don't know, because I said once to my Dad that I've got two mummies, and he said, 'Amanda's not your mum.' I told my Mum about that, and she said that it's probably just because he knows he's my Dad and he doesn't want Amanda to take his place. My Mum said that he's always been all right about Mum being a lesbian, and she knows him well. I still love him as well.

What about your mum's parents?
Well, my Mum's mum wasn't all right about it, but she's got used to it. But my Mum's dad doesn't like it at all very much. He lives in France and they write letters to each other. My Mum got a letter off him after she wrote to him telling him about being a lesbian, and it was a horrible letter.

Are there any other children of lesbian mothers at your school?
Not that I know of.

Do you know any other children who have lesbian mothers?
I know a girl whose aunt is a lesbian. But that's all. I know many people who are all right about it, like some of my Mum's friends who are lesbians.

What are your favourite after-school activities?
I love playing with Brodie. At weekends I try to make constructions with cardboard boxes, but they never work. I tried to make something like a bingo machine, but it just fell to pieces. When I was little, I always used to find containers and I would ask my Mum if I could use toothpaste and shampoo and mix them up in a big saucepan. I used to love it. I would have it in my bedroom for days and my Mum used to say, 'Gretel, it stinks.' And it would be all over the carpet. My Mum didn't like me doing that. I used to play out in the garden as well, mixing mud and grass together. I would stay out there until about six o'clock and just create. We didn't have a huge garden.

Do you take any classes after school?
On Thursdays I go to choir with two friends. We sing a mixture of songs. We've got a song about getting to a football match late because the car breaks down and they have to go on a bus. When they get there, they just see their team score a goal and they were cheering but they got a funny feeling that something was wrong and they look around and see that they were on the wrong end of the pitch, cheering the other team. I really like that song. I really like choir. I have swimming on Thursday morning at school and choir at school. I play the flute and I really like art. I like quite a range of music from *Swan Lake* to Take That and Bad Boys. I like to watch ballet, although I don't do ballet. I recently saw *Swan Lake,* and my Nana bought me the soundtrack. Every year, round about Christmas, my Nana (my Dad's mother) takes me to the ballet.

Do you think about having kids when you grow up?
I don't know. I used to really want to have them, but then I realized how much pain they are. We've got photos of Amanda and Brodie when she was just born, and Amanda is looking at Brodie in a daze, like she's

saying, 'Wow, it's a baby!' She is really tired. You have all the nights that you have to stay up.

Do you have ideas of what you want to do when you grow up?
I used to want to be a teacher, but with all the homework that my Mum comes home with, all the books to mark, I've changed my mind. I don't want to go and do loads of work after school, like I don't want to have a baby because it's too much work. But I probably will have one, I might do. I'm not sure. I didn't think Amanda was going to, but she has.

Do you envy any of your friends or wish you had a different family?
Yeah, there's one girl who used to be in my class at school. She has a huge house with loads of rooms about twice the size of our living room. And she's got really nice long blond hair as well. She hardly ever seems to wear the same thing again, so she must have a huge wardrobe.

What do you think about lesbian families compared to your friends' families?
I think it's absolutely fine. I've been in all different situations and they're all fine. I've had a dad and a mum, then my Mum had a boyfriend, then it was just me and my Mum and then she's been in a lesbian relationship. They're all fine. I really like my family, I know that. It's a happy family. I wouldn't really want to change. Sometimes I think that I'd like to be someone else for a day or just be someone else, and then I realize that I won't have my Mum and Amanda, that I'd have their parents, and I don't really like any one else's parents.

FOUR

Katrina

Katrina is seventeen and lives in London. She has a brother, Andy, who's three years older. She was brought up by her mother who has been a lesbian as long as she can remember. Her mother identifies herself as a black lesbian.

Background

My father left when I was three. My parents split up because my Dad had lost all their savings through gambling. My Mum didn't know anything about it until she opened a letter by accident one morning and discovered a repossession order. They had a big row and Dad said, 'Right, you're the one who wants to leave. I don't want to leave you really. Leave the kids with me.' Mum said, 'No way, Jose. You leave.' So he left.

I then had a stepfather for a few years. He was nice and we got on really well. If anyone has been a dad to me, I would say it was my stepfather. He asked Mum to marry him, but she didn't want to get married again and they split up over that. When I was about six, Mum met Carol and they were together for the next seven years.

There isn't any landmark in my life to mark my Mum becoming a lesbian. For me, it's always been that way. My Mum took me to a lot of women's functions and it was never hidden from me. I don't remember her sitting down and saying, 'Katrina, I'm a lesbian.' She didn't need to. I knew that I would never have a mum and a dad the way everyone else had. I don't know what it's like to have a mum and dad, so I suppose you don't miss what you don't know.

Mum's partners

Carol had two children of her own, a daughter who lived with her and a son who lived with her ex-husband. Sometimes we'd stay at Carol's house, sometimes at ours. I loved Carol so much. We were very close.

She was the soft touch in our family, while my Mum was the stern one who wouldn't take any feistiness. Carol was easy and docile, not the argumentative type. Whatever Mum suggested, she would say, 'Yeah, OK, that sounds good, we'll do that.' Whatever Mum wanted to do was OK by her.

I was eleven when they split up, and that was a shock. Not only was Carol a big part of my life but her daughter was as well. My Mum was very upset, but I didn't understand why at the time. I think Mum found Carol boring and went looking for excitement. She found Teresa.

Teresa was very different from Carol. She was about six foot two, almost masculine in her shape. She was a lot older than Mum with grown-up children, but very young at heart. She had a house in Hastings that we would go down to in the holidays. At first, I thought she was nice and I used to give her a cuddle when I saw her.

But Teresa was scary. They had a big fight in the kitchen when I was thirteen. I'd been away for the weekend at my friend's house and came home to find Mum and Teresa in the kitchen, silently picking dirt off the floor. There were pieces of broken chairs and broken plant pots all over and the sink sideboard was bent. I walked in cautiously and said, 'Hi! What's going on? What happened to the sink?' Mum said, 'Hello Katrina. Oh, nothing. Why don't you go upstairs?' 'Why, what happened to the sink?' And she said, 'It's OK, there's no problem here, everything's fine, just the chair's broken.' I said, 'Is it? The sink's broken too.' She said, 'Yeah, it can be fixed.' I said, 'OK then.'

It was obvious they'd had a fight. I'd never seen such damage and I didn't like it at all. After that incident, I became very wary of Teresa. I wouldn't go near her. I'm not going to blame my Mum. The way I saw it was that Teresa was hurting my Mum. I never witnessed any violence myself. I only ever saw Mum's tears, not Teresa's. That made me dislike her. They finally broke up.

Then my Mum met Rita, whom I now hate with a passion. She really did cause my Mum a lot of hurt and pain. I liked Rita when I first met her. We had a lot in common, but soon the arguments started and all I could see was my Mum being upset. I blamed Rita totally. I got standoffish to a point where she won't come here, which I'm pleased about.

My Mum was selective about what she told me, and I knew that. She wouldn't tell me things that she thought would make me turn against Rita totally or go after her with an axe. But from what she did tell me, I could guess the rest. If I did see her on a dark night, I probably wouldn't hesitate in beating her up.

Rita was like a spoilt child. I overheard some phone calls and know she used to say to my Mum that I was spoilt and that I just wanted Mum to myself, that I wanted attention. I do love attention. I thrive on it, but my Mum has always had partners, and I can accept that. Mum has her own life and wants someone she can be with. I wouldn't have had any problem with Rita if she'd been nice to my Mum, but she wasn't. Every time Mum used to come back from seeing Rita, she'd be crying or angry. She'd go and sit upstairs and wouldn't want to talk to me. I voiced my opinions on it. Perhaps I should have kept my mouth shut a bit more, but that's not in my character. Mum went out with Rita for five years. Because of me, they never stayed here unless I was away.

They split up last year sometime. It's been off and on. They get together, they break up, they get back together. I get sick of it. I say, 'Oh, get rid of her.' Mum says, 'Well, it's not as simple as that, Katrina.' I say, 'Yes it is. Tell her to go away. She's no good for you.' But Mum loves her. I guess Mum likes women who are a challenge. She definitely found her match in Rita. Mum is a dominating type, but Rita was even more so. They certainly clashed. Rita would say, 'I don't want to do what you say. I want you to give, give, give and I'll take, take, take.'

My Dad and I
Dad has been around on and off. For a while Andy and I used to see him every weekend. Then it seemed to get less and less. As we've grown older, he's become more out of touch with us. I did get a birthday card from him on my fifteenth birthday. He'd written 'Happy 16th' on the card. I was really upset about that. Four months ago, he turned up on the doorstep after not seeing us for about four years. That was a big shock. He did his usual thing, which was, 'I haven't seen you for ages. I'll start seeing you more regularly. I'll give you a ring in a couple of weeks and we'll go out.' But the phone call never comes. Mum was annoyed because he does it all the time, but there's nothing she can do.

I don't know if I want to see more of him. I'd like to know he was there, but I don't need him and I don't miss him, though I miss the idea of a father. I worry when I haven't seen him for ages. I wouldn't even know if he had died. Once I rang his family and asked if they knew where my Dad was. They'd seen him a couple of weeks before. I thought,

'Wow, I'm his daughter and I haven't seen him for three years.' He moves around a lot, and because he stayed away so long, it's too hard to be in contact. I may have wished for a father-figure in my life, but that was a dream really. I never had one. A dad is the word for the person that is the other half of my genetic make-up, but he's not my parent.

I don't like men really. I go out with men, but I wouldn't pick men for friends. The longest relationship I had was for two years, and he was my best friend as well. He was everything to me. But I came down to earth with a bump when I lost him. He was my best friend and we can't even hold a conversation now. I thought I'd be with him for ever. He knows everything about me, and me about him. That's hard to deal with, because I hate people knowing things about me.

I think I go round looking for a dad in the men I go out with. My boyfriend's mum wasn't there for him. And my Dad wasn't there for me. I wanted a dad. He wanted a mum. It was perfect. We parented each other and it was great. But that worked out only for a short time. I must admit I do like it when some male gets all protective over me. It's great. I never had it from my Dad.

My Mum and I

My Mum was the mother and the father of the family. She played both roles and was totally dominating. Once she's made a decision she'll stick by it, even if she later discovers that it was the wrong decision. She isn't a vindictive person, but because I'm the baby of the family, she wanted to mollycoddle me. She wrapped me in about ten inches of cotton wool to protect me from everything and everyone. She was worried that I would be treated the same way she was. She was very strict with me, though not with Andy. Andy wouldn't listen to her anyway.

I got fed up with her telling me what to do and not letting me out. She got into this grounding thing when I was between fourteen and sixteen, when I started wanting to stay out later. She wasn't joking either. Once I got grounded for six months for being two hours late. Only three weeks ago, we had an argument about going out. I wanted to go to a party on the Embankment which went on till six o'clock in the morning. I told her I'd be coming in at half-past seven in the morning at the earliest. She said, 'No you're not. Be back at 12.30!' I stuck to my guns. Finally, she said, 'If you think you're big enough and bad enough to come in whenever you want, then you can start paying your way. I want £60 off you for rent. When you're under my roof, you live by my rules. Either come in at the agreed time or move out.' She was being totally ridiculous. So I said, 'Fine, I'll move out.' Friday night came. I went out and came in at half-past seven. I'm still living here. I used to lie about where I was going, but now I tell her exactly where I'm going and what time I'll be in, and I always get home at the time I say.

Coming out about Mum

Other than my friend Jenny, who also has a lesbian mother, I don't think I know anybody else with a lesbian mother. There was Carol's daughter, but I didn't stay in touch with her after Carol and Mum split up. I don't think my mother really knew that many lesbians with children. If she did, I'm sure she would have introduced us.

Lesbianism is so taboo. As I was growing up, I would hotly deny it if my Mum was accused of being a lesbian. None of my friends ever knew, apart from Jenny and a girl who was like a second daughter to Mum. Mum was aware that I didn't want everyone to know, because it wouldn't have been acceptable in the circles I moved in. You can't give people a reason to get at you, especially someone like me who needs to be liked by everybody. If someone doesn't like me for something, I've got to know why. My Mum never jeopardized anything for me. Mum told me in recent years that she also kept it quiet because she was worried that my Dad might file for custody of me if he found out, even though he'd shown no interest in me whatsoever since he left. As soon as I was sixteen, that was no longer a worry.

I think some people did know, but didn't say anything. They must have had an idea, because the house used to be plastered with lesbian and feminist posters. There's a poster upstairs showing two black women sitting on a road sign that says 'Black Dyke Lane'. If anyone had taken a look at the books on the bookshelves upstairs, it would have been a dead giveaway – *Black Women in Love*, *The Joy of Lesbian Sex*, all the Women's Press books, and more. I found that actually people aren't very observant.

There's a photo of Jenny's mum and my Mum sitting on the kerb together with their arms around each other, and both with short hair, earrings, khaki jackets, big boots, dungarees and pink triangles on their jackets. You'd know they were dykes if you saw them. When we'd been going out for about a year, my boyfriend looked at this photo and asked, 'Who's that?' I thought about it and said, 'Oh, that's Jenny's mum and my Mum there.' 'Oh! Are they like best mates?' I went, 'Yeah, they are.' And he went, 'Oh, right, OK, right.' I was with this boy for two years, and he did know but he didn't say anything until then. Eventually he said, 'Katrina, about your mum? Is she?' I said, 'Yeah, she is.' That's all we said about it at that time. But later on he was curious. People really want to know. He asked if I'd ever seen anything. I did elaborate on it, because we were quite close, and he wasn't homophobic. So there was no problem.

Occasionally people say, 'So, has your mum got a boyfriend then?' I'd say, 'No, not at the moment.' They really don't know what to say next. I think they know, but they don't want to say, 'Oh, is she a lesbian?' No one would say that to you.

When I was about fifteen, I started to hang around with some kids, one of whom had known my brother and had been to our house. He was a malicious, conniving little git and would do anything to hurt people. He knew about Mum and he told everybody. I was at the youth centre and he came over to me with another boy. He said to the boy, 'I hear oranges aren't the only fruit?' I didn't click straight away what he was getting at. I tried to ignore him, but he then said, 'Katrina, what do you think about that?' And then they started making jokes against lesbians and sort of skirting around the issue. They said, 'Katrina, you know your mum?' When I said yes, they just burst out laughing. God, that was really scary! I don't know what I expected to happen – the house fire-bombed, bombs posted through the letter-box. Finally they said they knew my Mum was a lesbian. I denied it and only said she was a feminist. He didn't get one single syllable out of me about it, and after a while he got fed up with asking me about it.

Lesbianism was a big issue at the girls' secondary school I went to. Some girls were so stupid. They thought that if they're in a girls' school, they must be lesbians. They had to show how much they were into boys, just to prove that they weren't lesbians. As a result, our school has the highest teenage pregnancy rate in the borough. In the changing rooms, during shower time after PE, they'd squeal, 'Ooh! She's naked. She's looking at me! She's a lesbian!' I used to play along with it. It was almost fun, to act that stupid and pretend I didn't know about it. I knew lesbianism was nothing to be afraid of. I would revel in their stupidity. When they pointed at a girl and said, 'Ooh, she's a lesbian,' I'd ask them how they knew. They'd answer, "Cos she looked at me.' I'd have a great laugh at these stupid girls. It used to be really funny.

My sexuality

Carol's daughter is the same age as me, and Mum told me that she's a lesbian now. She used to be boy-crazy. We were both tomboys, but I went all girlie at some point. Hearing about Carol's daughter made me question my own sexuality. Mum says that if you are homosexual, then you're born with a gene for it. I had my first boyfriend when I was about thirteen and have always had boyfriends. I've never had a lesbian experience. Andy's very strongly heterosexual. Although he has been chatted up by a couple of men, he's definitely not interested.

I am the sort of person who thinks about things very deeply, and I think perhaps I might be a lesbian. I've pushed myself to be hetero-sexual because I know my Mum wants me to be a lesbian. She would love it. She'll joke about my boyfriends, 'Oh, I don't like that one, Katrina. Why don't you bring a girl home?' I feel OK about that. She can want what she likes, but I'm going to be what I'm going to be. I don't know if I'm set in my sexuality yet. I don't think I am. Mum says that when she was seventeen, she was strongly het and wanted to get married. Things change and I'm open to it. I'm not a homophobic person. I'd like to have a lesbian experience, because otherwise how will I know what I want?

Issues of race

My Mum identifies herself as a light-skinned black woman. She was born in Trinidad, in the Caribbean. She came here when she was eleven with her family and has been here ever since. A lot of people have problems when she says that she's black. Everyone denies it. They ask if she's Hispanic, or Latin, or Mediterranean, or Turkish or the latest is Apache. No one will accept she's black.

Being of such a light complexion with all the usual white features has given me a lot of problems with the way I identify myself. My Dad was white, but his mum was Indian. So he was half-Indian. My Mum's Trinidadian. So what the hell am I? I don't know. I call myself a person of mixed race. On job applications where you have to tick your ethnic origin, it will have boxes for Black, Afro-Caribbean, Asian, White UK, Oriental or Other. I always tick 'Other' and write 'mixed race'. At a job interview once, the interviewer said, 'I think you've made a mistake here. Why didn't you just pick White UK?' I explained that my mother is Caribbean, so I'm not really White UK. I couldn't bring myself to tick 'White UK'. But people have a hard time with that, because they look at me and see this white person, and say, 'No way'.

What is family?

I have my family who are blood-related, and we are all colours of the rainbow. There is a very strong bond there because of our biological connections. We went away to the Caribbean last year for a month and stayed with my cousins on my mother's side. We became very close immediately, because we are family. I don't know anyone on my father's side.

Mum stayed away from her family for a long time. I don't know the reason. We just didn't go over there, that was the way I saw it. We would only see them once in a blue moon, maybe twice a year. She felt so different to them. It's only been in the last two years that Mum has started to have a lot of contact with them and to be open about her lesbianism with them. They've had a hard time dealing with that, because they're so het. But she won't be quiet about it now.

They were here for Andy's birthday and Mum made some comment about a woman's bum. They all gasped and looked at each other. And she went, 'Well, come on, you all must know by now.' And they admitted that they did know. She digs Uncle Claude and says, 'So d'ya know any nice women then?' You can notice their uncomfortableness about it still when she mentions it. There will always be that.

But then I've also got a lot of other people I call family, like Jenny. Mum, Andy and I have adopted people over the years, who have become part of our family. When I say family I use it as a broad term. I don't think it's something that is only to do with blood. A child can be brought up by anyone. You don't need to have a blood-related parent to make that your family. Family is whoever. It can be two lesbians. I think it's perfectly OK for a child to be adopted by two lesbians. A family includes anyone who's going to love and care for you unconditionally. That doesn't necessarily have to be your biological mother and father.

Pros and cons

Growing up with a lesbian mother is not the easiest life. It would have been easier with a mum, a dad, two point four children, two cars and a chalet. But it would have been boring. I never would have met Jenny and I wouldn't be the person I am now. I wouldn't know the things that I know. Having a lesbian mother has enabled me to have a head start on everybody else emotionally, psychologically, intellectually – in every way. Other seventeen-year-olds are so naive and ignorant. I know things that other people don't know, and it's because my Mum's different.

People say you need a heterosexual mum and dad and it's all got to be just right, otherwise you're going to be fucked up when you're older and will have to spend thousands of pounds on therapy. That's not true at all. Everyone has their problems, but as a result of my upbringing, I'll be able to cope with more. I'm very stable. I'd say I'm more emotionally stable than many of my friends who are living with both their mum and dad. I feel sorry for some of the girls at my school. They've got to live with parents who fight all the time. I don't have to deal with fighting parents or with men. My Mum takes care of me. She doesn't bring anyone she meets home.

I think I wouldn't be as assertive as I am now if I hadn't been brought up by a lesbian mother. I wasn't brought up to be a passive woman. My Mum has drilled it into me since I was small that you stand up for yourself, you say what you want and you don't let any man tell you what to say or do. She's as good as her word. When I was eight, I was being bullied at primary school by two nine-year-old boys. They used to get me in the corner and kick me black and blue. I went home bruised and crying. My Mum went absolutely mental. She went up to them in the playground, grabbed them by the scruffs of their necks and threw them up against the wall. She told them if they ever touched her daughter again, she was going to cut their balls off. I never had any further trouble at that school. It is great when someone comes in and stands up for you. I loved it.

My Mum is assertive and strong. She just won't be pushed around. I've learned that from her. I might not be as physically strong as my Mum is, but I can talk my way out of anything. I'm diplomatic. I've got the gift of the gab, and I've got confidence in myself. Other girls my age aren't able to hold their own, because they've been brought up by dominating fathers. They can't stand up to boyfriends that bully them. When I tell boys where to get off, these girls go, 'Ooh, how can you say that to him? That's a bit strong, innit? She's like one of the lads, she is.' I'm glad that I am the way I am.

FIVE

Kieron Wild

Kieron is fifteen and lives in east London. He has two mothers, Carol and Helen. Helen gave birth to Jamie, and then six months later Carol had Kieron. Carol conceived by self-insemination using an anonymous donor. Helen and Carol separated when Kieron was four, and now he and Jamie live in both households. Kieron has cerebral palsy and goes to a special secondary school. His main concern is the rights of disabled people. Carol helped with this interview.

People in my family

I have two mothers, Carol and Helen. Jamie is my brother. When I was born, Helen and Carol were living together. After they split up, one part of the week Jamie and I are with Helen and the other part of the week with Carol. Carol and Helen have had relationships with other women.

Now Kathy is Carol's girlfriend. Kathy has three children, the youngest is an eighteen-year-old daughter, Sophie. This is how me and Sophie became brother and sister. On 15 August 1991, we were having a barbecue. Sophie came up to me and asked if I wanted to be her brother. I said yes, and so we adopted each other. I really think she's a good sister. Sophie used to live in the house with us, but now she's at university in Liverpool. That's a long way away. I miss her. We don't see each other very much.

Self-insemination

Self-insemination is something that a woman can do to get pregnant without having sex. I feel fine about having been conceived in that way. It's really good not having a dad. I find it fine. Nobody teases me. Some teachers have said things like, 'You can't have two mums.' There's one teacher who said, 'Everybody has a father.' I said, 'I don't have a father.'

He kept saying, 'But everybody has a father.' I just kept saying, 'No, I don't have a father.' I was twelve then and was at the first special school that I went to.

Some of my friends asked if I had a dad, and I said no. Nobody asked anything about a dad when I was at primary school. I think all the teachers knew I'd got two mothers. And they were fine about it. But they didn't talk about lesbians or have any positive images of lesbians. They didn't talk about different kinds of families or about how babies are made. I knew that from before I started school, because Carol taught me. It never seemed strange to me. It's what I've always known. It's very ordinary to have two mums.

I feel fine about having lesbian mothers. I know lots of other children who have got lesbian mothers and no dads. Some are my good friends. And that also made it very easy.

At school

I've been to three schools, first of all to a mainstream primary school and then to two special schools. When I was eleven, I went to a school for people with physical disabilities. I was there for three years. I was so unhappy there. Those three years were the worst time of my life for lots of reasons. We had this woman helper who was horrible to me. She knew my mother was a lesbian. She made fun of me, saying things like, 'Ooh, you're wearing those clothes.' About lesbians, she would say, 'Actually they are disgusting.' I just hated her. I did complain about her to the headmistress, but nothing was done. The headmistress was very nice, but she never dealt with anything.

A cookery teacher was horrible to me and I hated her too. I still hate her. She forced me to put Cape apples in a fruit salad. At the time, there was a boycott of South African apples and I respected that. I stand by Nelson Mandela. She said, 'Don't bring your politics in here.' She also forced me to cook meat sausages even though I'm a vegetarian.

When I was in the first year, I was forced to do a sponsored silence for *Telethon* [charity fundraising event] by one of my teachers. The problem for me is that *Telethon* portrays disabled people in a horrible way, showing us as poor pathetic victims all the time. So I was upset about that. Lots of my friends have been involved in organizing actions against *Telethon* such as blocking the roads. I never did that myself, but I supported them. My teacher said, 'You've got to do the sponsored silence for *Telethon*.' I refused and she said, 'Oh no, you can't do this. Oh no.' I wrote 'I want rights now' in my drawing book and I got told off for it. When they gave me the sponsorship form, I tore it up and threw it in the bin. When she asked, 'Where is your sponsorship form?' I said, 'What happens if you didn't get any sponsors?' 'Is that what you're telling me?' she says. She's not disabled and has no right to say that to me. I left that school.

The school I'm in now is a special school for young people with disabilities. Some have physical disabilities, some have learning difficulties, and some have medical problems. They all need more support than they can get in a mainstream school. I'm the only person with my kind of physical and learning disabilities in my class. It's a lot better than my other special school, and I have felt supported there. I'm much happier. I'm just starting to study GCSE subjects – art, science, maths, English, social studies, craft design and technology. I might not take the GCSE exams, because they're quite hard.

The teachers are really nice. I haven't talked to them about having lesbian mothers, though Carol told the headteacher when we went for the interview and my teacher knows. In fact there are a number of lesbians working in the school. That makes a difference. I've been bullied in this school and the staff are very supportive. The school's very good in that way. At my old school I never ever got any support for anything at all. So I feel a thousand times better being at this school, because I know that I can go and tell someone and they'll go and talk to the bully. They're very strict and make it very clear that they won't tolerate bullying. The teachers have talks to the whole class about bullying. They don't name me, but they say that some of the students have been giving one of the students a hard time. They say it's completely inappropriate and they make it very clear that it won't be tolerated, and that privileges will be withdrawn or they might be excluded from school. They're incredibly supportive.

Telling friends

When I was thirteen, I told my friends at school that I had two mothers. They found it very hard to believe that. One girl felt like having a go at me, probably because she is quite unhappy generally and saw that this was a way of stirring things up. She knew it would affect me. When they came to my party, this girl cornered Carol while another girl went to

Kathy. They asked if it was true that I have two mothers. Carol and Kathy said it was. And then they asked, 'How come?' Carol said, 'Well, we're lesbians and we had Kieron and we are living together.' Just after the party, this girl started being horrible to me at school. She made a point of telling another friend of mine that Carol is a lesbian, and that made it harder for me to have a friendship with her.

At my new school, I've made the decision to tell friends about having lesbian mothers. Most of my friends know now. Just a few don't know. The first friend I told was fine. The next person I told said that she will keep it secret, and I think she has. Her parents don't know. Another close friend of mine said, 'You shouldn't tell anybody, because they'll go and blab to everyone.' And then I told a friend who was fine about it because her mum works with lesbians. Several other friends have been fine about it too. One asked, 'Do you mind having them?' I said no. I'm glad I told my friends. I feel better with the friends that I've told.

Disability rights

I've been involved in lots of disability rights protests. I was on the TV protesting against *Children in Need* when I was in the second year. Last year, in September 1994, Carol and I went on a march. I saw a news item on TV about a protest against inaccessible transport, where people were chaining themselves to buses. It also said that there was going to be another action the next day. And it said where it was going to be. So I came rushing down the stairs saying, 'Yes, yes, yes! Could we go, PLEASE?'

Carol and I went, but we definitely did not want to get arrested. We went to the meeting point at Central Hall, Westminster, and there was absolutely no one there, apart from a few people. But then people started arriving. I brought a pair of handcuffs so I could chain myself to something. First of all a policeman came in to the organizing meeting and he said they were going to give only two warnings. He said, 'Yesterday we were very lenient towards everybody and we tried not to arrest you, and we gave you lots of warnings. But today I'm telling you that we are going to be harder and we are just going to give you one warning if you chain yourself to any buses. And if you don't move on when we've given you a warning, we'll arrest you for obstruction.' So he gave us that warning and then he went away.

We went up to the Mall, walking and singing and waving. We were shouting, 'We want disability rights now!' We started weaving in and out of traffic looking for accessible transport, but we didn't find any. Then Carol turned around and saw a line of policemen and white vans. They started arresting absolutely everybody. They didn't give us a warning. They were lifting up all the wheelchairs and putting them in the vans. They said to us, 'Right, now. Get on the pavement you two.' And Carol said, 'That's our warning. Come on. Let's do as he says.' And we got up on the pavement. And this policeman said, 'All right officer, arrest these people.' I said, 'But you haven't even given us a warning.' I was crying. He apologized for arresting us. He said, 'I'm sorry about this, but ...', as if he were apologizing for breaking a cup. He charged us with behaviour likely to cause a breach of the peace. They told us to get into the van, so we did. I was in tears and was very upset, because I didn't think we'd get arrested. The policewoman who was driving the van asked us, 'What are you being arrested for? Was it behaviour likely to cause a breach of the peace?' I stopped crying and said, 'No. We're being arrested for fighting for our rights.' And then I burst into tears again.

They took us to Charing Cross police station and booked us. They looked in Carol's bags and found my video camera and handcuffs! They took the handcuffs away as evidence, and put a place of safety order on me and put us in a cell together for about two and a half hours. They were nice to us once we were in the police station. They did bring us sandwiches and tea. I was scared at first, but then I was bored. We hadn't got any books.

SIX

Mary

Mary is twenty and grew up in London. Her family includes her gay father, the communal household she lived in all her life, as well as grandparents, other relatives and friends. Her mother died when she was five years old.

My household

I have a huge family. All my life, I've lived in a communal household in the same house. Different people have lived in the house during my life. My parents went to art school with their friends, Ted and Emma, who bought a big house in south London. My parents moved in just before I was born. When Emma moved out, she stayed part of the household. I'm godmother to Emma's daughter.

At the moment, I live with my Dad, Ted, Lucia and Sylvia. Lucia is my foster sister. She first moved in with her mum when she was eighteen months old and I was three. Sylvia has lived with us for nearly fifteen years. She became Lucia's legal guardian when Lucia was eleven. At that point, Lucia moved in permanently and has been here for seven years.

After my parents split up, my mother had a child with another man. My half-sister, Marigold, was eleven months old when our Mum died. She lives with her dad and we don't see much of each other now. My parents split up when I was two and a half, which means I have no memory of them in a relationship together. I stayed with my Dad and spent the weekends with my Mum. She died when I was five, but even before that, it was always just me and my Dad.

My Mum

Because my Mum left when I was two and died when I was five, I never got to know her very well. All I have of her are a few photos and her belt buckle. She was a very creative woman – a painter and a writer –

but I don't have any of her paintings. Ted and other friends of my Mum are good sources of information about her. Ted sometimes says, 'You look just like your mother. She used to pull that face.' We don't talk about my Mum much, mainly because it's been such a long time now. My Dad doesn't say when I remind him of my Mum. It's too painful for him.

When I was in primary school, it was embarrassing not having a mum. I couldn't say things like, 'My Mum won't let me do this,' or 'My Mum made my sandwiches.' I once had an argument with a girlfriend which ended when she turned on me and said, 'At least my Mum's not dead.' It shocked me, but I had no answer.

Ideal family fantasy

A few years after my Mum died, we had to draw a picture of our family at school. I drew a picture of my Mum, my Dad, a little sister and a dog and cat. The reality was that I didn't have a mum, my half-sister didn't live with us and we'd never had a dog.

In my teens, I had an ideal family fantasy. My fantasy was that I lived in this house with my Dad, my Mum, Lucia and a little brother. I was aware of how boring it would be, but I was still into having it. In the last few years I've become a little more realistic about my family situation.

Dad being gay

After my Mum left, my Dad never was with a woman. All the time I was growing up, the fact that my Dad was gay was a normal part of my life. I never thought about it as a phenomenon. I wasn't aware that there might be other children with gay dads or that people would want to write books about it or interview me on TV.

There never was a particular point in time when I realized that my Dad was gay rather than straight. I don't remember him sitting me down and discussing it with me. As I grew up and learned that there are different kinds of sexuality, I began to put two and two together. The way I felt about it was, 'All right, so he does it that way rather than this way.' It wasn't a big deal for me. My Mum's death is the most traumatic thing that's ever happened to me in my life. It overshadows any problems I might have had about my Dad's homosexuality.

When I was growing up, my Dad identified himself more as a single parent than as a gay father. He was worried about coming out, especially to my Mum's family, because they had been keen to have me when my Mum died. My uncle offered to take me to live with him in the States, because he's got a child three years older than me. My Dad categorically refused, saying, 'No. You can't take her. She's mine.' They recognized that he was doing a good job, but they were worried about him being a single father, even though he had already been for several years before my Mum died. I don't think they knew then that he was gay. It was settled within the family that I would stay with my Dad. Once it was sorted out, they were fine about it.

After that was dealt with, my Dad had a generalized anxiety that I would be taken away if someone official discovered he was gay. He was worried about what I might say at school and what would happen if a teacher got hold of the information. I don't know if my Dad told me to keep quiet about it or if I just picked the message up.

I don't see much evidence that my Dad suffers from being gay. Maybe it happens more in his work life, but even there it's easy for him to deal with it, because he works mainly with women. There are no men who could be threatened by him as a homosexual. The main problem he faces at work is that the women get annoyed that he doesn't find them sexually attractive.

My Dad's been more active in the gay community since he's been with his current boyfriend, Mark. He and Mark go out to clubs a lot more than he did with the boyfriends he had when I was younger. Then it was hard to get a baby-sitter and he didn't go out as much.

On the whole, it's a straight world, with heterosexuality pushed on you from every direction. Like everyone else, I've been influenced by that. But because my Dad's gay, I've also had the added benefit of a positive experience of homosexuality. As a result, I feel comfortable with gay men and can enjoy myself at Gay Pride. I can spot gay men a mile away, which I suppose is useful when I'm looking to pick up men. The fact that Dad's gay means that he and I can talk about men in a slightly more equal way, and I think he understands me more than a straight man would. It is not a big thing, but it's some sort of solidarity. His homosexuality influenced me to question my sexuality more than I might have done. Until recently, I would have said I was straight, but I'm not sure at the moment.

Coming out about Dad

My first coming-out experience was when I was still in primary school. One day my best friend and her cousin were playing with me in our garden. During the game, the cousin happened to appear at the front of the house just as my Dad and his boyfriend were kissing on the doorstep. When the cousin reappeared in the garden, he whispered something to my friend, who asked me directly, 'Is that your Dad on the doorstep?' I nodded. She said, 'He's with a man.' I replied without even thinking about it, 'It's my Dad's boyfriend.' To that casual remark, she said, 'Oh, all right, OK.' At that age it wasn't relevant to us. We were ten years old and about to begin puberty. It was enough to be thinking about our own lives, let alone what our parents were up to. After that, I didn't think any more about coming out until I was in secondary school.

When I was twelve and just starting at secondary school, I felt nervous about revealing my secret. I was worried that people would hold it against me. I chose a few apparently trustworthy people to tell – my best friends at the time, a girl we hung out with and a boy whose mother was a lesbian. Although I was so careful about who I told, when I left school five years later, I discovered that the entire school already knew. My 'best friend' had made it her business to gossip about me to everyone. I think she was hungry for attention and wanted to show how perfect she was by pointing out what she thought were imperfections in other people. By the time I realized that she'd done this, I was sixteen and wasn't bothered.

Although I was shocked that my best friend had betrayed my confidence, she actually made life easier for me. No one was surprised when I told them, since they already knew; or else they already knew, so I didn't have to make a special point of coming out to them. I found it amusing that everybody had known and not said a word to me. They probably kept quiet because they figured it was nothing to do with them or maybe because they were embarrassed by it. People have a hard enough time asking me where my Mum is without querying my Dad's sexuality.

I became aware that having a gay dad might be a problem for some people when I was eighteen and on holiday with my girlfriends for the first time without my Dad. There I met a man who'd been adopted at the age of four. He was twenty-seven and was looking for his birth mother. We had a heavy conversation about our backgrounds, and I told him about my father being gay. He wanted to know how I dealt with that. He said, 'It must worry you that people will think you're like a freak show. They might think of you and your dad as something strange and be quite scared of it.' I said, 'Yeah, I suppose so, but I've never experienced anything like that. I just get on with my life.'

Dad's partners

Shortly after my Mum died, my Dad met John. John never lived with us but was around a lot. They were together for about eight years from the time I was six. It was important to me that my Dad had a stable relationship after my mother died. John is a really nice guy. He used to spoil me. He gave me my first job when I was sixteen. After John, it was a long time before my Dad had another long-term relationship. There were a number of other men messing him about, which upset me.

Then two years ago, my Dad got together with Mark. At first Dad was happy and I really liked Mark. I was happy for my Dad because Mark made my Dad feel good. But then I started getting jealous. I wanted more attention. Last summer my Dad broke up with Mark. I was annoyed with him. I saw a different side to my Dad. He acted like a love-sick puppy who wasn't dealing sensibly with breaking up. I gave him a lecture about how he was better off on his own, how the relationship with Mark wasn't going anywhere and anyway he'd got me. That decided him. In twenty-four hours, he was back with Mark. But Mark spends less time here now. I think my Dad could do better in a relationship and have more fun with somebody else.

Relationship with Dad

My Dad is a strong man and very hard-working. I would describe him as masculine and powerful. Within our household he holds a lot of power. He's Dad in our family and at his work. Many people find him intimidating, but he doesn't intimidate me. I think he sometimes wishes that he could.

My Dad and I have always had a solid parent-child relationship. He's a good listener and he gives good advice. Throughout my teenage years, I could talk to him about anything. When I was fourteen, I told him the day after that I lost my virginity. I had no doubt that I could go and talk to him about it. There were a few times when I didn't want to talk to him about boys, so I found a woman or a girlfriend to talk to. If I did go to somebody else, it was only because I wanted to clarify the issues in my own mind first. I'd usually end up talking to him about it anyway, even if I had decided I didn't want to.

In the last six months, tension has grown between me and my Dad. He's worried about me because I haven't been very happy recently. I'm at a strange point in my life where I'm changing a lot, becoming an adult and a woman, and I'm not quite keeping up with myself. I'm more in tune with how I feel about my Mum dying. My feelings have become recognizable as anger with my Mum. I'm also angry at my Dad and confused about my feelings towards him.

My Mum used to be an angel. I thought she was perfect and had done nothing wrong. Now I feel angry with her, which is slightly better than being angry with myself. But I'm not handling my grief very well. It makes me feel that I'm a weak person. I'm angry with Mum for putting me in the position where I have to make a choice between being strong or weak.

I also resent my Dad for coping with my Mum's death in such a way that I can't be upset without feeling that I'm a weak person. He's very strong and it seems to me that he can handle everything. I'm angry at him for making me be the kind of person who manages and keeps everything under control. I can't blame my Dad entirely for that, because I think it's down to me as well. Even though my Mum died fifteen years ago, I feel that I'm going through the worst of the grieving process now. I find it very hard to be upset about it with my Dad. When I do get depressed about my Mum, I'd rather cry with my teddy bear than with my Dad.

I resent Dad for not being my Mum. I wish my Mum were alive for me to talk to. I'm finding it hard to talk to my Dad about what I'm going through now. It's not because he's gay or because he's my Dad – it's because he's a man. I don't want anything to do with men. I've been having a hard time with them. Last year when I did my A levels, my boyfriend was unfaithful to me and we broke up. Then I had a week-long fling on holiday and fell hopelessly in love with a seventeen-year-old boy. I didn't hear from him when I returned to England and I felt devastated. I said to myself, 'I've had it up to here. I am not putting myself on the line any more for anybody.'

I'm sure my Dad would be sympathetic if I did show him my feelings. There have been a few rare occasions when we have talked about my

Mum and we've cried together. It made me feel even more desperate to see him crying. I want him to be able to make things all right. But when he cries, I know how sad it really is and that it can't get any better. It scares me that he's still so upset by Mum dying. But really, there's no reason he shouldn't be.

Because my Mum died, I understand that one day my Dad too will die, like everyone will. I'm scared that I won't get as much love and support and caring from him as it is possible to get while he is alive. When I am angry with him, I feel guilty, because he's the only parent I've got. I don't want to take it out on him. He has done his best and it's not his fault either. I should say something to him about it, because I want to save our relationship.

Wanting a feminine influence

There have been times, especially recently, when I've wanted somebody to take the role of mother. I have my Dad. He does everything for me. He is a perfect parent. He couldn't possibly begin to make up for the things that a mother could – just because he's a man – but that's not his fault. I sympathize with him about that. But my biggest thing is lack of a female.

My Dad wasn't much good when I started my periods. A lot of my friends had already started and I knew about it from them, but I didn't really know what to expect. My Dad hadn't told me anything. The day I started my periods, I came home from school and my Dad was the only person in. I thought, 'I've got to tell him because it's really exciting.' When I told him, he said, 'Oh, no, what are we going to do? What do we do? Do you want to go to the chemist?' And I said, 'No. Go away.' There was a woman called Katie living here then and she took me down to the chemist. She bought me the full range of sanitary protection. We spent half an hour in the toilet trying them on.

For a while when I was seventeen and eighteen, I felt insecure about my femininity. I started feeling that I was too masculine in my mannerisms, attitudes and dress. In my early teens, I was often mistaken for a boy. People in my household assured me that my Mum wouldn't have been much of a feminine influence. She was a very strong feminist and used to wear Doc Marten boots in 1980. My best friend helped me come to terms with the fact that there's nothing wrong with not being feminine and that, anyway, I probably am quite feminine. My friend is feminine, but at the same time very independent. She's got a mum and an older sister, so she's had feminine influence in her life. Talking to her made me realize that I don't have to change myself to be more feminine, that I can accept myself as I am and that I'll probably blossom in time.

Sylvia could have been more of a mother to me, but for a long time I pushed away anybody who tried to mother me. I had my Dad and I felt I didn't need it. I thought Sylvia wanted me to be her daughter only when it suited her. I was resentful towards her because she doted on Lucia. The day after we'd had an argument, Sylvia said, 'So Mary, I hear you've got a problem with me.' And I thought I can either brush this off and let our relationship deteriorate further or I can try to sort something out. I decided to be upfront and said, 'Yeah, I do. You're not giving me what I want when I want it, and as a result we're really angry with each other. And we've got to deal with it. I live with you and I love you. And you're part of my family.' I was as honest as I've ever been with anybody in my life. Up to that point I hadn't actually told anybody that I wanted Sylvia to be my Mum. But that was why I was feeling so jealous of Lucia and of their relationship. Since then our friendship has blossomed. I feel more at ease with Sylvia.

Out and proud about gay dad

When I was nineteen, I was asked to speak at a public conference about lesbian and gay parenting. I wasn't sure whether or not I wanted to put myself on display, but I decided to go to support my Dad. My Dad and I were both overwhelmed and overjoyed by the interest in me. At first I thought, 'Oh my God! What have I done? I should have kept my mouth shut.' But I realized that I could change people's attitudes and I felt good about that. One man asked me if there is anything wrong with me, if I felt that I wasn't normal because of having a gay dad. I can't remember how I answered him. But he seemed to believe me and understand what I was saying.

I also appeared on a Scottish TV chat show. A woman in the audience told me that it's not right for gay people to have children and that it shouldn't be allowed, because it's unfair on the kids. I was very angry but because I was on TV, I couldn't say, 'You're a fucking bigot.' I calmly said, 'Well, I don't know if you're a well-educated person or not, but I think I'm fairly normal. And I don't think I've suffered from it. I'll leave it to you to decide.' At the end of the show, a middle-aged woman said, 'Well, I think it's a bit strange and I don't know that it's normal. But she seems a well-adjusted and happy child, so there's nothing wrong with it as far as I can see.'

Some of my black friends are anti-gay. I argue with them and say, 'You shouldn't be against gay people, because you are also discriminated against, if not as much, then maybe less than gay people are.' They turn around and say, 'Yeah, but you can't tell if somebody is gay or straight just by looking at them. You can tell that I'm black.' That is a valid point – no one can tell that I've been brought up by a gay man unless I let them know. To the outside world, I'm just another person. But that doesn't mean that gay people are not discriminated against.

People need to hear that it's perfectly acceptable for gay men to be parents and that it doesn't make any difference to the child. What's important is how much the child is loved and how well the parents look after their child. There are so many parents out there that are not doing a decent job of bringing up their children, while my Dad, without exception, has done a good job for me. I am really proud of him for being what he is.

SEVEN

Fiona MacNeish

Fiona is nineteen and grew up in rural Scotland with her brother, Stuart, and her sister, Sheila, who are two and three years younger respectively. Her parents were together until Fiona was eleven. Since they split up, her father has had two gay partners. Fiona went to live with him when she was sixteen.

I grew up in a small rural community in the north of Scotland. Where we lived wasn't a town. It couldn't even be called a village, it was just some houses scattered about. Everyone belonged to the Free Church, a strict Christian sect. The congregation was small and close-knit. They were kind people but not worldly wise. My family didn't have a TV. My Dad was a minister in the Free Church and my Mum was a minister's wife. My brother and sister and I were brought up religiously. Now I'm not at all religious and neither is my Dad.

Homosexuality was never mentioned in the Free Church. I've read verses in the Bible which says it's wrong, but no one preached against it. Where we lived, no one knew anything about it. Nevertheless when I was nine or ten, I started to think that my Dad was gay. I don't know how I worked it out. It wasn't a logical process, because he didn't do anything obviously gay. We were living in the depths of the countryside and he didn't have a gay lifestyle or a male partner. One of the things that made me certain was finding a book he'd hidden in the house called *Homosexuality and the Church*. I had a look at it, though it didn't help me understand him any better. I put it back where he had hidden it. Somehow I understood deep inside me that he was gay and I totally accepted it, right from the start. Even though I was brought up so religiously, I've always had my own views about things. I didn't mention what I knew to anyone.

It was a difficult time for me. I used to find myself crying, mostly because of the responsibility of knowing my Dad was gay before my

Mum did and knowing they were going to split up. Not being able to talk to anyone about it was hard. I wasn't meant to know, but I don't know why I didn't talk to my Dad. I think I wanted to protect him. At some level I knew he wasn't ready to talk about it.

I didn't and still don't know anyone else with gay parents. I didn't know any gay people then. It would have helped me if I'd been able to talk to someone who understood and who could explain what homosexuality was. I couldn't talk to anyone in the community where I grew up. They were nice people, but they were all in Dad's congregation. I couldn't have talked to my Mum's family, because they're even more religious. It might have been helpful if I could have got in contact with someone through my secondary school.

When Dad and I were in West and Wylde, a gay bookshop in Edinburgh, he found a children's book about a gay father and his roommate. Dad asked if he should get it for Stuart and Sheila, but I said it was a bit late as they were fourteen and fifteen at the time. It would have been good for me to have had a book like that when I was younger, but only if my Dad had given it to me and said, 'Look I'm gay. Here's something to read to help you understand it.'

When I was eleven, things started to go badly wrong between my parents. My Dad had been having doubts about his faith and decided to leave the church. The reason he gave to his congregation was that he was having a nervous breakdown brought on by stress. But during this time, I overheard an argument between my parents, during which Dad told Mum that he was gay. Mum was very upset. I didn't tell anyone that I'd heard that conversation, not even my brother and sister. Shortly afterwards, my Mum and Dad split up. My brother and sister weren't told why. Even though I knew, I kept it to myself.

We moved to Aberdeen and Dad moved to Edinburgh. Leaving the place where I grew up traumatized me just as much as the divorce. It's a beautiful area. I love it there and miss it terribly. I still think of it as my home. But neither of my parents felt they could stay in the area any more. No one in the congregation knew why they split up. My Mum thought they blamed her, and they probably did. Dad was their minister, and to this day they still call him Reverend MacNeish and ask him to say grace when he goes to visit. He's never been out to them and thinks there's no point telling them. They don't say anything against gay people, but they just wouldn't understand. It would give them too much of a shock.

After the split, I lived with my Mum and Stuart and Sheila. My Mum wouldn't let us visit my Dad's house in Edinburgh. Dad used to come up to Aberdeen or meet us at my Gran's house. When I was thirteen, I learned that Dad was living with a man named Andrew. I met Andrew at my Gran's house when he came with Dad, and for some reason I didn't like him at first. I think I was jealous that he was with my Dad and I wasn't.

One day, when my brother and sister were still getting over the trauma of the breakup, my Mum was in a bad mood and said to us, 'Oh by the way, your father is gay.' Because of the way she said it, they were very distressed about it. Part of the reason I hadn't told them was to protect them, because I knew they wouldn't understand. It wasn't the right time. Anyway it was up to my Dad to tell them, not my Mum or me.

It affected my brother most. He'd met Andrew before and really liked him, but he hadn't worked it out for himself that Dad was gay. For some reason, he focused on the fact that he'd held Andrew's hand. He kept saying, 'But I held Andrew's hand', as if he would be contaminated by that. He cried himself to sleep every night for weeks. He was confused, because in the playground the kids call gay people perverts and he thought that meant Dad was a pervert. However, after a few months, he came to accept it and he was happy being with Andrew. He never said he didn't want to see Dad. Both my brother and sister have totally accepted Dad's sexuality now. They don't even think about it any more.

After my Mum told my brother and sister, I said to Dad, 'By the way, Mum's told Stuart and Sheila that you're gay.' He looked at me and asked, 'Did she tell you then?' I said, 'Yeah, but I've known for about three or four years.' He was very surprised and asked how I'd worked that out. I said I just knew. Later, I asked him if he'd always known he was gay and why he went into the Free Church and why he got married. He said he was trying to hide it from himself. He knew when he was really small, but he didn't admit it to himself.

I wish that I'd talked to my Dad about it at the time to give him some support. I don't think he had much. It would have been easier for both of us if we'd talked about it then. He came out to Mum first, then to Gran and his family. He didn't get any support from them. He was in a gay Christians' group, which must have given him some support. That's where he met Andrew. There wasn't a long time between Dad coming out and meeting Andrew.

It gradually became intolerable at home with Mum. I left for good when I was sixteen and stayed with a friend for two weeks, because I didn't know whether or not Dad would want me with him. I went to visit him in Edinburgh and I was so happy when he asked me to come and live with him. He and Andrew had to find another flat, because their flat only had one bedroom. I moved in with them and that was great. We got on really well. My brother and sister stayed with Mum. They have more divided loyalties than I have because they get on better with Mum than I ever did. They're quite happy living with her. I don't think her sulking really works on them. They come down as often as they can to see Dad and me – about every two weeks.

After they split up, Mum didn't want us to see Dad, but complicated things by changing her mind all the time. At first she said we couldn't come to Dad's house and could only see him when he came up to visit. Then she allowed us to come down for the day, but we couldn't stay the night. When I was living with Dad, she tried to get a court order to stop Stuart and Sheila seeing Dad. It was horrible, because it would have stopped them seeing me as well. In court, the sheriff testified that they shouldn't see Dad because of Dad's gay lifestyle. Dad appealed and won, and then they were allowed to see us.

When Dad and Andrew split up, Mum tried to prevent Stuart and Sheila from staying with Dad, saying that Dad was between partners and that they'd be corrupted. She thought he would make us gay. It didn't make any sense, considering that she didn't want them to stay when he did have a partner. She never even met Andrew. Her main objection to letting my brother and sister see my Dad was Dad's sexuality. That's the reason she gave. However, I'm sure she would have found another reason if he hadn't been gay. I don't know what she thinks. They haven't said one word to each other for years.

Having a gay father has not influenced my sexuality, apart from the fact that I can be more open with my Dad than most people can with their parents. I can talk with him about my relationship with my boyfriend. If I do fall in love with a woman, then I wouldn't be particularly bothered about it. At the moment I'm heterosexual.

When I came to live with Dad, I met his gay friends. I thought they were all really friendly. I liked being around them. There was a nice atmosphere and I felt comfortable. I was never worried about being around gay people. Sometimes I go with my Dad to gay bars. There are some women there, but the bars are for men really. I feel fine there. My Dad doesn't go to many things, but we went to the Gay Switchboard ball and the World AIDS day events. There are a lot of gay people on those.

I don't remember ever having anything against it. I don't know why I accepted Dad's sexuality so easily. I've always been accepting like that. When something happens, even if it's a shock, I always think there's nothing I can do about it, so I may as well accept it. Because I love my Dad so much and have always been close to him, it's been no problem for me. My Dad doesn't try and say what I can and cannot do. Dad and I are very close. We have a good laugh together. We can talk openly about many things. I think we're closer now than we would have been if my parents had stayed together. We're good friends as well as being father and daughter. I always hold hands with my Dad. People probably think I'm going out with a much older man.

A year ago, Dad and Andrew split up. Dad's with Gordon now, who's really nice. They don't live here all the time. They live between Gordon's and here. I still see Andrew as much as I can. It's sad they've split up. I started to feel that Andrew was a parent to me. I didn't ever foresee Dad and Andrew splitting up. I saw Andrew as family. We're the only family that Andrew has besides his brothers and sisters. Andrew was really upset, because it's so difficult for a gay man to find a family and have kids round. My brother and sister still see him as well.

I don't necessarily think of family as blood relations only. I think of family as people that you love and trust and who are friendly to you. My father, my brother and my sister are definitely close family. But so are Gordon, Andrew and a lot of my Dad's friends. I think of them as family more readily than I think of my relations and my Mum as family. I don't think of my Mum as family, not now.

Gordon really likes having us around. I suppose it might put off some gay men who want to go out with my Dad if they knew he had children. I can't think of any of my Dad's gay friends who are interested in becoming fathers. But Dad's been lucky with both Gordon and Andrew. It's a bit easier, because we don't live with Gordon and I'm with my boyfriend most of the time.

Being a father isn't great for my Dad's image. Dad likes to look good. When we go together to the supermarket and I call him Dad, he tries to shush me up, saying, 'Don't call me Dad.' He's serious when he says that, but he can laugh about it too. He thinks men won't look at him if they know he's got a daughter, that they won't think he's gay.

Dad has a different kind of problem when he's out with my brother. Stuart looks older than he is and is very good looking. Dad looks obviously gay. He and Dad walk down the street holding hands and give each other a kiss goodbye in the train station. My Dad said himself that he can see people looking, and thinking, 'That's dodgy, what's that man doing with that little boy?'

I never thought it was necessary to go around announcing that my Dad's gay. With anyone I've been close to, I've let them know. The only person I told at secondary school was my best friend. I wasn't particularly close to anyone apart from her. I didn't make a big thing about it. I just let people know naturally. When friends came to the house, I'd say, 'That's Daddy and Andrew's room.' I'd talk about Dad and Andrew living together, about going places with them. I let people work it out for themselves. I thought of it as pretty normal, so I talked about it as if it were normal. I've always got upset when people make jokes about gays and I'd say, 'I don't want you to talk about it in front of me.' Surprisingly, there weren't a lot of jokes, probably because people did work out the situation. No one was really shocked.

I've had some bad reactions. My best friend from Aberdeen has a horrible boyfriend. I don't know what she's doing with him. She told him a funny story about Gordon and Dad, making it obvious that they were gay. The boyfriend jumped up and said, 'God, your dad's a fucking poof.' I was shocked and went out of the room. I didn't like him anyway, but after that I didn't want to be around him at all. He made it even worse by saying, 'I know there's some people around like that, but I thought it only happened in America.'

This year I'm working in a little cafe, just me and the two owners. They've made a few derogatory remarks about gay people, but stopped when I turned away and started doing something else. What bothers me is that they're such nice people. I don't know how to deal with them being nice and being bigoted all at the same time. I don't how they didn't work out that Dad's gay. They must be so naive, as Dad looks obviously gay with his short hair and moustache.

My Mum's family don't know and it's pointless to tell them. They don't even have a TV. If you iron on a Sunday, they go mental. They're just like that. They'd either shut it out or say my Dad was wicked and forget about him. I see them occasionally, but he doesn't have contact with them.

In my Dad's family, none of my aunties and uncles like my Dad since he's come out. They think we are both weird. My Dad and I don't have much to do with them. They're polite to my Dad, except for one cousin who has had a violent reaction. She's spiteful and ignores him. If they're eating dinner together and he asks her to pass the butter, she pretends she hasn't heard. He used to try and give her a hug or touch her. He would deliberately talk to her and look her in the eye. She just looked away. My Dad doesn't make an effort now.

My Gran, Dad's mum, has only come to Edinburgh once to visit my Dad since he has been living here, and then only for an hour. I persuaded them to come to the house. My Gran came with my aunt and they sat in the kitchen with their coats on. She doesn't feel she has to make the effort to come here. It doesn't upset me that I don't see Gran, but it upsets me that Dad's relations ignore him.

Some of my friends try to prove that they don't mind about my Dad being gay. Out of the blue, they will say something like, 'Oh, isn't it terrible the Church won't let gays be priests.' It just makes it worse. It's patronizing. I don't want people to condone my Dad's lifestyle. If they accepted it, they wouldn't say anything about it. I wouldn't say out of the blue to a friend, 'I don't mind that your parents split up and that you live with your mum.'

My boyfriend really likes my Dad. He's met both Andrew and Gordon. He accepts them completely. Or if he doesn't, he keeps it to himself. He's not used to being around gay people. Once we were going to a ceilidh for Gay Switchboard and he did say, 'Oh no, what do I do if a man asks me to dance?' I said, 'Don't worry. A man won't ask you to dance.' It's obvious that he's not gay.

Even though I tease my Dad about being a granddad, I don't particularly want to have children myself. I don't think I'd like to get married. I would live with someone. I lived with my boyfriend for about six months, but I don't think there's any point in getting married. I don't really agree with marriage.

The only disadvantage to having a gay dad are those people who can't accept it. It hurts me when people are homophobic, because I think how much I love my Dad and Gordon and Andrew and all those people I know who are gay. Sometimes I get upset and feel like I've betrayed my Dad if I don't say something to challenge homophobia. But I can't go round being a crusader all the time. My Dad went on Gay Pride and I would have liked to go with him. I feel a sense of solidarity with my Dad and I want to show people that I do.

Everything about having a gay father is an advantage. I've met lovely people. I wonder how many people with straight parents have as much love as I do and are as happy as I am with my Dad. I've always been broad-minded, but having a gay father has made me even more broad-minded. I can accept people for what they are. I don't worry about people's sexuality. Whether you love a man or a woman should not affect the way people think of you. I don't see how people can say who you should love or try and define love. Having a gay dad has made me realize that love can manifest itself in so many different ways. I vaguely felt all this before, but the reality of having a gay father has undoubtedly shaped my views.

EIGHT

Emily

Emily is twenty-one, the oldest of four sisters. Her parents separated when she was eleven. A year later, her mother came out as lesbian and has been living with her partner, Stasha, for the last ten years. Emily went to boarding schools and didn't have the experience of living in a lesbian family. Emily herself is a lesbian and is in a committed relationship with a woman.

Do you know what a lesbian is?

Mum came out to me and my sister, Jai, when I was twelve. We were sitting in the car and Mum said, 'Do you know what a lesbian is?' We didn't have much of an idea at all. Mum then said, 'Well, I'm a lesbian.' Jai and I just said, 'Oh right, fine.' Mum went on to say that we shouldn't talk to school friends and people in the village about it. She was trying to protect us, but I didn't understand the social significance and stigmatization attached to being a lesbian.

We were living in Hampshire in a small village. My Dad was teaching at a posh boarding school in the village. All the members of staff lived in the village and their kids went to the school. Everyone knew each other. Dad was the favourite schoolteacher and a surrogate father for many of the kids at the school. He was seen as a jolly and helpful man.

We had a different view of him within the family. He had had a couple of mental breakdowns and was abusive towards Mum, which no one in the school or village knew about. Mum tried to leave him three times. Each time he pushed himself to the edge of a nervous breakdown and she went back to him. When I was eleven, Mum finally left for good. Dad was seen as the victim by people in the school. My sisters and I were left with my Dad, but six weeks later Dad had a nervous breakdown and disappeared for several weeks to a mental hospital. My two youngest sisters went to live with my aunt. Mum collected Jai, and

I stayed on at Dad's school as a boarder. We were spread out round the country and it was very confusing, because we were unsure of each other's whereabouts.

I went through a short but intense phase of hating Mum. As far as I was concerned, she was the cause of my family falling apart. I felt very alone – I didn't have a home any more, didn't know where my parents were, didn't know where my sisters were, didn't have any friends left. This phase of anger with Mum passed and I got very angry with Dad. This was the context in which I naively told some staff at the school that Mum was a lesbian. It was a big mistake and turned into a major village scandal. I ended up leaving the school because of the homophobia that emerged, though there were other reasons as well. I came north to live with Mum for a year.

The five-year-long custody case

Dad initiated a custody case after he got out of mental hospital. He wanted us back and thought he was in a position to care for us. He didn't believe he'd ever been mentally ill. He claimed he'd just been reacting to my mother, that she'd pushed him over the edge.

The case turned into one of suspected abuse. Mum was scared of what Dad might do to us, based on her experience of his abusive behaviour towards her. He'd never abused me, but I've always been worried about his relationship with one of my sisters. Mum told the social workers how worried she was about us and when I was about thirteen, we were put on the at-risk register.

Up until the last year of the case, it had felt like the authorities were on our side – on the side of Mum and us four sisters. Even though they weren't coming up with revolutionary results, they were supportive. While they were investigating the allegations of abuse made against Dad, they were concerned about our safety and hadn't been interested in what Mum was.

When I was nearly sixteen, a court welfare officer came along and interviewed all four of us sisters as well as Mum. She then said she'd better go and interview our father. Mum tried to dissuade her, saying, 'He's three hundred miles away. As soon as you meet him, you'll be charmed. You'll take his side, and you won't believe a word the kids told you.' As far as I was concerned the authorities were meant to be representing my view in court, which had nothing to do with what my

Dad thought. I knew he thought I'd been brainwashed by Mum and that I was in danger from her. I was in a lot more danger when I was around Dad. He is emotionally unstable and a big emotional manipulator, a real guilt-tripper.

The court welfare officer went off to talk to Dad and came back with a report which predictably said the major issue was the risk to our safety from Mum being a lesbian. She used words that my father had already repeatedly said to me – that I'd been brainwashed by Mum and that my sisters were at risk of being influenced by both of us. She wrote that I was idolizing my mother and that I was gay because Mum was, and that if I were taken out of Mum's care, I would no longer be lesbian. I became sceptical about authorities and people who claim to help.

There were a lot of controversial issues involved in that court case – suspected abuse, lesbianism, Dad's mental health. Mum says that her sexuality was a minor issue, which is probably a more accurate analysis than my memory. But the way lesbianism was dealt with had a major effect on my acceptance of my sexuality. That is why I remember it as a big deal in the custody case. After hearing the welfare officer's report, I started feeling that my sexuality was subversive, that I was different because of my sexuality.

The custody case went on for four years. In the end, Mum got sole custody when I was nearly seventeen. Dad got access rights. She never contested his right to see us.

My own sexuality

I was about nine when I started thinking that I was attracted to women. My first affair was with a woman at Dad's school in Hampshire. I'd gone back from the north and was a boarder for two terms, because I was on the at-risk register and wasn't allowed to live with Dad. The whole school knew about my affair. It was a huge scandal. The custody case was going on and the headmaster felt he had to protect Dad, so I was asked to leave. I was indignant at the time, but looking back, it was actually the right decision for me.

I left that school and went to a boarding school in Yorkshire with my sister, Jai. I was not out at school. I was terrified of anyone guessing my sexuality and covered up as much as I could. Evidently I was successful, because none of them guessed at the time. One of the typical sixth-form conversations the girls used to have was what if one of us was a lesbian.

I used to think it was directed at me, but I realize now that it wasn't. I was so worried about discovery that I made sure one girlfriend called herself by a different name every time she rang. I was also extremely heterosexually promiscuous. That was the way I coped at the time. I don't judge myself about it. I'd much rather have been brave enough to come out, but I couldn't have done at the time. Since I left school, I've been determined to be out. My old school friends have all been great about it. Most of them were upset that I'd deceived them.

Now I'm in a long-term committed relationship. Joy's the first person I've made plans with. We have a level of security that you get when you know you're going to be together for a lot longer. I've never felt that kind of permanency before.

On the edge

I've been to places in my head where I felt like I was on the edge. When I left school I went through a hard patch. I was very lonely, made suicide attempts, ended up on different medications and had to go and see a shrink at the hospital. I used to self-mutilate. I got addicted to cutting myself up. It lasted for four years, when I was about fifteen till about nineteen. I'd never do it again, though I still think about it. It was a coping mechanism. I have an addictive personality. Most of my addictions have been self-destructive, but that's the nature of addiction. A lot of my life I've had it really hard and sometimes the only way to deal with it is to express it in unconventional ways.

Most of it was to do with different forms of abuse that I've experienced. I wouldn't say that any of it was to do with my Mum being a lesbian. But some of it was to do with internalized homophobia. I was really angry that my sexuality had caused so many problems socially. I couldn't do anything about being a dyke and I couldn't change my situation. I couldn't make people listen. I didn't have any other outlet for that anger. I'd had one experience of homophobia and there was no way it was ever going to happen again. The only way that I could ever get rid of any of those feelings was to take it out on myself. It's something that you only understand if you've actually done it. There's a feeling of relief and a sense of letting something go when you cut yourself. It's masochistic, but it's really relieving, it feels good and it's effective. It would have made a huge difference if I'd lived with Mum, but my philosophy of life is that I don't wish anything had been any different, because I like who I am now and I like where I am – take away any part of my life and I wouldn't be here. There's no point wishing for a different life.

The reason I stopped cutting myself is that I woke up and realized it wasn't helping me at all. My girlfriend at the time was incredibly unsympathetic. It was a very short, relatively insignificant relationship, but her reaction made me wonder why I was doing it. In addition, I got a job where I had to wear a short-sleeved uniform. People used to see the scars and I was mortified. That motivated me to stop.

Lesbian daughter–lesbian mother

I'm a dyke. I define myself as a dyke. If Mum were forced to classify herself, she would say she is a lesbian or that she is gay. But given the choice, she would prefer not to label herself. That's a cop-out to me, but I can't judge her for it. I'd rather that she call herself lesbian, because it's important for me to have that identity. Mum's not into categories. She believes that everyone is fundamentally bisexual. I think there is no clear-cut divide. Sexuality should be on a continuum rather than put into distinct categories, but I'd still rather she called herself a lesbian. It doesn't matter so much any more and when it did really matter to me, she did call herself a lesbian.

Because of the way lesbianism was dealt with in the custody case, I needed to prove to myself that my sexuality was my own, that it wasn't to do with Mum. In the welfare officer's report, Mum was accused of influencing me. I was told that it was just a phase, that it wasn't my decision. It's been important for me to realize that I was attracted to women before I even knew about Mum. As early as age nine, I was on a primary school wildlife trip and I wrote a love note to one of the female residential teachers there. That's a bit of evidence that I'm not a lesbian just because Mum is.

I know a lot of people with lesbian mothers and I've done research on it for my women's studies course. You can't generalize about what effect it has on kids, but I've never found any evidence that it influences the sexuality of the children. It really helped me accept my sexuality. It's made a big difference. I am happy with my sexuality and I feel really calm. I don't feel I've got anything to prove any more.

Having a lesbian mother has made it easier, because there's an acceptable role model for me. Mum has always been my ally. She is like me and she understands me. Her life experience is similar to mine. For quite a while, she was the only out lesbian that I knew. She's been a good mother, has done brave things and deserves to be happy. She says she is happy. I have felt really close to her. In the last three years, Mum and I have been away for two weekends together and had a really good time. Both times we went out and searched for the lesbian bars in the area and went dyke-spotting.

Whenever my friends, most of whom are dykes, find out I've got a lesbian mother, they always think I'm really lucky, which I am. But there are downsides to it when you're a lesbian yourself. It doesn't mean that she has no problems with my sexuality. She said recently that a lot of satisfaction in her life has come from having kids. She believes that having children in a straight relationship is an easier experience, and that it's very difficult to have them in a lesbian relationship. She's lived for a decade as a heterosexual family and a decade as a lesbian family. In the heterosexual family, she was not as happy personally but it was better for raising children.

I've had a few problems getting Mum and her partner to recognize the commitment and seriousness of my relationship with Joy. I tell them, 'This is someone who is going to be in my life for a long time. Treat her as a daughter-in-law.' They're backing off, because every time they've got to know one of my girlfriends, six months later they've had to meet a new one. They find it hard to take me seriously.

Mum admitted to being more critical of my girlfriends than she is of Jai's boyfriends. Because Jai is straight and Mum is lesbian, Mum feels she's got to prove to Jai that she's not anti-men or hostile to her and her boyfriends. It's important to Mum that Jai feels able to talk to Mum about her relationships. Because I'm a lesbian, she can be very critical of my partners in the same way Mum would be with Jai if Mum were straight. It's a weird kind of logic. At first I thought, 'Oh great, cheers Mum. Thank you!' But it was good to hear her spell it out. I don't like it and I wish that she wouldn't do it, but it makes sense and at least she is honest with me. I appreciate that. That's the most that she can give me. She's trying to protect me when she criticizes my girlfriends. I know that she'd support me and help me as much as she could, if needed. Still, it would be nice to hear her say how great it is being a lesbian.

Mum and I have such different lifestyles and such different political views now. Mum's become a lot more liberal. I've got to respect it but I don't like it, and it's put a bit of a wedge between us. Mum used to be what I would call radical. She was very politically active, especially in the years before she came out, when I was about ten or eleven. I admired her for that and I wanted to copy her. She was a role model for me then. I took on that political aspect and got into all sorts of left-wing and human rights groups.

Mum has spent eight years working her way up the social services ladder. She's become a career woman, a professional. I've watched her lose a lot of compassion and political awareness that she used to have. She was never on the scene, which I can understand because I hate it myself, but she used to be out and proud. She doesn't smile as much as she used to. She doesn't have as much fun. She doesn't go on Gay Pride. One day I want to get her there. That would be an uplifting experience for me, and I think for her as well. She won't go while she's working, I know that. She has made mistakes and often says that she wants me to be angry with her. She worries about my lack of anger and thinks that I should be expressing some. There were times when she wanted to protect me but didn't. I think she blames herself a lot.

Mum and I have grown apart, but my relationship with her hasn't fallen apart. There's no big event that's made it deteriorate. I used to rely on her and be really close to her. When I was addicted to self-mutilation, I felt like I could not turn to her. I then lost the only support that I'd ever had. It's through no fault of hers or mine really, it's just the way it happened. Her partner moved in and they built a home together at the same time as I went away to a new boarding school. I felt really excluded from that. However much they tried, spending only three months of the year there just didn't make me feel part of it.

A married couple
Mum met Stasha about a year after she left my Dad. They've been together for nearly ten years now. I started getting to know Stasha the year I lived with them when I was twelve, but I've never lived with them since. They're madly in love and are good for each other. They make each other happy. They're a family. It is difficult for me to feel comfortable in something I've never felt a part of.

Stasha was a straight feminist. Mum's the only woman she's ever been out with. It was love at first sight and about two years later they moved in together. Stasha never expected to be going out with a woman or to have a family. I've really appreciated her generosity and commitment to Mum and the sacrifices she has made. However, my relationship with Stasha has not been good. We have big communication problems, which has put Mum in a difficult position. I'm not blaming anyone. It's just circumstances – the fact that I wasn't there and Stasha was. Stasha thinks that I was jealous because she took my place in Mum's life. That is a pile of crap, because I wasn't there anyway. I was close to Mum, but I didn't have the experience of living with her that Stasha's had. My version of it is that I went through an angry, rebellious phase, during which I was suspended from school several times, ran away from school and used to cut myself. I would come home with huge scars on my arms. Every time I did it, it hurt Mum, though that wasn't my objective in doing it. Stasha was the one who was there dealing with Mum's tears and anger. She's protective of Mum and it seemed to Stasha that I was doing it on purpose. Stasha's been making more of an effort to get to know me now that I'm no longer hurting Mum. Equally I've had more time for her as I've matured and become less self-engrossed.

It was too late for Stasha to take on a parenting role with me, but she has with my two youngest sisters. She is their parent, financially and emotionally. Abby has lived with Stasha since she was six. For Abby, Mum and Stasha are her parents. She thinks they're a pain in the arse most of the time! That's just the way it is! I envy Abby having grown up in a stable, woman-orientated household. That is totally alien to me. I've moved around so much as a kid.

I respect Mum and Stasha's relationship and their commitment to each other. But they've turned into a closeted couple. They want as few people to know as possible. I can understand it, but I don't really like it. I know lesbian couples who've been together for many years and who lead a lifestyle which I would aspire to much more than I do Mum's and Stasha's. I admire a more lesbian-orientated lifestyle, not necessarily on the scene, but just more out.

Who counts as family?
I count my Mum and Stasha and my three sisters as my immediate family. When I talk about going to see my family, I mean my Mum and her partner. Their home is the family home, even though I don't feel an integral part of it.

My Dad has got to count as family, though I don't like him very much. He's a prat and not a particularly likeable or harmless one. I don't count his new wife, Joanna, as family. Joanna is older, extremely Christian and does not understand lesbians and gay men at all. She knows that I'm a dyke and she knows that Mum's a dyke, but she's never acknowledged it.

I'm consciously working on getting closer to all my family apart from my Dad. I haven't lived with Abby since she was four, except for a year. Beth and I are getting on better now. I used to be much closer to Jai than I am now. She was the only one I've lived with more than I haven't. We went to the school in Yorkshire together for three years. I still find being apart from her very hard.

Having kids

One day I'd like to have my own family. If I were straight, I would probably end up pregnant accidentally within the next few months. I have an irrational desire to be pregnant now. However, I'm only twenty-one and Joy's twenty-three. I'm in the middle of a degree and poor. I console myself with 'one day'. The main problem is that I only want a girl. I don't like myself for it, because I can't justify it ethically. But that's what I know about myself. I've thought about adopting or fostering children, if I can find somewhere that's open-minded enough to let lesbians foster. I hate heterosexual sex. When I'm ready to be a biological mother, I'll have a good male friend donate his sperm rather than have sex with him.

Joy and I have very different ideas on lesbian parenting. Joy thinks the kid will have enough to deal with not having a dad. She wouldn't want to make her lesbianism explicit outside the home. I'd want us both to be known as the parents, but I'd be sensitive to what the child wanted. My sister, Beth, is proud to have both Mum and Stasha go along to her school and be out, whereas Abby would rather avoid the situation. It's a difficult one. When Joy and I get closer to agreeing, that's the time to have the kid.

NINE

Claire and Jane

Claire is thirty-three and grew up in a small Sussex village with her two younger brothers and her sister, Jane. Their parents divorced when Claire was eight. They lived with their mother and visited their father on weekends and holidays. Her mother had relationships with women, but didn't tell Claire she was lesbian until Claire was sixteen. Claire has four children and lives with her partner, William. They've chosen not to be married.

Jane is twenty-five and is Claire's younger sister. She has always lived with her mother and has never had the experience of living with a mother and a father. Although there were women living in their house most of her childhood, she didn't know her mother was lesbian until she was fifteen. Jane lives on her own with her two children who are aged three and eighteen months.

The divorce

Claire: My parents didn't have a very happy marriage. My Dad was a strong, dominating character, just like Mum's father.

Jane: I can never understand how my Mum and Dad got together. It's completely alien to me to think that they were attracted to each other. After they married, Mum got stronger and developed her own ideas that weren't the same as Dad's. Before I was born, Mum fell in love with a woman friend who lived nearby. When they'd go out for the day, Mum found that she wanted to be with her all the time. She talked to Dad about it, because she didn't understand what was happening to her. They tried to work it out together.

Claire: Dad believed strongly in marriage, and at one time considered trying to keep it going under any circumstances. But my Mum felt that the marriage wasn't working and that it would be best to end it. Years later, she told me that she felt that her relationships with women had always been happier and more satisfying than her relationships with men.

My Dad insisted on joint custody, which gives him some legal rights. My Mum had day-to-day care of us, but she was happy for Dad to see us. We had a lot of contact with him. For our sakes, they always managed to get on and be friendly. When they first divorced, he used to come back home and Mum would go away for the weekend. He and his new wife had the spare room, which they decorated to their own taste. The next stage was a caravan in the woods, where they'd come and stay. My Mum might or might not be around, but we were under Dad's care. We started visiting my Dad in London, because he and his wife didn't like to stay in the caravan in the winter. For a long time, my Mum used to drive us to an arranged point halfway between home and London, where Dad would pick us up. When we got old enough, we used to go up on the train and my Dad would meet us at the other end.

My Dad is very honourable and supported us financially for twenty-one years. He gave the house to my Mum and then he maintained us and her. She never worked. We were very lucky, because a lot of women get no maintenance payments.

Jane: I blamed myself for years. I was the youngest child and I thought they got divorced because four kids was just too much. It wasn't until I was sixteen that I realized that wasn't the case.

Claire: I spent a lot of my childhood wishing that they would get back together. Even though Dad remarried shortly after the divorce, I didn't accept that they weren't going to get back together. I couldn't understand why he didn't live with us all the time.

Jane: Dad took the blame for the divorce. He kept Mum's secret, if you like, from her family, who didn't really know the situation. Looking back, I think that was a noble and decent thing for him to do. He cares a great deal about her and that's why he didn't want to cause any unpleasantness.

Claire: My Dad never once mentioned anything about my Mum's sexuality. He and my Mum both felt that it was in our best interests for us not to know. They decided not to tell anyone the real reason the marriage had irretrievably broken down. At the time, she hadn't told her own parents that she was lesbian and it wasn't his place to tell them. My Dad suffered a lot at the hands of people who thought he was irresponsible for abandoning his wife when she was pregnant with his fourth child to go off into the arms of another woman. While still married to Mum, he started a relationship with his secretary. He was open about it with my Mum, as she was with him about her affair with the woman across the road. Once Mum told me about her sexuality, I let Dad know that I knew and he was pleased to put his side of the story across.

Secret girlfriends

Jane: There were always women living in our house. I didn't think anything of it until Mum told me she was lesbian. I'd thought they were Mum's friends or lodgers. Now that I'm much more aware of sexual relationships, it seems strange to think that I didn't ever wonder.

Claire: Mum allowed us to assume that the women living in our house were paying guests, lodgers or friends. She took a lot of trouble and time to make sure that we didn't become aware that there was more to their relationship than that. We had a big house and it was set up so that they appeared to have separate rooms. In one arrangement, they had adjoining bedrooms connected by a door at the back of a walk-in cupboard. In another, my Mum had the bigger room and the 'lodger' had a smaller box room off it with a bed in it. We were told the lodger slept there. But in reality it wasn't like that at all.

We were never allowed into my Mum's bedroom in the early morning. If we knocked, eventually the door would be opened a crack and she'd say, 'Yes? What do you want?' At the weekends when there was no need to get up early, there was an unspoken tension about disturbing Mum in her bedroom. It was different at my Dad's home, where we all jumped into his bed in the morning and lay there for as long as we could keep still. My Mum wasn't self-conscious about herself, but her bedroom was a private off-limits place. I couldn't understand it at the time, but now I know why.

Some of Mum's girlfriends I remember with more fondness than others. My Mum was our mother, but they were fairly involved, especially when we were younger. In lots of ways it was nice for Mum to have somebody around the place and to have support. We might have suffered more if she'd been a single mother of four children without emotional support.

Jane: Some of Mum's partners played an important role in my life. When I was quite little, there was one woman who I considered as part of the family. I remember her singing me songs and rocking me to sleep. Later on when I was seven and eight, there was another woman who was sweet but also stern. She had a brusque, jolly ha-ha, stiff-upper-lip personality. My brother and I got stroppy with her, because she used to be possessive about the garden and didn't allow us to have swing-ball games in the front. My Mum was never like that. She was very relaxed and we could do what we wanted. I don't remember the others well enough to say what sort of role they played in my life or how they acted with me. By the time I was at an age where I might have remembered it more, Mum didn't have permanent partners, just women who stayed a couple of nights a week and went out with her.

Claire: When I was in my early teens, I didn't understand why one of the women had such protective and jealous feelings towards my Mum. When anything happened, she was always right there, pushing us onto the sidelines, while she protected my Mum. We weren't able to comfort our Mum, because she was there first. I felt resentful of her and kept wondering what the big deal was. It's only with hindsight that I realize the depth and nature of their relationship and can put it into perspective. Perhaps her behaviour was natural within the terms of their relationship, but I didn't know that.

Jane: I'm not quite sure whether what Mum calls a lesbian is what I do. She always seems shocked when I suggest that she's having a sexual relationship with somebody. So I don't really see her as a practising lesbian. Her friends don't often stay over any more. It seems to me that she's got close girlfriends as I would class girlfriends, friends she spends time with, rather than one sexual partner.

Coming out to daughters

Claire: My mother didn't tell me she was lesbian until I was sixteen. We'd gone out for lunch to celebrate me leaving school and I was relating some wild rumours that were flying around about the school secretary and the youth club leader's wife. I didn't think there was anything much to it and was just gossiping. She thought I was hinting and leading her on to see what she would say, so she decided to take the plunge and tell me she was lesbian. But it was totally out of the blue for me. I hadn't been leading her anywhere and hadn't had an inkling that she might say something like that.

Jane: My Mum first told me she was lesbian when I was fifteen. She'd been out at a party and I'd been at home watching TV. At eleven o'clock I found myself in tears, though the film wasn't in the least bit sad. When Mum arrived home, she came in to talk to me and I asked her if she'd had a good time. She said she'd had a fight at the party at eleven o'clock and was in floods of tears. It all came out. She said, 'Have you ever thought there's something funny about your old mum?', and then told me that she was a lesbian. I'd never had a clue. I knew she had a lot of friends and that they stayed over, but I hadn't placed any significance on it. I thought it was like my own friendships with my best friends.

When she told me, I didn't think anything drastic. I was concerned that she was so upset, and anyway the word 'lesbian' didn't mean much to me then. It wasn't something I'd given any thought to. I had a brief dramatic reaction and wrote an entry in my diary which read: 'Oh God, what am I going to do? Why can't this family be like everybody else? God help me.' But really there are so many differences about our family that it just felt like one more. I didn't dwell on it and it didn't upset me.

Claire: Once she said it, a lot of things fell into place. She told me that the reason for letting us assume that her girlfriends were lodgers was to protect us. What we didn't know couldn't hurt us. I can see why she did it. We lived in a small village where rumours fly round and people get hurt. So she was doing it with our best interests at heart. I didn't blame her for not telling me earlier. It was her private thing. I think we were better off being protected. That's not necessarily the way I think things should be for people in that situation now. It's up to the individuals concerned. I don't really know what difference it would have made had we known. I might have felt burdened by it a bit.

Jane: Attitudes in our village were very conservative and small-minded. My mother stuck out like a sore thumb. She didn't want anybody to know except for her close friends. What she didn't like was the gossip, that all the village would be assuming things about her. People had stereotypes in the 1970s about vegetarians – that they would wear sandals, support CND and be butch, macho lesbians.

Telling others

Claire: Mum's sexuality doesn't come up with close friends very often. It's only when a friend confides in me something that's relevant that I would share something about Mum back. I've talked to my partner and other close family, but generally I don't drop it into the conversation. I got the feeling from Mum that it wasn't something that she wanted known about.

Jane: It's not something I would talk openly about with friends until they were close enough to be trusted, because there is so much prejudice against lesbians.

Claire: When she told me, it was a relief to her to have somebody to talk about it with. I don't really know if it was a secret. It's not a secret for her any more. Most of her friends and acquaintances probably know. She's not living with a partner and I don't know how many people would think twice to see a nearly sixty-year-old woman out with another woman.

Relationship with Mum

Claire: Soon after she told me, I went to live with my Dad to go to college in London. I was no longer at home for it to have a day-to-day effect on me. Eventually I had my own family and lived further away. As my sister grew older, she became Mum's confidante and support.

Jane: I'd always lived with Mum and never had the experience of living with both my parents. I was at home on my own with Mum since I was twelve. I was eight when Claire left home, one brother was at boarding school and then my other brother left when I was twelve. That's why Mum and I got so close. We're quite similar in a lot of ways and I agree with many of her beliefs. Finding out she was lesbian certainly didn't affect our relationship, which was strong anyway by the time she told me. I've accepted that my Mum is lesbian, but it's a slightly uncomfortable subject, if I'm honest. My mother is completely accepting of who I am as a person, and what I do. She doesn't want me to be anything that I'm not, which is really important to me.

Claire: Mum was relaxed and free and easy with us. She was a very loving, caring, accepting mother. She wanted the best for us, and she wanted for us what we wanted for ourselves, rather than imposing her own aspirations on us. This was in contrast to my Dad. If we didn't live up to his aspirations, then he found it difficult to accept us. She was a good mother, though sometimes a bit distracted by things in her life.

Being different

Claire: When you're a child, all you want is to be the same as everyone else. It's only when you're an adult that you revel in being different.

Many aspects of Mum's lifestyle that weren't anything to do with her sexuality made our family different from the norm. If I'd known she was a lesbian when I was a child, it would have been one more thing that made us different. I probably would have found it a burden knowing she was lesbian. I was already uncomfortable that my packed lunches were radically different from all my friends!

Jane: From an early age I knew that we were odd. It was odd in our village to be a macrobiotic and a vegetarian. It was odd to be into CND. Mum went on all the marches. It was odd not to have a TV when that's all everyone talked about at school.

Claire: I didn't have friends over, partly because of being away on weekends visiting Dad in London. But I wasn't totally comfortable bringing friends home because of Mum's lifestyle. She was heavily into diet, macrobiotics, wholefood, alternative lifestyles and self-sufficiency – a treat for Sunday dinner was a boiled egg. We ate what we were given, but I hated being different from my friends. I don't want my children to go through what I went through. I want them to feel comfortable inviting friends for tea and to feel that the food I'm offering is acceptable to their friends. That's important to me and I'm sure that's directly out of my childhood experiences. But I do want them to grow up respecting the fact that not everybody is the same and people do eat different things and live different lifestyles and that we must be accepting of that. I don't want them to suffer, but I want them to learn the right attitude.

I always wished that I had a family with a mum and a dad together like the majority of my friends. At the time, there was only one other girl in my school whose parents were divorced. Once I realized that my parents weren't going to get back together, there was a time when I wished for a different family. I didn't know then that Mum was lesbian, so I can't say it was anything to do with that.

Jane: All my life I've known that my family was not going to conform and be the same as my friends' families. I don't remember ever being singled out for being from a single-parent or divorced family when I was at school. Claire always says to me that when I was little I used to think everyone had a mum and a dad and an Emma – Emma being my Dad's wife's name. That was my norm. I was aware of being different, but I don't remember it ever being a problem for me.

Relationship with Dad

Claire: I always felt very close to my Dad and we enjoyed a loving relationship. If I confided in him about problems at home that I was unhappy with, such as not being able to take the right ingredients to school cookery classes, he tried to find a compromise solution without sitting in judgement on Mum's lifestyle. It's very easy for parents with different views to use their children as pawns in their own battles, but I think both my parents did a brilliant job of avoiding that sort of situation. I know my Dad felt very frustrated sometimes.

Jane: I never had a loving relationship with Dad and grew up without a father's love. That was the hardest thing for me to overcome from my growing up. I thought that he didn't care for me. That happened, not because he lived apart from us, but because of the kind of person he is. He was permanently disapproving, telling me that I was irresponsible and immature and that I wasn't reaching my achievements. Anything I did was wrong. That's how I interpret it.

If a girl doesn't have a good relationship with her father, it's quite hard to adjust to adult relationships with men. I would have liked the same type of love from a man that my Mum gave me. I don't know what it's like to be loved by a male. If I'd experienced that as a child, then I wouldn't have had so many problems with men. Now I feel that it's not so important and I can get on with him and just be myself. I'm not that concerned whether he approves of me or not, because I approve of myself. In recent years our relationship has improved as we've begun communicating better and sorting things out.

Effect on sexuality

Jane: After my Mum told me she was lesbian, I wondered if I was too. My mother's brother is gay as well. I did think that it could be hereditary and maybe I was going to be like them. When I was a teenager, I had lots of boyfriends. As soon as one got keen on me, I'd move on to the next one. I wasn't interested. In counselling, the theory was that I was trying to replace the love that I felt my Dad hadn't given me, that I was using sex with men as a way to find this love. Perhaps I was also trying to prove to myself that I wasn't a lesbian.

My Mum was cool about my sexual experimenting. When I was at college, from age seventeen, I was lodging above the garage at home and was quite independent. The first time I told her that I had slept with someone, she asked me if I'd been careful. Her theory was that she would rather I was safely doing it at home than in a ditch somewhere. She was understanding about everything. I suppose I did abuse her trust. I can remember instances where I was out all hours and didn't ring her and she was worried.

Claire: Mum told me she was lesbian in July. By September, I had met a boyfriend who was keen to sleep with me. I'd always said that I'd wait to have sex until I'd found the man I was going to marry. At first I said no to him, but very soon agreed. It's hard to know whether I would have held off if Mum hadn't told me, but knowing about her sexuality made me feel the need to find out about my own. I lost my virginity to him and found out. Perhaps all people wonder about their sexuality at times in their lives – it was definitely something that I wondered about at that time.

My Mum's sexuality has returned to haunt me with both my partner, William, and Dad. After I gave birth to my second child and my first was eighteen months old, sex wasn't high on my agenda. This caused a problem for William. One of the things he said to me was, 'You're not turning out like your mother, are you?' I think he felt rejected because our sex life wasn't all that it had been. It was a knee-jerk response to a situation he found difficult to cope with, but it hurt me a lot at the time.

About five years ago, my Dad and I were having a late-night heart-to-heart talk. The business of when I was living with him as a teenager came up. He had never allowed me to have friends, either girls or boys, in my bedroom. I had to entertain them in the living room with him sitting there behind the newspaper. He told me recently, 'With a mother like yours, what did you expect?' I was very upset by that. He couldn't trust me alone in my bedroom with a woman, because I might end up the same way as my mother. The only excuse I can give him is that he was much the worse for drink.

Repeating family patterns

Claire: I've never plucked up the courage to marry William. The marriage myth was blown apart in my childhood and I don't have any faith in marriage guaranteeing relationships. Having four children together, we're obviously committed to each other, but I don't feel that marriage as an institution has any benefits for me. It let me down as a child and I'm not prepared to go with it as an adult.

Although I never planned it that way, at times I've ended up being the only adult in the family, taking on all the roles and being there for the children. Circumstances have forced William to be away from home quite a lot for work. The children see him at the weekend when he's home, but then he's like a sugar-daddy, taking them out and buying them treats. I work part time from home, which means I'm never not at work. So when William is away, I have a lot of responsibilities and things don't happen unless I do them. I get to the end of my tether and the children suffer. If William were around, we'd be sharing the load and the children would get a better deal. It wasn't something I wanted for myself or for the children. It's interesting the way history repeats itself.

Jane: It's interesting that I'm on my own with my children just like my mother was. My first child was the result of an accidental pregnancy. I didn't want to be with the father. After I'd been on my own with the baby for six months, the father and I decided we'd try and live together. That lasted long enough for me to get pregnant with the second one. By the time I discovered I was pregnant, we were fighting all the time and we split up while I was still pregnant. He believes that the woman should do everything, while the man goes to the pub. Since I didn't grow up with a mother and a father, I don't really know what a father does in a family, because I've never witnessed it firsthand. I'd like it to be equal, not just the housework but everything. My dream is that the kids can go and talk to their father same as they talk to me.

I'm great friends with my kids' father. We see him often, but we get on better when we're apart. I'm not scared about bringing up children on my own without a dad. It happened to my Mum and I had a glorious upbringing. I don't relish being on my own for ever, because I need some love as well and somebody to love, other than children. I get flashes of the future and picture myself there, like Mum is, on my own. I wouldn't want to get so independent that I wouldn't be able to live any other way.

Lesbians having children

Claire: I'm not aware of lesbians with children apart from my mother, so I haven't had to think about it. I don't really see problems with it. In a lesbian partnership with children, there are two caring parents. What you haven't got is the male role model, same as in a single-parent family, but extended family or friends can perform that function for the child.

I've always had a relationship with my Dad and it's been important for me, so I guess there would be issues for a child who didn't have a dad at all. There are so many variations of the family today – the family itself is evolving. Life is complicated. But that's the way things are.

Jane: As long as it's a secure and steady, ongoing relationship that's going to last, I can't see any problem for the children. There are no guarantees in normal relationships. These days, they don't seem to last five minutes. In some ways, it appeals to me to have two women caring for a child. That child's going to be really loved.

Benefits of a different upbringing

Claire: The experiences of our childhood and our family environment has made the four of us more accepting of people generally. There's not much that we can't take on board. Compared to most children's lifestyles at the time, ours was wild. We got used to it, though it probably did take its toll. We had to adapt to two very different lifestyles. There were good and bad things about both.

Jane: It must have been good for me to have all those people around as a child. I got more adult attention than my Mum alone would have been able to give. There were always people around and they were interesting people as well – students and foreigners, with a mixture of lifestyles that I wouldn't have seen otherwise, living in a little village. Meeting a range of people gives you a wider outlook on the world. Having had such a different family has put me in good stead for life, really.

TEN

Kate

Kate is twenty-four. She has a younger sister, Claire, and a younger brother, Alistair. She grew up in the north of England and moved to rural Gloucestershire when she was a teenager. Her father left when she was seven. She didn't find out that both her mother was lesbian and her father was gay until she was fifteen.

Not one but two gay parents

My experience starts at the age of fifteen when my Mum told us that my Dad was gay and, two weeks later, that she was too. I'd had an inkling about my Dad. He had left us when I was seven and had never remarried. But I hadn't had a clue about my Mum.

Dad was always with men. When he came back at Christmas or when he came to see us for the day, there would always be a man with him. He used to have guys living in his house as lodgers. He never introduced them as partners. Once when I was thirteen and was staying the weekend with him, one of the lodgers gave up his bed for me. When I went down to wake Daddy in the morning, the lodger was in my Daddy's bed. I sensed that I was disturbing something when I walked in on them. I was mortified, but I denied it to myself.

But there was never any reason for me to believe our mother was lesbian. She'd always been a normal mum. She'd been married twice, she was interested in men and she'd had babies. When she was married to my father, she had me and then my sister, Claire. After my Dad left, my mother married Ken and had my brother, Alistair. Unfortunately, Ken died.

Before I learned about my parents' sexuality, my sister and I were already the oddest kids in our village. No one else had an upbringing like ours. After Ken died, we moved to Berkeley in Gloucestershire. It was so small you could drive past, blink and miss it. I hated it because

I'm a city girl at heart. We'd always been Northerners and I'd grown up in Yorkshire, Durham and Newcastle. We had no connection with Gloucestershire. Mum moved us into a mobile home, which was a terrible strain after living in houses all my life. At school, we were the only kids living in a mobile home and the only ones who were poor. We couldn't have what everyone else had, and I vowed to myself, 'I am not going to be like this when I grow up, never.' On top of all this, our family life wasn't great. There were a lot of arguments and we were always going to family counselling.

One day in the midst of a terrible argument, Claire shouted as usual at Mum, 'I'm going to phone Dad.' Out of the blue, Mum blurted out, 'He left. That's how much of a father he is. Didn't you know he was gay? He was off having affairs with men when I was pregnant with you, Claire. So much for him being truthful.' I violently denied it. I was saying to my sister, 'Don't listen to her, Claire. She's only trying to get at you.' Deep down I knew it was true, but I tried to pretend it wasn't. I wanted my father to be that perfect dad that all the other kids have. I didn't want a dad who's different, who's gay and who sleeps with men. I didn't know a lot about homosexuality then. We discussed it once with Mum after we'd calmed down and everyone was thinking clearly and not making irrational statements. She told us that he was born like that and that it's in his genes. She said he tried to be a father but he has always liked men, and that's just the way it is sometimes. We didn't talk about Dad being gay any more after that conversation.

Two weeks after she told us about our father, she sat my sister and me down. We'd just got in from school and were still in our school uniforms. She said, 'Claire, Kate, I've got something to tell you. Now, you've taken the news of your father so well, I want you to know that I'm gay too.' That was just too much. On top of everything else that made me different, I suddenly had two gay parents. It was just about tolerable to have one gay parent, but not two. The whole thing embarrassed me. I felt angry with both of them, especially my mother. I thought that they didn't have to be gay, that they'd chosen this lifestyle because they'd had so many letdowns. I was shouting at my Mum, 'How can you do this? Why do you have to put us through so much crap? Here I am, living in a mobile home, got a gay father, and now you're telling me you want to be gay as well. God, how much do I have to put up with you!' I wanted to punish and hurt her.

I couldn't talk to Mum about it when I was still living at home. I was hoping it would be a phase she'd get out of quickly. I was trying desperately to reassure myself that it was all right and to be calm about it. I was trying to persuade myself that it's my parents and there's nothing wrong with it. My Mum introduced us to Danny, her girlfriend. We were having a normal conversation, but all the time, I was looking at my Mum and Danny and thinking, 'Oh God no, not my Mum, this is so weird.' Now I realize, through talking to my Mum, that they didn't choose to be gay. That's just the way they are. Mum explained that when she and Dad got married, it was the 1960s and everyone got married at that time. Being gay was quite a hard thing then. So they didn't admit it to themselves.

Seeing mum and her partners

I got to understand Mum's sexuality by talking to her and seeing her with her partners. She and Alistair moved in with Danny and they lived together for four years. I never lived with them, because I moved out at the age of sixteen. When I went to visit, I'd see Danny and Mum sitting there in their armchairs, like very good companions. There was no discussion about their love for each other and how they were feeling. They were polite to each other. They didn't hold hands or kiss in front of me, which I don't think I could have dealt with straightaway. They broke me in to the lesbian lifestyle very gently over a period of four years.

Mum's relationship with her current partner, Jude, couldn't be more different. Jude and Mum are very open and they discuss their relationship with me. Mum will say, 'We don't see each other all the time, because I need my independence. Jude needs hers. Oh, we haven't seen each other for a week, have we darling?' They kiss and touch each other in front of me. Jude says, 'Hasn't your mum got lovely hair? Your mum's wonderful.' And they talk to me about my life, ask me why I want to get married. A few years ago, I had to live with my mother for a month, and that helped me learn an awful lot about the lesbian lifestyle.

Am I one too?

When I learned that both my parents were gay, what I needed to clarify was whether I am gay. I didn't ask Mum until I'd moved out of home and I was getting on much better with her. I asked, 'What about me? Are you sure it's not going to hit me when I'm twenty-five? Am I suddenly going to turn round and go, oh my God, that's it, I want a woman.' I was worried, because initially she'd said it's in your genes. I reasoned, 'Well, my genes are made up of you two, and you two are gay, so why aren't Claire and I like you two?' Then she said that both she and my father have known since they were young. She said you just know. She used to have a crush on her schoolteacher. I've never had anything like that, so that was some reassurance for me.

I think she'd be quite chuffed if I turned round and said, 'Mum I've met a woman.' I go through patches when I haven't got a man around, and I say, 'Oh God Mum, I'm sick of this boyfriend. He was a pain. I'm sick of men.' She always tries it on, 'Kate, why don't you try women?' It's all tongue in cheek, but I think she'd be quite pleased if I did.

Give me an old-fashioned man!

Call me old-fashioned, but I like a man who takes charge and looks after me. Because of the lack of a father-figure, I want a man to be a bit stronger than me. I always go for the same type – a man who's larger than life, has a big personality, is self-made and is very successful. Perhaps because my father was a failure and a pauper, I find such men highly attractive. It's what I want for myself. I'm completely materialistic.

My mother is not at all materialistic. I'd even say she's anti-materialistic. She has strong opinions about domineering men. She doesn't approve of the way I am with my boyfriends and is disappointed that I choose men so different from the people that she socializes with. I think she wants me to take a more leading role in my relationships with men, like the perfectly balanced equality she has had with Danny and Jude.

My Mum has influenced my views about men. She hated my last boyfriend. They're both domineering people and they clashed terribly. He was a pig, but he was a wonderful person as well. There were two sides to him, as there are to most people. When my mother criticized him to me, I began to think the way she did about him. That's when it finished. We would have been together a lot longer but for her. I'm glad I'm out of it, and I'm a better person for it. My Mum is good at making me more independent and teaching me that life isn't so bad without a man.

My mother at the front of Gay Pride

It is interesting to see how differently my parents handle their sexuality. They are absolute extremes. On the one hand, there's my mother who is flagrant about it, and even encourages me to try women, because she claims they're so much easier than men. On the other hand, there's my father who never says a word about it.

Since she's become a lesbian, Mum fits the dyke image perfectly in her dress-sense, her views, her personality. Every year, she goes on Gay Pride, and she's there at the front, with the biggest banner and the loudest T-shirt. She loves it. She's finding her youth again, doing these wacky, wild, off-the-wall things. It's a reaction against the boring, normal life she led for so long.

She's always been strong and independent. She had to be ever since Ken died and she found herself on her own raising three children. But since coming out, she's that much stronger. She's calmer as well, at peace with herself almost. She's got herself sorted out. A lot of women still think they need a man for fulfilment in life, but she doesn't. She's been so happy since she came out. For the first time in her life, she's had two very good, steady relationships. That's why I am genuinely happy for her. My one objection is that she's now far too opinionated. She's become an ardent feminist, and I think she goes overboard. She's become anti-men. She can't understand how other people feel. I'm not the same as her and she can't accept that I have different views.

Dad with blinkers on

When I was a little girl, I thought my Dad was great. I looked up to him. He was always saying, 'Let's go out and party. Let's go shopping. Come on Kate, we'll go and buy you a dress or do your hair.' My relationship with him deteriorated when I found out about his sexuality, mostly because he wasn't open about it. He's only ever talked about it once, when he came to pick us up shortly after my mother told us. He took us for a car journey and all he said was, 'I believe your mother's been going on about me. I did want to tell you myself one day.' I don't think he ever would have done.

I think that he feels a failure as a father-figure. He's very poor and can't provide for us money-wise. We're all doing much better than him. He probably feels that being gay has let us down in some way. He may be thinking, 'These girls must look at me and think I've got no money and I'm gay, what sort of father is he?'

He's quite camp. I don't think he's got a problem accepting he's gay in his own society. He's been doing it this many years and it's the way he is. He's happy being gay. He's clocking on fifty. By that age, you must have accepted yourself. On the other hand, Dad isn't the type to go on Gay Pride. He's a man with two heads. He puts a different one on for different social occasions. Perhaps he can't put the two together. He can be a gay man and he can be a father, but he can't be a gay father. My heart goes out to him. He's a very confused man. I don't really feel angry at him for being gay. I understand that that's not his fault. That's the way he is.

I do feel angry with the way he's gone about it. It was a terrible thing to have affairs when my mother was pregnant. That's very selfish. I don't understand why he took on the responsibility of a family if he knew he was gay. I don't understand why he wasn't prepared to fulfil the role of father once he had us. Every child needs a father and he never really has been a father to us. I feel disappointed in him. I don't think it's anything to do with him being gay, but emotionally he can't sort himself out. He's in turmoil all the time. He's never been settled in himself.

Except for that once, we've never talked about who he is. I tried to tackle him on it and he didn't want to talk about it. It's very sad, but I thought, 'Well, that's the way he is.' He doesn't talk about it to anyone. In nearly ten years of silence on the subject, I realize he is never going to say anything. He's going to pass away, without ever opening up to us. I only see him about twice a year, so it's easy for him to get away with it. It's not a real relationship. How can it be when he only gives part of himself to the relationship?

Coming out to friends

I don't go around shouting about my parents' sexuality wherever I am. Not everyone can take on board the fact that I have two gay parents. Initially I thought it was going to put people off me, so I used to not say anything until I had to. I've found that it's like a big secret that I'm keeping. If I'm seeing someone and there's a chance they may meet my parents, it's a big hurdle and I worry how I am going to get over it.

Danny was such a handy name, because Danny could be a man's name. I lived with one girl for ages and we'd talked about many things, but I hadn't told her my Mum was gay. One day, my Mum was coming to visit. While we were tidying up, I said to her, 'I've got something to tell you. You know I mentioned my Mum's partner, Danny? Well Danny's not a man, it's a woman.' This girl was so nice. She acknowledged how hard it was for me to tell her.

I only mentioned it to one person at the schools I went to in Gloucestershire. They're all very small-minded there and had no understanding at all. No one at my school even knew anyone who was gay. They used to joke about gays. They saw gays as people out there somewhere – as other. So to tell anyone would have been impossible. My boyfriend was the only person I told and he was great. It was lovely to have a bit of support, because it was a massive burden I was carrying. It wasn't until I'd moved into cities where people are more liberal that it became easier.

I went to Birmingham to go to university, where I met Brian who became my best friend. He is gay and I went to gay pubs with him and his gay friends. They thought having two gay parents was cool and trendy. Whenever Brian introduced me, he'd say admiringly, 'Kate's parents are gay. She's great.' Brian came to my graduation with my Mum and Dad. It was the first time I'd seen my father with someone else who was gay. He got on with him really well. I probably learned more about my father's lifestyle through going out to these gay pubs with Brian than I have from my father.

The burden has got lighter as I've grown up and talked about it more. I told my last two boyfriends on the first night – just got it over and done with. They were shocked for about five minutes and then that was it. There was no big build-up to telling them. My boyfriends are interested in me, not in my parents.

I'd like to get married
I want to get married, because I want to have something that I didn't have. I do want a conventional family. There's a deep feeling inside me which comes from growing up in a society which values marriage and the traditional family. At the same time, I admit I like my off-the-wall family. We're very different and unique, and I like that.

I would never get married unless I was completely sure, and I'd lived with the man for a very long time. I've been through a divorce, and the aftermath is horrendous. But my mother's opinions have certainly influenced me. She questions the reason for marriage. She can't see any point to it. With the high divorce rate, I can see what she means.

I'm only twenty-four. I couldn't even contemplate marriage for another five years. I couldn't give my life up yet. In my twenties, I want to be spoiling myself and making the most of my own time. What I plan to do is learn about myself emotionally. I want to be completely selfish, get my own things, and do what I want to do when I want to do it. When I've done that and worked really hard, I'll probably have some children and then go back to work.

What I've learned

The main thing having gay parents has done is help me understand gay society and changed my view of gay people. There isn't that much to understand, because they're normal people. It's just that they experience a lot of prejudice. If I hadn't had gay parents, I would have been carrying on like the rest of society, thinking they're in gay clubs and I'm not, and if it crosses my path then so be it. I wouldn't really have understood. My parents have given me hands-on experience, so to speak.

I watched Gay Pride on TV and I saw some people there with their parents, saying, 'My Mum's gay and I'm proud of it.' I'd like that to be me. I'd like to go and show my support for gay people. For most of my life, I thought my family was a real disaster and that having two gay parents was the ultimate embarrassment. While it's not your conventional kind of family life, it is a family. It's just a different kind of family. Gay people do have stable relationships and I can see how much happier and calmer my mother is now that she's lesbian.

ELEVEN

Mandy Allen

Mandy is twenty-four. She grew up in London, the only child of a lesbian mother. Her mother and father separated when she was one and Mandy's father had little to do with her as a child. Her mother has been open about being a lesbian throughout her life.

Everything was fine in my life until I was ten. Although my Mum and Dad had separated when I was one, I was too young to know about that. My Mum apparently told me that she was a lesbian when I was four. They were just words and I didn't understand what they meant. All my life my Mum's lesbianism has been normal to me.

I felt I was a special child. I had lots of mummies and people who loved me. I had loads of friends and loved playing and being with people. I was secure and confident, happy and bubbly, artistic and creative. Although I got on with a lot of people, I've always been very independent and even a bit of a loner.

From TV to court

When I was ten, Mum had been active in the women's movement for years and had been fighting hard for what she believed. She was one of the few lesbian mothers who were out at that time. This was 1980, and the subject of lesbian mothers was very hush-hush. Mum was invited to appear on a BBC programme called *Gay Life* to talk about being a lesbian mother. She asked me if I wanted to go with her, and of course I did. Ask any kid if they want to go on TV and they'll say yes. My participation in the programme was to swing on a swing and be Mum's daughter. I remember her sitting on a green corduroy cushion talking to the interviewer.

The TV programme changed my life. Three days later, my father started a custody case to take me away from my Mum. He'd found out she was a lesbian by watching the programme. Mum had never hidden it, but she had avoided the subject with him. My world went to pieces. It was the first time I'd seen my Mum out of control, in real pain. She was so frightened.

Mum did her best to keep some stability in our lives while this was going on and to protect me so I wasn't connected to the real craziness of it all. She never made me fear my Dad or tried to alienate me from him. She tried to explain the danger to me, because she knew it was possible that he would come and take me. Mum also warned the headmistress of my school that my Dad might try something.

And he did. He arrived at my school out of the blue. It was like a dream to me. I thought he'd come just to see me. I wanted to go out with him and have an ice-cream. But we were put in the library and he wasn't allowed to take me. The headmistress phoned my mother to say that my Dad had just arrived and was trying to take me out of school. She phoned the police, but found that she could only keep me in the building for an hour and then she would have to let him take me. They couldn't stop him legally.

I couldn't understand why they would think my Dad was doing anything wrong. I didn't realize he was trying to take me away from my Mum. There was no way I would have considered going with my Dad. I loved my Mum. I wanted to stay with her and I would have fought to be with her. Obviously I was very afraid. I didn't understand what was happening. Eventually the police got there. I stayed at school and he went off. He gave me 50p, and that was the last time I saw him until I was about twelve.

It was very frightening to see my Mum so distraught. The day Dad filed suit for custody, I came home from school and found Mum hyperventilating and crying. She had a look of desperation and crushed me in her arms. She was devastated. I had never seen her like that before. Mum is so well controlled and balanced. She has always taken responsibility for herself and introduced that to me at an early age. But at that point, I felt I had to protect her. I didn't see her as weak but as human.

My Mum was so determined not to let my Dad get me that she took me to America, intending to live there if she had to. But my Dad dropped the court case about three weeks after we got there. He must have realized that he didn't really want me to live with him. His motivations were not very clear and it was never that likely that he would succeed. He had had no real involvement with me for the first ten years of my life and had never paid any child maintenance. That was Mum's choice too, because she wanted to be independent and didn't want his money. My father's second wife certainly didn't want me. She was hostile to me throughout my childhood.

I flew back from the States on my own and stayed with Nan, my Mum's mother, for about two weeks. The stress of the court case had exhausted Mum so much that she needed a break, and she stayed on in the States. My Nan loves me very much, but she was naive and said some painful things to me, threatening to call me a lesbian if I mentioned Mum's lesbianism. Hearing that as a ten-year-old child from my Nan was really scary. I thought she was saying there was something wrong with my Mum. It alienated me from her. I went through seven years' struggle with her on that. It doesn't matter any more now. I'm much stronger and I'm no longer affected by Nan's opinions about Mum's sexuality. I never did stop loving her.

At school

The TV programme had a major effect on my school life. I left school on Friday evening a secure and happy child. When I went back to school on the Monday, I'd lost all my friends. I was picked on. I imagine that my friends' parents were scared by the TV programme. I don't think the kids knew what a lesbian was. In heterosexual society, it was scary to admit that there were gay people in this world and to believe that it's OK to be gay.

Some of the teachers were supportive. But some didn't know how to deal with it. My form teacher was fantastic and acted like a friend. I was very emotional with her. She helped iron it out with my class, and my class very slowly adapted. But it never was the same as it had been when they didn't know about Mum's lesbianism.

I grew up overnight because of the custody case and people's reaction to the TV programme. It was like a whoosh from my guts – it was that physical. I changed from feeling safe and happy to feeling scared, from nothing being wrong in my life to suddenly being alienated for something that I didn't understand. The world that had been mine until I was ten suddenly wasn't there any more.

After the custody case, I became frightened of being rejected. I didn't want to tell my friends. My best friend at secondary school didn't know about Mum's lesbianism for three years, because I was so scared I would lose my first long-term friend. I was not ashamed of Mum's lesbianism. It was purely about my fear of being rejected. I'm very alert to rejection even as an adult. Losing everything – Mum's happiness and my happiness – had such an impact.

For about three years after the custody case, we had a rule that my Mum and her lover didn't hold hands or make any display of their relationship when we went out or were near my friends. I loved her lover at the time. We were all very close, a great family. But I needed boundaries and rules to protect me when I started secondary school. My Mum supported that. I was never angry with my Mum, just frightened of reactions after her sexuality came out into the open.

Dad – the wish and the reality

Since I was one and until I was ten, I'd probably only seen my Dad about six times, as far as I can recall. My Dad has always been the deepest, most painful issue for me.

I saw my Dad when he tried to take custody of me when I was ten, and then I didn't want to see him for a couple of years. When I was twelve, I went to my Mum and said that I'd like to see my Dad. It was a nervous day for both of us. But she didn't deny me. She got in touch with him. She was nervous about what shit he would feed me about what she was. She couldn't afford to have too many situations where people could play with my child mind to alienate me from her. Children are vulnerable.

My Dad and I went for a walk in the woods. Neither of us said much. He held my hand and we walked and talked, but about nothing deep or heavy. He'd bought me an expensive gold chain, which terrified me. He let me open the box and he took it out and put it on me. It was as if he were buying me. I have never liked that kind of thing anyway. Give me a skateboard and I'd be fine. He was scared that because my mother was a lesbian, she would corrupt my life and I would become a lesbian. I knew he was thinking, 'My girl's going to be a little girl. She's going to be feminine.' Little did he know that I thought he probably would have corrupted my life a lot more than she ever could have. I cried when I had to leave him.

I haven't got a clue why I asked to see him. He has always been a mystery to me. I have moments when I don't want to deal with him or even to know him. But then there are moments when the daughter in me comes out and says, 'I've got a dad.' And I get this immediate pang to meet him. I grieve over him. I wish my Dad could give me a big cuddle and sit me on his knee. But that desire doesn't last, because it is only fantasy. It's about my image of a father. I never had him as a father. I don't know who he is, really.

Now I see him maybe once a year. When I am with him, he's suppressed. He's threatened by me because I'm very open. I'm not swayed by other people's opinions and I'm not naive and innocent. If my mother had stayed married to him, we would have had such a limited life, with far fewer choices.

A strong mother

There was a unity my Mum and I had when I was ten, a bond between us. The custody case enhanced our relationship. We became friends. There was just her and me. She's a strong and dominant woman and she fights for what she wants in her life. Seeing my Mum like that was partly what got me through. I fight strongly in my own right now, because I know what she had to go through just to be herself. For many years I felt empowered by her strength. To me, she was like a goddess. I had her on a pedestal. To this day, I've never rebelled, though I've had my difficulties with her. We've talked about this, because there probably should have been some sort of rebellion. There was a lot inside me that needed to be expressed.

Our relationship is based on talking. Even from the age of three, Mum would ask me something and I'd say, 'Why?', and she'd tell me. Whenever Mum and I had problems we needed to deal with, we talked them over. I've always listened to her. She taught me about being female in this society, about loving your body in a positive way, but being aware of the need to protect yourself from abuse by men. She was very good at introducing periods and going through the bra syndrome with me.

Mum was a well-known feminist, fighting for women's rights. She was always open about her sexuality. I was involved in her political activities and went on marches and demonstrations. I was like a little child star, because I was one of the very few children well known in those circles. Because of Mum's lesbianism and feminism, I've had lots of women around who loved me, who put their arms around me, and who talked to me. I was surrounded by adult conversations. Many of

Mum's friends took an interest in my upbringing. Jane would take me out to fly kites, another would take me out for a boat ride. I had lots of love and support. As a result, I love people and I'm very talkative.

Mum's lesbianism and her strength of character have given me many choices in my life and so much freedom. It has been tough for us both, but my life has been spectacular. I didn't see that my friends at school had that kind of support. My Mum brought me up so that I can take care of myself and so I'm confident enough to be myself. She made me aware of racism and other important issues at a very young age. I learned to believe in myself. I'm a separate person from my Mum. I stand as myself now.

Other mothers

Mum had had relationships with men until she met Jane when I was three. Mum said that it took me a couple of days to get used to Jane. One night after I'd just met her, she came to my room to put me to bed. I must have been thinking, 'You're not going to put me to bed. My Mum's going to put me to bed.' So I bit her foot. She was howling and jumping about and my Mum was shouting, 'What is going on?' But from that point on, I bonded with Jane. She was loving, so I took to her very easily. Since then, Jane has been my surrogate mother. At a very young age I was dependent on her. I loved her very much and still do. Jane and I are very close.

Mum and Jane had a relationship for two years. When they separated, Mum let Jane be part of my life. It would have had a major impact on me if somebody of Jane's significance in my life had disappeared at that age. They both went their separate ways. When I was eleven, Jane separated from a long-term lover, and came to live with us for six months because she was so distraught from the relationship ending. Mum then sold her house and Mum and Jane bought a house together as friends. They have always remained close friends. My Mum and Jane lived together for six years in south London and they were the best, most secure years of my life.

I didn't accept two of Mum's lovers. One woman had two children, and I'd never had to share Mum. I never got close to the other one, but luckily it was a short relationship.

When my Mum got into a relationship with Susy, I was a teenager and knew what was what. I understood that it was a sexual relationship. Susy was a big kid, and she was great with kids. We did things together all the time. She was into the music I liked. She accepted me, which made me accept her. I loved her so much. So there was Mum, Susy, Jane, and then Jane's lover Janne – we all became a close unit. There were four women who became my family.

But my world fell apart again when I was sixteen. Mum and Susy separated because Susy wanted to have another relationship. That was the second time I saw my Mum in pain and out of control. And then three weeks later, Jane separated from Janne. Suddenly I lost two major figures in my life. That was all very peculiar. One minute the relationships were fine and the next minute they were over. And they both went out of my life completely. Plus neither Jane nor Mum would talk about the separations, for whatever reasons. I was really isolated. I'd invested a lot in them. That was probably the one time when I really felt bad about all the shit that I had gone through in my life. Eventually, Janne and I started seeing each other again. We're really close now. But I don't see Susy very often.

I was seventeen when Mum got together with Lynn. We have a beautiful relationship, but it's taken many years to get to the point where I can say that. Mum had never lived with a lover, so I'd never had to deal with that before. I think that the relationship with Lynn is the only one of Mum's relationships I've really had to challenge. I've had to accept that I've got to share my Mum, because Mum really loves Lynn. I've never seen that woman love someone the way Mum loves Lynn. And that is saying something. Seeing Mum so happy with Lynn has reinforced my respect for her. At first, I resented Lynn because I still loved Susy and I couldn't love both Lynn and Susy. I didn't like Lynn. Lynn is calm, reserved, stern, a lot older in maturity and attitude than Susy, who was very bouncy and young. Lynn is political and active intellectually, while I'm artistic and carefree. I saw my fun Mum gradually start changing on me. I think Lynn had a lot of difficulties accepting me. It's hard to take on board somebody else's kid, especially a teenage kid. I tend to be overpowering sometimes. Lynn and I are family now.

My sexuality
I'm not sexually attracted to women. I know my sexuality. It's more that I have an emotional attraction to women. I've always been very close to

women. All my life I've been loved and protected by them. Mum talks a lot about the emotional side of lesbian relationships – about being taken care of and not being challenged with sexuality, but still being challenged as a person. For Mum, lesbianism isn't just about sex. It's about sensuality – the beauty of being able to touch someone and have contact. You don't really see that same affection in relationships between men and women.

Relationships with men

There weren't many men around during my childhood and I feel fine about that. There were the odd few that I saw with some continuity, but nothing in comparison to the colossal number of wonderful women friends that Mum had.

At the age of fourteen, I had my first boyfriend. Not having much awareness of men, I went for someone I wouldn't go near now – the typical down-at-the-pub-with-his-pint kind of bloke. I lost my virginity on my fifteenth birthday. I was emotionally pressurized into it, although I made the decision. I remember crying and crying afterwards. I felt dirty, unappreciated and unloved. But I stayed with him for four years, engaged in a massive power struggle. At a young age, I knew about my rights and what I wanted for my life. I wasn't suddenly going to tie myself down to a bloke and have kids at the age of sixteen. I wasn't a raging feminist, but I was aware and outspoken. By the age of sixteen, I was also open about Mum's sexuality.

He felt threatened by me and we had a very aggressive relationship. It ended before I went to America. When I came back, I got straight into another relationship with one of my closest friends. That was a nightmare as well, two years of turmoil. But there were some benefits and some security there.

My Mum was great about both these relationships. She let me do what I needed to do, which is why I got out unscathed, never having had a kid or been married. I think she was very concerned about both men, because all they ever tried to do was suppress me and put me in a pretty little box where they could own me. She felt that they fed off of me and that I was lucky to get out with my strength and my independence intact. As a teenager I didn't see that. I thought that I was in love. I wasn't, of course.

I was out of a committed relationship for four years. The last two years, I've been on a journey of self-awareness, getting everything into perspective for myself. I've learned about being alone, about not needing to depend on anyone, men or women. I've learned to be in a relationship because you want to be there, not because you have to be there.

After four years on my own, when I met Tom I fell absolutely madly in love with him. He's American and we don't actually spend that much time together. But it's great, because we communicate well and that's important to me. It's OK to cry, to talk, to ask for support and for both of us to show our human side. I need somebody who understands that I'm a big kid in a lot of ways. I think a lot of that has to do with the fact that I felt my childhood sweep away from me when I was ten. As an adult, I slip back into being a kid, where all my insecurities, my fundamental issues are. Tom loves me and is able to support me.

It's been a hard battle with men and me. I've been in stereotypical male-dominated relationships. I had to go through that because I hadn't had much experience of different kinds of men. Now, at the age of twenty-four, I know it's OK to look for what I want in the person. One of the meaningful things I've learned from Mum's relationships with Lynn, Susy and Jane is to respect your own space and to be aware of other people's needs too. I see how Mum and Lynn give each other a tremendous amount of support. They are inseparable individuals in a very bonded relationship. But they respect their individuality. They can agree to disagree. I want a man who can hold me, who can talk to me, and who can have intellectual conversations. It's important to have the option of individual bedrooms and to have your space and independence noted and appreciated. I don't think I would have got that growing up in the heterosexual world. My values are all down to my Mum's choices.

I doubt very much I'll ever get married. Marriage represents absolute pain. All I've ever seen is breakups. Most of the marriages in my family have broken up. All of my friends at school have single parents. Marriage seems to ruin the commitment. My Mum always emphasized her mistake of getting married and having a child so young. She was really scared that I would do the same as she did. She's never regretted having me, and she's fought very hard. But it took a lot away from her life. I see that.

TWELVE

Mark

Mark is a gay man, aged twenty-nine, whose mother is a lesbian. He comes from a white middle-class family and followed in the family tradition of spending much of his childhood abroad. Keith, Mark's father, was abusive towards Mark, causing much unhappiness. Mark and his mother both came out within a year of each other when Mark was fifteen. Mark's mother had been married twice before she met her first woman partner, Liz. Mark lives in the West Midlands with his partner, John, and their cat, Ron. He sees his mother, whom he counts as one of his best friends, several times a week.

The non-biological father

My mother got pregnant with me at the age of eighteen after a holiday fling on a Mediterranean cruise ship. Her parents were quite enlightened for the times and gave her the option of an abortion, but she decided not to. She returned to her family in Uganda, where she met an older man called Keith who knew that she was pregnant and asked her to marry him. Throughout my childhood, I was led to believe that Keith was my biological father, but I never loved him and I've got very few good memories of him. He was a control freak, often putting my mother down and expressing his dissatisfaction with her hair, weight, clothes, make-up, etc. However, despite his shortcomings, he did attempt to be what he thought of as a good father. My mother remembers him being tender to me as a baby.

When I was three, we all moved to Australia. Soon Keith started seeing another woman whom he later married. So at the age of six, my mother and I returned to live in England. I went back to Australia for a summer holiday when I was eight, but got kidnapped by my father, who persuaded (or manipulated) me to stay with him against my mother's will. He felt that my mother was incapable of being a good mother. It had nothing to do with her being a lesbian, because she wasn't at that time. He thought he could give me a better upbringing with a higher standard of living and a stable relationship. During that period my mother had a nervous breakdown, largely attributed to my absence.

I spent a very unhappy three years in Australia. I did the only things a powerless child can do – alternately withdrawing and rebelling. In their frustration, my father and stepmother both beat me with their hands and belts for minor indiscretions. We lived in a small country town where it was the norm for kids to be beaten by parents and teachers, but to this day I still find it hard to forgive. Finally my father realized that I was becoming increasingly disturbed – I had nightmares, phobias, permanent bed-wetting, and nervous twitches and habits. At my and my mother's insistence, he allowed me to return to England. On my return, my Mum said I was virtually devoid of a personality. I'd been cowed and wouldn't say boo to a goose.

I still have a shallow and tense relationship with my father, even though I've tried since I was seventeen to broaden and improve our depth of understanding. I've come out to him. I've opened my heart to him. I've told him about the anger I feel for the things he did to me in childhood. He has written back and apologized. I find it very sad that he's a man who has not learned to cry, laugh and express his emotions. It explains a lot about him.

I didn't find out that Keith wasn't my real father until I was fifteen, around the time that both my mother and I were coming out as gay. Mum and I were in the kitchen one afternoon and I asked her about Keith and how she'd met him. Something about her replies didn't make sense. My mouth opened and out came, 'Keith's not my real father, is he?' I don't know where that came from, because I'd never suspected it before. She just looked at me and said no. It was a shock, yet it made a lot of sense and was actually a relief. I'd spent all my life trying to love this man who was a wanker to me. I was so upset and angry that she hadn't told me that I ran off to stay with a friend for a few days.

I wish I'd known right from the beginning, but if Keith had acted as my social father properly, there would have been no need to tell me. Because he didn't treat me right and I didn't express any love for him, she decided to tell me. I don't hold it against my Mum, because I think she did the best that she possibly could. She was a young woman in the

1960s who did what her husband and parents told her to do. When she finally had the strength, she made her own decision and told me. I'm glad she did. You can't write it down in stone and say that every child has an inalienable right to know who its biological father is. It depends on the circumstances. Telling a child at an inappropriate time may not be good for the well-being of both child and family.

'Mark, I've got something to tell you'

When I got back from Australia, I lived with my Mum and her boyfriend. Eventually she married him in order to give me a stable upbringing. I was thirteen by then. However, he didn't like kids and I didn't get on with him. My stepfather was pretty strict. He hit me a couple of times, but he didn't beat me.

When I was fourteen, my mother started spending nights away from home. It soon turned out she was seeing a woman named Liz, who was twenty-three, a student and dynamic. My mother was thirty-three. In the space of a week, we left my stepfather and moved in with her new female lover in a tower block in Birmingham! Eventually we bought a house and all moved in together.

I knew that my Mum and Liz were lesbians, but they didn't tell me for about four months. My Mum called me into the bedroom and said, 'Look, I've got something to tell you.' Liz turned bright red and ran out of the room. I burst out laughing and said, 'I already know, Mum. You're a couple of dykes.' I don't remember this, but they said later that for months I was completely fascinated by lesbianism and that they couldn't get me out of the bedroom. I wanted to know what they were doing in there!

There's a big lesbian community in Birmingham, and from fifteen onwards I was around a lot of lesbians. One time, I came home and there was a woman-only party with forty dykes in the living room. I walked in and the whole room came to a standstill. Everyone stared at me until someone said: 'Oh, it's only Mark. Come in.' Many of Mum's friends were nice, supportive people, but I had mixed feelings towards dykes. After all, I'd been brought up to be a heterosexual male. I was into being right-on, but for a while I was just playing at it. Some of the lesbian separatists found me difficult, because I was becoming a man. I really disliked those who saw me only as a man, not as a person.

Mum's partners

When my Mum met Liz, Liz was twenty-three and I was fourteen. She was like the big sister I'd never had. To start with, we used to have some stomping arguments. Once when Liz and I were screaming and throwing things at each other, my Mum came downstairs and said, 'I'm going to move out and leave the two of you to live together.' We both shut up, terrified at the thought of it. Although we were very close, we were like sibling rivals for my mother's attentions and affections.

Liz grew into a parental role over the next couple of years. She was concerned about my well-being and she encouraged me to do lots of things. At the same time, she thought I was a little brat provoking her all the time (I was too!). Liz and I used to go up and down a lot, but we grew to love each other.

When my mother began living with Liz, it was great for me. It was the first time in my entire childhood I'd been in a happy home environment. My mother was in love. There was no heavy, brooding male presence around the house. She says herself that she had chosen two very inappropriate men to marry. They were both a lot older than her and were useless as fathers. They were emotionally boxed in, uptight men, not at all supportive of her.

My mother and Liz were together for eight years. Liz is still a big part of my life. She introduces me to straight people with, 'This is my son Mark from a previous relationship.' At first, I didn't get on well with her current partner because I was dead jealous. I thought Liz ought to be with my mother. I think her partner was jealous of me as well. We both saw each other as a threat, but now we get on really well.

My mother's been with a new partner for three years. We don't have the relationship Liz and I have, but that is not surprising as my Mum's current partner did not help to bring me up. However, we are close and I am very fond of her. She has a great sense of humour, is very supportive and I think she's great for my Mum.

I was gay first

I'd been having sex with other boys at school, on and off. The first kind of playing-around sex happened when I was in Australia. I started cottaging when I was thirteen years old and was promiscuous for fifteen years. Mum didn't know that I was gay and I didn't tell her until I was fifteen, because I was young and frightened. I'm not gay because my

Mum is a lesbian. I was gay first. I had no idea my Mum had slept with women when I was having sex with boys. People say, 'Oh, you picked up on that.' They also say, 'You had two horrible fathers.' So what! The fact is that I am gay. I don't care why. Whether it's nature or nurture is irrelevant.

During the year I was fifteen, I met a man in a toilet in Birmingham who was thirty. He was the first man I'd ever met and I fell head over heels in love with him. I was with him for about four months until he dumped me unceremoniously after he got an anonymous phone call warning him off young boys. Because of our ages, he could have gone to prison. I tried to explain to him that my parents would be fine about it, but he was very frightened. So I told Liz and my Mum that I was having a relationship with a girl and they let me stay out overnight. Being good lesbian-feminist mothers, they sat me down, gave me a packet of condoms and told me that if I got her pregnant, they'd chop my balls off. I took the condoms to my boyfriend and we nearly wet ourselves laughing.

I confided in a friend who was living with us at the time. Even though I'd asked her not to, she went and told Liz. Liz persuaded me to tell my mother. Over a period of a weekend, it reached crisis point and I finally went upstairs to my mother's bedroom. I said, 'Mum, I've got something to tell you. You know this woman I said I've been seeing? Well, I haven't been seeing a woman. I've been seeing a man. I'm gay.' She looked at me, went quiet and then started crying. Finally she wrapped her arms round me and said she was really proud of me for being different but she was worried about me. She didn't have a problem with me being gay, but she felt that I was in for a hard life. Although she'd been a lesbian feminist for a year and a half, I think she still had some homophobia of her own to overcome. When she found out he was thirty, she was even less happy.

Teenage queens
Having a lesbian mother meant I wasn't isolated or cut off from the gay community. I also had my own support network of young gay men at the Gay Youth Club in Birmingham. I went through a camp phase, along with all the boys at the club. We were 'out' in a big way – I'm talking lipstick, make-up, long burgundy hair and loud clothes. There would be ten to fifteen teenage screaming queens terrorizing

McDonalds, having milk-shake fights, bitching, shouting, swearing, being really camp and causing a riot.

Compared to most of my friends, I had it lucky. They were getting beaten by their parents and at school. Some were in care. We were very angry and confused. We took our revenge whenever we could by being vile and loud and hateful. Coming out is one of the biggest things in your life. It's the self-consciousness of walking down a street knowing that I had just sucked a man's dick in a toilet, thinking that people know and despise me, that there must be something wrong with me. It's a mixture of being proud to be gay at the same time as thinking I'm a disgusting pervert. I'd had fifteen years of indoctrination by straight society to overcome.

Superficially, having a lesbian mother helped me to come to terms with being gay very young and to be quite vocal about it. It helped that I was surrounded by lesbians and gay men who seemed to be happy. I've come out whenever I could and in every job I've ever done since I started working. But even up to the age of twenty-four, there was still a part of me that occasionally thought, 'If only I had a nice, normal, quiet life and had kids.' If I'd known when I was coming out that it was OK to have a lesbian mother, I think I would have had a less bumpy ride through adolescence. That is why I want to help other young lesbians and gays. Queer kids should be living in lesbian and gay households, where they can grow up to be normal, happy people with positive role models. I really like the Albert Kennedy Trust (see Appendix A). Liz and her current partner have done respite care for lesbian and gay teenagers over the years. Perhaps in the future, John and I will be able to foster lesbian or gay teenagers. It's a nice thought.

My Mum, my friend
My relationship with my mother is better than it's been for a long time. She and I have always had horrendous rows. I'm still angry towards her for lots of things in my childhood, especially for leaving me in Australia. And she still resents being pregnant with me at eighteen. We can deal with it now, but when I was a teenager, I was very rebellious. My Mum and Liz had lost control of me by the time I was fifteen. Basically I did what I wanted and I stumped around the place being an obnoxious prat. I would push and push until there was an explosion. They didn't know how to handle it. My mother hit me a few times out of exasperation. At

the same time there was a lot of laughter and fun in our house.

We are very different. Sometimes I think she's a neurotic closet job and her politics are shit, and she thinks my politics are over the top. We have rows about lesbian and gay politics, because she's of the Stonewall variety and I'm of Outrage. I don't think she's ever been totally comfortable being a lesbian. She said to me about five months ago in the middle of a row, 'I've been learning in co-counselling that being lesbian and gay is just an expression of distress from childhood.' I felt completely betrayed. Luckily she realizes now how silly that is.

My mother is a good friend. We see or speak to each other nearly every day. If she weren't a lesbian, she wouldn't be such a big part of my life. She's completely accepting of me being gay, of me having male partners. She's met my partners and she likes most of them. Everybody says, 'What a fantastic mum you've got,' and she is. She's easy to talk to on many levels and she's young as well. A lot of my friends say, 'God, I wish I could have a relationship like that with my parents.' The downside is that I get jealous. When I have a row with my mother, my friends always take her side. She is a wonderful mother, but she has her faults which other people don't see. When my friends see her out walking the dog, they go and talk to her and I'm left out. But then again, she gets pissed off when she gets introduced as my Mum. She says, 'I'm a bloody person in my own right.' Of course, she can laugh about it afterwards. I think it's great.

Straight understanding
Social services got involved with my family when I was sixteen. While I was on a Youth Training Scheme, I confided in the scheme's facilitator that I was rowing with my Mum and that Liz had hit me. Without asking my permission, she got social services to arrange a meeting with my parents. My Mum and I ended up having a row, with a social worker present as a referee. Then we both calmed down, went home, had a big cuddle and everything was great. I twigged early on that the social worker thought I was gay because my parents were. She said, 'If you don't like living with these two lesbians, you can come into care if you want to.' Because I was angry and confused, I did toy with the idea for a couple of weeks. Then I remembered all my friends who'd been in care and I thought, no way.

It makes me angry when 'straight' people say they understand and then interfere in our lives. They think they're doing the right thing, but actually they have no idea of why we're living our lives the way we do. They don't know what it's like to be oppressed. I often feel oppressed and threatened by heterosexual society. It's important for gays not to turn the other cheek but to educate people on their heterosexism, to challenge them in a direct and positive manner, to let people see that we are strong and powerful. I like to go on Gay Pride and be a gay separatist for the day. It's part of my liberation. Once a year I need to feel angry but proud. I want to be able to walk down the street holding my partner's hand knowing that I won't get my head kicked in or get arrested.

From angry to OK

Growing up in a 'dysfunctional' family can be held responsible for my unhappiness as a child and as a teenager. From the ages of fourteen to twenty-two, I was out of control, depressed, attention-seeking and very unhappy. I made a couple of fake suicide attempts. But how many people can claim to have had a wonderful childhood? I've still got problems, some of which I attribute to my childhood (though who hasn't?). But presently I'm happier than I've ever been and I don't regret any of it. Looking back, I think that the pros outweigh the cons – I've met many different people, lived in a different culture, and in a different country. The cons were the unhappiness of my teenage years and the pattern of instability I've repeated all my life, moving from one relationship, job, school and house to the next.

Now, I feel I'm an OK person and it's OK to say that, though there's still a part of me which doesn't believe it. I'm English after all – we're brought up to hate ourselves! I've had a couple of years of therapy and I got some benefits from it. My therapist pointed out that I showed in my behaviour the classic signs of childhood abuse. We soon worked out that I had been physically and emotionally (but not sexually) abused.

I'm grown up now. I've lived in this house for three years, learned to drive, and held down jobs. I've got a partner who is the first and only man I've ever lived with. I have a feeling that we're going to be together for a long time. Partly because of a spate of queerbashings in Birmingham, I took up a martial art, which has given me a discipline I've never had before. I have to work hard but I love it, and it amazes me that I've actually stuck something out for as long as two years.

Gay families

In my use of the word, my family is my partner, my Mum, my Mum's partner, Liz, Liz's partner and quite a few of my friends. We're a family and we're part of other families as well. I use the word 'family' on my own terms, not the way heterosexuals use it. Close support or community doesn't give it the oomph that I'm trying to convey, so I say family. Family doesn't necessarily have to mean biological relationships, but it can involve them. It's a family of our own choosing, which is important.

In 1988 when they brought in Clause 28 (see Chapter 19), I said to my Mum, 'Look, they're trying to say that we have a pretend family relationship. How outrageous!' We both felt that it was a real infringement upon our lives. I was so angry that I wanted to go on the march against Clause 28 and appear on TV. I wanted to stand up with my Mum and say, 'Look, she's a lesbian. I'm a gay man. She's my biological mother. So what! We are not pretending a family relationship.' But I didn't, because my Mum didn't want to be 'out'.

I'm delighted that my mother's a lesbian and that I know Liz and that they were together for eight years. I've been parented by lots of lesbians and gay men. It's been fantastic for me. I don't think that all lesbians and gay men would be good parents, but I think we should have the opportunity, like everybody else. We are human beings and we have as many rights as they have. Many of us make fantastic parents.

THIRTEEN

Rachel Bellos

Rachel is nineteen and grew up in Brighton where she lives with her daughter, Hannah. At the time of the interview, Hannah was just two weeks old. Rachel has an older brother, Max, now twenty. Rachel's mother, Linda, came out as lesbian and left their father when the children were three and five. After a long custody battle, their father was awarded custody. Linda has been active in community politics in London, was leader of Lambeth council in the 1980s, and became publicly visible as a black lesbian mother.

My Mum's always been lesbian. She came out when I was two or three and I've accepted it as totally normal. Her sexuality was just one other fact about her. It wouldn't have occurred to me to explain that my Mum had a girlfriend, any more than it would to explain why my Dad had one. I wouldn't have thought that needed explaining. I can't imagine what it would be like for either my Dad or my Mum to have anything but women partners. It's always been that way in my life.

My parents got married when they were nineteen. They were living in London but decided to move to Brighton so their kids would have fresh air, the sea, culture and a sense of community. My parents were staying with my uncle when my brother, Max, was born. But once I came along, they bought a house and we moved into it. I've lived in that house all my life until just a few months ago.

When I was three, my parents split up. Mum moved out and lived down the road with her first girlfriend. Six months later, Dad's new girlfriend, Liz, and her daughter moved into our house. Mum stayed on in Brighton while she completed a politics degree at university. When I was four, Mum moved up to London. Until I was six, I didn't see her much at all because of Liz.

My Dad's partner, Liz, was an evil, twisted woman and used to hurt us. She didn't lose her temper. She contrived reasons for doing it. She treated her own child like a princess. I don't understand how anybody can inflict pain on another person, let alone on a child. She must have been mentally disturbed. Liz had a great amount of power. She was a clever woman who knew how to manipulate to get what she wanted. Liz sent Max away to a boarding school for mentally handicapped children, claiming he had learning difficulties, which wasn't true. He was only hyperactive. My Dad took him out of it.

Liz used to make it impossible for my Mum to see both me and Max at the same time. If Mum had arranged to see us, Liz would take one of us away from school so that Mum couldn't take both of us. Liz also stopped us from seeing our grandparents. Before Liz moved in, it had been a regular occurrence to go to my grandmother's house. Liz claimed they were interfering with the way she was bringing us up. My Mum and grandmother knew what was happening but couldn't do anything. Their hands were tied.

Dad was pretty messed up by the divorce and didn't know that Liz was abusing us. He felt inadequate as a male because my Mum was gay. He has nothing against gay people, but it made him question whether he was such an awful sexual partner that she had to turn to women. All the things that he could think, he thought. So when he found a new woman partner, he felt like a man again. He was blinkered and didn't look at what was happening to his children. He believed at the time that women know what they're doing with children and left her to it.

I didn't talk to my Dad about it. I didn't see much of him during those three years. He was working full time and as we were so young, it was bedtime at five. Anyway, it's very difficult to tell your parents about bad things that have happened to you, especially if you love them a lot and you know they love you. I would rather be hurt than see him hurt as well.

My Dad found out what was happening three years later. He was devastated at what he saw and finished with Liz. Then our life became a lot nicer. Now, when I think about what happened to me and Max, I'm appalled. But when you're a child you take everything as it comes, and you don't realize how horrific it is. My brother has never talked about what happened. He's very shut up. He's got deep sad eyes, which show a lot of pain. Max was worse affected than me by the whole thing because he doesn't talk about it. I've always talked with friends, since talking about it makes it easier to live with. Keeping it to yourself never helps.

My parents had a custody battle from the time I was three until I was about seven. They went to court and my Dad got care, custody and control. Max and I weren't aware of what was going on at the time. Our parents sheltered us and were careful not to involve us. We just went to school and saw our Mum whenever she came by.

I've always wondered why my Mum didn't get custody. It would have been sensible for us to be with her. She applied for custody immediately after she moved out, but the fact that she left and didn't take us with her counted against her. More significantly, she was out as a lesbian and never hid the fact that she was gay. I guess the judge didn't think lesbians should be mothers. What I find horrific is that the judge must have known about the abuse that was going on. Throughout the custody battle, my Dad was living with Liz. The social services knew about our situation, and we were on the at-risk register at that time and until we were thirteen and fourteen. The court would have seen reports from social services about us. The judge must have thought that we were better off with someone who was abusing us than with someone who was gay.

I don't know how the judge could ever question my parents' love for us. Both of them created us and both of them love us. You don't have to be of a certain sexuality in order to love your children and to bring them up properly. It's very frustrating how much the system failed us.

My Mum was blocked from being a full-time mother to us, and I feel for her. Because she came out and said, 'I'm gay', she lost her children and had to stand by and watch the abuse that was going on, powerless to do anything about it. Now that I'm a mum myself, I know that would have devastated me. The father of my child won't ever take Hannah away, because he doesn't really want the responsibility of parenting. But I don't know what I would do if anybody else, such as his parents, tried anything. I hope nothing like that is going to happen. I don't regret that my Dad got custody. He's always loved us so much. I don't resent my father for anything that happened. I understand. When I was younger I used to resent my Mum more, because she wasn't there and I didn't understand why she wasn't there.

Dad has had other partners since Liz, but no more live-in relationships. I was much happier when Dad's partners didn't live with us. I think he realized that partners could take over and that he was ultimately responsible for us. He was working full time, and ended up working nights as a taxi driver, so whatever partner he'd have would have been responsible for us when he wasn't there. Very soon after Liz left, he had a relationship with a woman until I was about ten. I couldn't stand her, but she wasn't evil, just fanatical. I don't think I've liked many of my Dad's partners. Eventually he had a relationship with someone I did like. He's single now. He decided to give up on relationships, saying they're too much hassle.

Dad and I have always been very close. I was a naughty child away from home with my friends, but I always had a good relationship with him. Last year I blocked him out of my life for a few months, which I'd never done before. He hated my boyfriend. I ended up leaving home because I freaked and went into a rebellious mood. I rebelled against everything he was telling me and thought that he was totally wrong and that he was being selfish. He probably was right. I told him I was pregnant when I was about four months pregnant and had been living away from home for several months. I feel guilty about what happened between us, but we're back on an even keel now and are getting along better.

From the age of six, I saw a lot of Mum. We saw her every other week or every weekend. She often came down for Sunday visits with her girlfriends. It was something to look forward to. Mum has always been fun and exciting. At first, when Liz was there, we only saw her for the day. Later it was the weekends. After Liz left, we'd spend the weekends and the holidays with her. Even though I used to enjoy going to see my mother, we were closed off from each other. Because of everything that had happened in my past, especially what Liz had done, we found it difficult to talk to each other. We were holding something back. When I got to the age of fifteen, it came to a head. At that point, I felt I didn't have a mum in the way that I needed. I needed her to understand me and to talk to. I wrote to Mum explaining how I felt. It turned out that she felt the same way. It helped us to make our relationship a lot better, and now it's very good. I'm so pleased that we could do that. I kept thinking, 'Oh my God, I've got my Mum back.' It was a real identity crisis for me, trying to communicate with her. Thank God we sorted things out.

Now I have a close bond with my mother. We just naturally know things about each other, we know if something's wrong, we know what the other is thinking. When I fell pregnant, I phoned my Mum on a

Friday and said that I needed to come and see her on Sunday. She asked whether it was urgent. I said it was quite important and she said, 'You're pregnant.' She knew immediately. It's a mother-daughter connection that happens because we're both females and because she carried me for nine months in her body. It's the same with Hannah. She's not two weeks old, she's nine months and two weeks old.

Some of the distance between my Mum and me was that I resented her for giving things to Max. I also resented him for asking when he knows that she's not able to say no. Mum sided with Max and gave in to him all the time. She thought of me as the winning little sister and felt guilty towards my brother because he was so much more affected by the abuse and the divorce. She did everything she could to compensate. There was a bit of favouritism towards him. She tried to please him. If he said, 'Can I have?', she'd say, 'Yeah. You can have whatever you want.' But I didn't like to ask for anything. I'm not the kind of person who likes to borrow. I've got too much pride.

My sexuality isn't influenced by my Mum's at all. My Mum encouraged us to have relationships, but she didn't mind whether it was with boys or girls. I had my first boyfriend when I was about thirteen. I went to France at Christmas time, where my Mum had a house with her partner, Lily. My boyfriend had bought me a gold necklace with a locket. We were playing bridge and my aunt asked who bought me the necklace. I replied, 'Oh, just a friend.' Lily started teasing me, saying 'Oh, what's her name then?' It was good fun.

My parents are liberals. They've been easy about me having sexual relationships with my boyfriends. As a result, here I am with a baby at the age of nineteen! I belatedly realized that there is nothing bad about being a virgin. Sex is very nice, but you don't have to jump into it so young. I felt pressure from my boyfriends and from my friends to be sexually active. We all lost our virginity at about the same time. It's pathetic. The pressure is mostly from the media. There's nothing on TV or in the teen magazines about young love relationships that don't involve sex. Even if they're advocating safe sex, they should be saying that you don't have to be into sex when you're young. Sex is portrayed as something you have to do, you have to get in practice. You're in if you do it, and you're out if you don't. That's totally wrong. I don't want my daughter to be sexually active so young. I want her to keep her innocence. I wish that my parents had been stricter. I didn't get any messages from them that what I was reading or hearing was wrong. My parents and a lot of my friends' parents were around in the 1960s and 1970s when the message changed from 'sex before marriage is wrong' to 'sex with everyone is cool'. But in fact they all have stable monogamous relationships now.

There have always been gay people in my life. My Mum used to bring me and my brother to gay events. In the early 1980s, there were Gay Liberation marches, because gay people were just starting to come out. I used to go on gay marches with Mum as often as I went on anti-racist marches with her. I went on a lot of demonstrations and I loved it. She also took me to all-women parties in Brixton at clubs and at women's centres. It was great fun.

I've never had any stick at school about my Mum being lesbian. When people say to me, 'Is your mum gay?', I say, 'Yeah'. That's it. I'm not ashamed about it, and if they want to make a big thing out of it, they can. I'm not interested in their opinions about it. It helps other people change their attitudes about gay people when they look at me and think, 'It's not such a weird thing, is it? Her mum is a lesbian and had children. She's a human being.'

I grew up with a boy whose mum was gay and I have a few friends whose mothers recently went off with women. A friend of mine hadn't told anybody about his mum being gay. One evening, he and I and a few other friends were sitting around talking and I brought it into the conversation that my Mum is gay. They accepted it as normal. Later he came up to me when we were alone and said, 'My Mum's gay too.' He was really pleased to be able to tell someone at last. He's seventeen. I just said, 'Oh, is she? Isn't that nice. It's not that special.'

Having a famous mum has meant that I've also had some media attention. When I was ten Mum was interviewed by the *Guardian* about being gay. She went too far and really slagged Dad off for no good reason. My Dad didn't know about it until a *Daily Mail* journalist came up to us and said to my Dad and me, 'Do you know you were in the paper?' He came and interviewed us and took photos of us children. It ended up being a slagging match between my parents about the way their relationship had affected them – how my Mum turning gay had affected my Dad, and how being gay had affected my Mum. It was ridiculous. But my Dad didn't mind doing it, because he got paid £250 and we all went on holiday.

Many years later I was going out with a boy and was invited to his house for dinner. His family were a bunch of Tories, himself included. For some reason I gave my full name. He said, 'You're not Linda Bellos's daughter?' I said, 'Yes, I am.' Then he said, 'Your mother had more publicity than Margaret Thatcher at one point.' Thatcher was his idol and he couldn't bear my Mum stealing some of her prime TV time. At first it was good fun going out with him, because I was trying to make him understand that the system the Tories had created was working against him and his family. But I didn't succeed.

The only time I've been recognized in the street was after appearing on the TV show *Richard Littlejohn – Live and Uncut* with my Mum and Max last summer [8 July 1994]. My Mum, her girlfriend Jane and I were getting on a bus. Everybody on the bus started whispering, 'That must be her girlfriend.' It was really funny. Everybody watched it because it was a new TV show. Max and I sat in the audience while Mum was on the stage speaking about lesbian mothers. Littlejohn asked me if I'd been taunted at school because of having a lesbian mother. I said that all my friends have been very open and that I didn't come across any taunting or stigma. I explained that having a heterosexual father and a homosexual mother has helped me grow up with no barriers against either sexuality. To me, all of it is natural. He was criticizing lesbians who have children by artificial insemination and claiming that those children need a mother and a father. I said that as long as you've got love from your parents and security, I don't see what the problem can be. Children don't need a dad and a mum. Children need love. And that's what I've had.

FOURTEEN

Rikki Beadle Blair

Rikki is a black gay man, aged thirty-four. He grew up in Bermondsey, south London, with his mother and his younger brother and sister. His mother is in a relationship with a woman who has had a child, Nathan, by donor insemination.

Not screamed from the rooftops

I don't have a clear memory of my mother's sexuality throughout my childhood. At no point did my mother march in and say, 'OK, I'm gay now. You've got a lesbian mother.' We don't explain things openly like this in my family. It eventually dawned on us that she was lesbian. I imagine I was the first to know, as I'm the oldest. Also being gay, I was probably more aware than my brother and sister.

My mother got pregnant with me when she was sixteen. I presume that she was leading a heterosexual life, at least until she had my brother at the age of twenty-four. We weren't brought up by a mother and father, and then the father went away. We each have different fathers. You could say my mother got sperm donors in her own way. None of us has met our fathers. We didn't stand out by being a one-parent family, as that was common in my area.

My mother always had lots of women friends. She was very sociable, and many women would stay over after parties. But there were some who were clearly more than friends. I could hear them making love when I got up early or woke at night. Gradually I realized that so-and-so was staying often, and then it became apparent that there was a relationship. My mother started to have long-term live-in relationships with women when I was in my early teens. I was quite grown up. I knew what lesbianism was and I knew that's what she was. It wasn't traumatic for me at all.

My mother never announced that she was lesbian when we were

growing up. I don't think she saw it as being in the closet. She's one of those people who says, 'I don't hide anything. But I don't scream it from the rooftops.' She never felt she had to explain herself to other people, and as she was the boss of my family, she never explained herself to us. And we never challenged her. I kept wondering how we could go on not mentioning it. But it remained unspoken for years. Now we can talk about it and she does say she's a lesbian. She's very active within the lesbian community. But it's still surprising to me to hear her use the word 'lesbian' about herself after all those years. It doesn't feel wrong, just unusual.

My mother had to have all her defences up, since she didn't get much support. There must have been gossip about her. She was a young black woman bringing up three children on her own in the 1960s and 1970s on a white estate. She came and went when she pleased. When she was younger, she used to love to dress up and go out and dance. They'd tut as they went off to the pub greasy-haired and dowdy, while she was whooping it up with her big wigs on. They didn't like it, because she didn't behave like a Greek widow and she wasn't answerable to any man.

Nobody would think my mother was a lesbian, especially a woman with three children. Lesbians were invisible in the 1960s and 1970s. It was OK for women to be friends, and she and her women friends were seen as tarty women who should have been at home looking after their men.

A mother with passion

I have great respect for anybody who can bring up three children on their own and not completely cave in under the stress of it. My mother is smart and that's worth its weight in gold. She knows how to get on in the world, how to assess a situation quickly and what action to take. She's always been right about people, about judging what their intentions are and about telling you what traps to avoid in life. She taught us to be smart. Of course, when you're a teenager, you think your mother doesn't know anything and we ignored her, but she was always right.

My mother is very demonstrative of her feelings. If she's angry, she throws things; and if she's loving, she hugs and kisses you all over. In fact she can't really control her feelings. That's either great or not so great, depending on what feelings she's having. In many ways, she was very open. She wasn't afraid for us to see her naked. But we never sat round and discussed things. As children we didn't question her about anything. It wasn't fear of what she might say. It's that we grew up in an atmosphere where we didn't talk about feelings. As a result, I don't know anything about her life before she had me, or about her life outside of her life with me. I don't know why she had children, or whether she was lesbian at the time. She's very different now. She works as a counsellor for young people and I'm sure she's very good with other people, but she wasn't a counsellor for us when we were growing up.

When we were children, my mother wasn't involved in feminist things, though she certainly was liberated. Now she is gung-ho into it. I used to be the politically correct one in my family, but she's way beyond me now. Luckily she's not a separatist, though she skirts with radical-feminist politics. When my brother teases her about being right-on, it's an acknowledgement of who she is. As she gets older, she becomes more willing to reveal who she is to us. I suppose the reason she didn't talk about things when she was younger is because she didn't know who she was then.

My mother wasn't perfect. She's a much better mother to Nathan than she was to us, because she wasn't happy when we were young. Her saving grace, and it's a considerable grace, was that she wasn't pretending to be somebody she wasn't and that she passed on passion to us. We never felt that she was cold toward us. As long as there's passion, the family bonds are strong. There's no chance that somebody could be disowned. We may deafen each other screaming but we won't shoot each other. From the outside, it appears that we're a cold family because we don't talk about feelings, but it's quite the opposite. We do communicate and we know each other well. We know every emotion. As a result, our family is strong.

I want my mother to be proud of me, and I think she is. When I was very small, she made it obvious that she was proud of my intellectual achievements. But otherwise she didn't act like she was proud of me or say it directly to me. I'm an entertainer – I write films. I've just written the movie of Stonewall for the BBC. I write my own shows and I act and sing. I've been doing a musical for the BBC, which I wrote and choreographed. We did a performance of it on stage, which my mother came to. People were saying to her, 'You must be so proud of your son.'

She said, 'Oh yes, I am.' I was shocked to hear it, because she seldom says it to me. I'd like her to be more gushy, to say how wonderful and beautiful I am all the time. But in my family, everyone does their own business and we don't ask anybody else's approval.

Mother's partners

Until my mother had a long-term, stable relationship, I was the second parent in my family, being the oldest and a take-charge type of person. Together with my mother, I helped bring up my brother and sister. When I was seventeen, my mother started living with Susan, who was the same age as me. I felt relieved, because my mother was very unhappy unless she was in a proper relationship. Also I wanted to get out and do things. I didn't want to be at home with responsibility for my brother and sister. Susan took on the role of mother with my brother and sister and brought them up. They grew up with a sense of having two mothers. They didn't call Susan Mummy, but definitely looked on Susan as their mother. She was more domestic than my mother, which they really liked.

The relationship lasted a good twelve years. When they broke up, my brother and sister were in their twenties. My mother was worried about telling them it was over, in case they took it badly, which they did. They are very family-orientated and wanted the family to stay together. It was like any divorce situation where children don't want their parents to break up and move on. They wanted to continue to have a relationship with Susan, but Susan drifted off and led her own life. It upsets them to think about it even now, because Susan was a mother to them. Susan didn't bring me up, because she was the same age as me. I saw her as a member of my family, but more like a sister than a mother. I moved out at the age of seventeen, so I never lived with them for any length of time. I was less sentimental than my brother and sister, though it still was very sad. We all loved Susan very much.

Before she met Susan, my mother had a sadness that we didn't understand and that she couldn't discuss. When real love came into her life, the sadness disappeared, the sun shone for her. She was complete and happy. My whole family was happier, because our mother was happier. Each successive long-term relationship was a good thing, and the one with Susan was fantastic. It goes to prove that a happy parent is the best parent. And that's partly why my brother and sister were so unhappy when the relationship with Susan broke up.

Being gay

I don't have a particular moment in my life when I realized I was gay. But I understood I was gay before I recognized that my mother was, and possibly before she even realized she was. I was very young, maybe six or seven. At that age, girls and boys of my own age seemed equally attractive to me.

As you get older, other children tell you you're gay by the way you talk or the way you behave. They tease you, insult you or just make observations about your behaviour. I got a bit of teasing when I was very young, and as I grew older, I got tons of it. But I was never pushed outside of my group of friends. All my friends were tough street kids, the kind who run around causing trouble. But all of them accepted me, because I was very creative, had lots of ideas and I led a lot of activities. So my friends excused me for not being as masculine as you're supposed to be. I had a vigorous personality and that got me by. Certainly there were other kids in the neighbourhood who gave me lots of trouble for being gay. Starting when I was ten or eleven, I was bullied often.

When you're young, you instinctively don't like the idea of being labelled. I still don't like labels. They're very limiting. I hated the idea of being what people said I was. If someone said to me, 'You're queer', most of the time I would say, 'Oh, so what if I am?' But actually inside I'd be thinking, 'I don't want to prove them right. How boring to be just what they say I am.' To this day I hate having to live up to a stereotype. Or even having to think about it. Why should I have to think about other people's imagery of me?

We all use these labels. I'm as bad as everyone else. But it's a scary thing to take on the label, especially at seventeen when you know that the world hates gay people. Even when somebody very sympathetic says to you, 'Are you gay? It's not a problem for me', I couldn't bring myself to say yes. It seemed too big a thing to say about yourself, even to yourself. I wasn't one of those people who looked in the mirror and said, 'You are gay!'

Coming out to mother

People often say to me that it must be so cool to have a gay mother, that she would be much more understanding. But in the end your mother is your mother, and you don't want her to know too much about you. You spend your whole childhood with her watching you, and you want to do things that she can't see. You just don't want to talk to your mother about sex when you're sixteen.

She didn't disapprove of me being gay. But telling her wasn't particularly easy. I was seventeen and she brought it up just as I was leaving home. She said to me, and not in a very nice way, 'You're gay, aren't you?' I knew that she wasn't going to throw me out of the house, murder me or drag me off to be exorcized. She'd have been mad to do that, as she was gay herself. But it still felt awkward, because she was uncomfortable talking to me about personal things. Now she'd be terrific about it. It's nice having a mother you can share things with. She always says to me, 'Are you coming to Gay Pride this year? I'll meet you by this tent. We'll do this. We'll do that.'

Being different

As a gay person, you learn that there's only one thing wrong with being gay, and that's that some straight people don't like it. The only possible drawback to having a lesbian mother is other people's behaviour towards us, but in our case it never was a problem. It sounds like a cliché, but it's more important to be loved by your parents than who or what they are. And to be taught common-sense by your parents is more important than to be taught to behave in an acceptable way.

There are only disadvantages if you care what other people think. Children are affected by what people say, it can't be denied, but it's impossible to go through your childhood and not have anybody say anything bad about you or your parents. Kids will always find something. My family was completely different from the other families we knew in many ways. There was only one black family where we lived, which made us very different. Although we had no money and were working class, I was well spoken and literate because my mother had taught me to read early. That made me stand out from the other kids. As I grew older, I came to realize that I had an unconventional family, but we didn't worry about what other people said about us.

That my mother was a lesbian didn't make us different in the eyes of other people. It wasn't something that we displayed to other families. My brother had more to lose by introducing his friends to his mother, as he's not gay, but he used to bring all his friends home. If any of my friends asked me if my mother was a lesbian, I would say yes. I never lost any friends because of it, though I don't know what they said among themselves. I had a boyfriend when I was fourteen and fifteen who used to stay over. My mother didn't know that he was my boyfriend. He knew that she was gay, because we could hear them making love in her room. But he seemed fine about it.

Her being lesbian didn't affect me, and it affected me even less as a teenager. I did want a more conventional mother, I have to be honest. I wanted a mother who would pick me up from school and make sandwiches and be domestic. My mother wasn't domestic. I didn't particularly want my mother to look like other mothers. I liked my mother standing out, especially with her big wigs, which I always liked.

Black community

My mother had lots of black friends, but I didn't. We didn't live in a black community. There was one other black family where we lived in Bermondsey and we immediately made friends with them. But otherwise all my friends were white, and we didn't have to deal with the black community accepting my mother's or my sexuality. Now I live in an area with lots of black people. It's always been the case that if you're gay and black, other black people who aren't gay react very badly to you. In fact, it's increasingly the case. I get more abuse now from black people than I did ten years ago.

It's because gay people are hiding themselves less, so of course if you're out, you are more of a target. Basically black people are not on top in this society. So the way you get a sense of being on top is by pushing someone else down. You can't fight white society so you choose other targets, and gay people are easy to assert your aggression against. Working-class people tend to be more vociferously homophobic, because they're on the bottom rung of society, and black people are even lower. Minorities always turn against one another. Obviously it's a foolish waste of energy and time for black people to turn against other black people who are gay or against white people who are gay. For people to turn against anybody because of who they are is mind-bogglingly pointless. But people do it. This is the world we live in.

We live in a society where you have to watch yourself all the time. My family has had trouble from white people putting fireworks through the letter-box, because we lived in a National Front area. As a black person you expect to be treated badly. You learn that very early. And as a gay person you learn that as well. Luckily my mother and I haven't had any abuse because of being gay.

Mother's influence

One thing people often say is that if you've got gay parents, you will be gay yourself. I suppose that can be said of me, but it's not true of my brother and sister. I don't really think it affected us at all. Not everything we do is due to her influence. You do rebel against your parents and when parents hide things from their children, you want to do them even more. There are many things I want to do now which are things my mother didn't want me to do.

In some ways, you become your parents, but I wouldn't say that I model my romantic relationships on my mother's relationships. With my friends, I recreate the relationships within my family, not my mother's relationships particularly. But I don't do that with my romantic interests at all. My mother's relationships used to be very volatile with lots of screaming and arguing, and I don't do that.

Family announcements

After the relationship with Susan, my mother became involved with Carola, who got pregnant by artificial insemination. When the baby was three years old, my mother suddenly announced it over Christmas dinner. She said, 'Well, I'm definitely with Carola and we've had a baby. We had him by artificial insemination. I consider him to be your brother.' It was a new way for her to do things, quite a middle-class way, really. My brother and sister looked as if they couldn't understand what on earth she was thinking of. And then they exploded. They were so angry with her and were determined not to accept this child or this other relationship. They felt that our mother had gone off and had another family and excluded them. It was a big mess. My sister muttered, 'That little boy's not my brother.' And I said, 'Well, let's keep an open mind. And let's be civilized.' I was told that we're not the Waltons and that being civilized has no place in our family. It's not as traumatic as it sounds, because screaming and shouting is bread and water in my family. There's never a whisper when someone can shout. There's never a tiptoe when someone can stomp.

In my family, everyone accepts everything eventually. Now, of course, my brother and sister love the new family. They see that Monica's happy and that Nathan's lovely. He's a year older than my brother's little boy. My mother, Carola and the two little boys go away together at least twice a year, and they're good friends. Nathan knows that Carola is his mother, and that my mother is the other strong parental figure in his life. They don't live together, though they certainly see themselves as a family. He definitely knows who his mother is, as opposed to having two mothers. It will be better for Nathan, because he's being brought up to be talked to. He'll expect everything to be explained to him. He'll find it very odd if they just do things without explaining them to him, because he's come to expect that – that's the currency he's going to be dealing with.

Others like us

What was missing for my mother and for us was a sense that there was a community of people like us. It would have helped us to feel normal. One of my mother's girlfriends had children and they lived with us for about two years. So we knew that there were other lesbians with children. But still we could never turn on the TV and see somebody with parents like ours. It is easier for kids like Nathan growing up now. There is a range of visible gay people and gay families. I want to make some films which show families where there are gay parents. When you're asking for equal acknowledgement, it's not just for gay people themselves but for all the people around them, their families, children, parents and friends. If you don't acknowledge gay people, you're denying a lot of other people as well.

FIFTEEN

Rosie

Rosie is twenty years old and grew up in Norfolk and London with her older sister and younger brother. Her mother is lesbian and brought the children up on her own after separating from their fathers. Rosie's parents are Buddhists and her father is gay. If forced to label herself, Rosie considers herself bisexual.

My story

My mother married an actor when she was very young and had my sister at the age of twenty-three. Her husband turned out to be gay – something he was trying to repress, being Scottish and it being the 1960s. My Mum left him for a lot of reasons, not just because he was gay. She moved in with my father, who also turned out to be gay, so she hasn't done very well with marriage. My father left us when my brother was only one month old and I was four years old. Both my parents were Buddhists by this time and he felt he had to leave so he could carry on with his spiritual life and not be hindered by family life. That was his choice. My Mum brought us all up on her own, which I'm sure was quite difficult for her. We lived in a big house in Norfolk and had a lot of support from the Buddhist community. I think my Mum had a relationship with a man then, but nothing very serious, because her main focus was looking after three young children. I don't think she had time for anything else.

I can't remember whether Daddy was involved with us or not at that time. He says he was and Mummy says he wasn't. I think we saw him occasionally. He certainly wasn't a great father-figure. We moved to a flat in London when I was seven and Daddy got back involved with us. We saw him every week and that was really nice. He always came to us to visit. I couldn't go to his place, because he was living in a single-sex Buddhist community where even seven-year-old girls weren't allowed in the building. It was pathetic. I had to have tea with him on the stairs outside.

First Dad, then Mum – two gay parents

When I was about ten, Daddy came to look after us in the flat while Mummy went away on a retreat. Daddy brought a beautiful young man with him who was about twenty. At the time, my Dad was forty. They were in bed together in the morning when I came in. I got on really well with his boyfriend, and it was never an issue for me that my father was gay. All it meant was that he had nice young men around who wanted to play with me. I'm not sure whether he had relationships. I think they were more like flings.

When I was thirteen, my Mum was spending a lot of time with the mother of a friend of my brother's. I wasn't quite sure what she was up to and didn't really want to know, but I ended up asking, 'So what exactly do you do with Joan?' I wasn't conscious of knowing, but obviously in that question I did know and I was asking her to come out. She said, 'Well, sometimes we kiss.' I was shocked and very angry, but not because she was kissing a woman. I think I would have found it much harder if it had been a man. It was just that I didn't want to share my mother with someone else. I'd never known her to have a significant friendship with an adult. All my life, she had devoted herself to us children. Suddenly she was very happy and in love. I said to her, 'You can't really do that. It's not on. You're my Mum.' It came out in homophobia, but the main issue was jealousy.

I didn't like Joan for lots of reasons and that relationship didn't last very long, less than a year. Her next relationship was with Maureen, whom I disliked intensely. I was fine about my Mum being a lesbian by then, but Maureen and I just didn't hit it off. It was one of those personality clashes. She used to stay the night and I got annoyed with her prancing around in the morning without her clothes on. I didn't actually want to see her body. It felt like she was taking liberties in my house. She was nice enough to us, but she wasn't interested in children and we only tolerated each other. That relationship lasted for a year.

Then the Catherine story – Catherine was an art teacher at my school when I was about fourteen. Embarrassingly enough, I had a tremendous crush on her. There was great intrigue in the class about her sexuality. Once we saw the little Gay Pride badge she wore, we knew for sure, and my friends and I used to go and talk to her about our crushes on other girls. She became our dyke counsellor. When she left our school, I gave her a leaving card saying 'Gosh, haven't you been fabulous. I'm going to miss you so much.' She'd seen my Mum at parents' evenings and we had a funny conversation where she was trying to suss out whether my Mum was gay. I let her know that my Mum thought Catherine was very attractive. So after a parents' evening, they arranged to go out for dinner and that was the start of a five-year relationship. They're still together.

It's lovely to have Catherine about. I get on with her so well. My friends are pleased, because they can still come and see her. I was embarrassed at first, but it wasn't like I'd really been in love with her. I just appreciated the fact that I could go and talk to her. Catherine calls herself our other mother. But that's a bit of a joke. She's seventeen years younger than my Mum, so she's more like an older sister. She's good fun and sometimes we go cruising together.

My Mum and I

I'm very close to my mother. I suppose she's my best friend, really. I tell her everything and if she disapproves or is not sure about something I want to do, then I take that very seriously. I used to be jealous of her relationship with my sister, who's six years older than me. My sister had to take on a lot of responsibility when first her Dad and then my Dad left. Because of that, she and Mummy were very close and I felt I couldn't be part of that. But that dispelled when we moved to London. Then everything seemed to be all right.

My Mum used to find me difficult when I was adolescent. I've always had a problem expressing emotion. I used to bottle it up and be very angry. I don't really know why. My Mum is quite straightforward. If something's troubling her, she'll say right out and that's it gone. Once I'd learned how to express myself and became more articulate, we got on much better and I was a lot happier. I never felt the need to rebel, because we've been brought up in such an open way. There was nothing to rebel against. We could do what we wanted. I suppose sleeping with a boy when I was fourteen was the biggest rebellion I could have done. My Mum wasn't very pleased about that, because she thought I was too young, not because it was with a boy.

My Dad and I

Dad is an impressive man – big, powerful and good-looking. We've never had an intimate relationship. In fact, I've been in awe of him, because he embodies a lot of things that I admire. I've needed his respect and his affirmation of things I've done. It was almost as if I had to earn his love and prove myself with him, which I never had to do with my mother's unconditional love. I don't think he saw that I needed to impress him. He loved me anyway, unconditionally. But because he wasn't around much, I needed every second with him to count. This is more to do with my parents having a broken marriage than with their sexuality.

I am angry with him for leaving, because it was so difficult for Mummy, but I think he has changed dramatically since then. He's supportive now and open to all of us. Mummy says he's unrecognizable from the man she married. Buddhism has changed him. He's undergone a spiritual transformation. He spends six months of the year in India teaching Buddhism, so he's not an all-the-time father-figure. When he's here, he's lovely, and when he's not, I don't miss him that much because I'm used to him not being around constantly.

He was a theatre director and I'm interested in theatre. I acted in two plays last term, and he came up to see me. He was very supportive, and that mattered to me a lot, even though I think I shouldn't really need the approval of my parents any more. Surely I'm old enough, but he's still my Dad.

Coming to terms with their sexuality

Coming to terms with their sexuality was a considerable business for both my parents. They did start out doing what society expected – getting married and having children. Then, through their spiritual development, they were able to step back and say, 'That's not quite where it's at for me.' It's a shame they didn't do it before they got married and had children, if it wasn't particularly right for them. I can't imagine what it would have been like if my Mum and Dad had decided they were gay at a younger age and had children within that relationship. That would have been interesting.

Coming to terms with his sexuality was particularly hard for Dad, because he was brought up in a working-class Irish Catholic environment where both homosexuality and Buddhism are absolutely beyond the limit. He struggled with it for a long time. He's fifty now and only recently has he come to terms with his sexuality, although he's been having sex with men for many years. He's been celibate for the last ten years.

Dad does identify as gay, very much so. He goes on Gay Pride every year with his little banner. Mum does too. They don't believe that a lesbian and gay identity is the most important characteristic about themselves. They're certainly Buddhists first and happen to be homosexual at the same time. It's all to do with integrating themselves, coming to terms with their sexuality in order to become a whole person, rather than in order to become gay and be political about that. Their sexuality is not such an issue.

My sexuality

I'm not a lesbian. I like both men and women. I say I'm bisexual if I'm forced to put a label on myself. Women are more physically attractive than men to me. But I've had my most significant, most satisfying relationship with a boy. That makes a big difference.

At secondary school, I became the school dyke and had quite a standing in school because of it. I wasn't interested in boys at all. I went out with another girl for two years. Quite a few younger girls fell in love with me and used to identify with me as a way of coming out. I fell in love with my history teacher when I was in the sixth form. She was new and it was her first teaching job. We got on really well, and used to go out for coffee together. The head hauled her up and said, 'Listen, you're new here, so I have to tell you a few things. Rosie is a lesbian and she's obviously therefore in love with you, and obviously you mustn't sleep with her because you're her teacher.' My teacher was angry, first of all that the head dared to interfere in her friendships and secondly, because she was straight the whole time. I was angry that the head had assumed that just because I was lesbian, I would fall in love with my teacher. However, I proved that assumption was true by doing just that.

If anyone at school had a problem with my sexuality, they probably assumed it was just a phase, since I was so young – the way I was almost aggressively out was a phase. I wouldn't find it necessary to be like that now. I kept trying to proselytize to little girls, saying it's all right to be gay. People got a bit annoyed with me over that. But it was never a problem at school and it hasn't been a problem at university either. I just finished my first year. I've been going out with a boy, but our relationship ended at Christmas time and I've slept with a couple of women since then. It's good fun.

That my parents were gay made it a lot easier for me to come out and to see that there could be a physical dimension to my friendships with girls. The way we've been brought up has been so open. We were encouraged to be what we wanted to be. I have experimented sexually, and my parents have created a supportive environment for that. It helped that my secondary school was a girls' school and was quite a hotbed of lesbian experimentalism. A lot of girls at my school who weren't necessarily gay experimented. I certainly don't regret having done that, even if I decide I'm not lesbian. It's been great fun.

When I call myself bisexual, I get bad reactions from some lesbians. I find it so annoying. I've been told that I'm sitting on the fence, that I'm dabbling and that because I have long hair and wear dresses sometimes, I'm not a proper dyke. Well OK I don't want to be a dyke then. It's a bit silly, and it's mostly young girls who are saying this. No one I've had a relationship with has had a problem with my sexuality.

My Mum was more supportive when I had a girlfriend than when I went out with boys. But she liked this last boyfriend very much because he's so nice. My Dad has been slightly disparaging about my lesbian relationships. His homosexuality is about pushing away from women – first from his mother, who was very domineering, and then from my mother. So when I told him that I think women are great, and that I'm going out with one, he wasn't very happy at the time. But on the other hand, he said get on with it. It's not appropriate for parents to interfere too much.

Being different

At school, I chose friends like myself, people who are very open. Some of my closest friends identify as lesbian now. They find it incredibly refreshing to come to my home and see my parents as role models. They like it in other ways, because you could do what you want in my house. We were allowed to smoke pot in the house when no one else was. So I've had quite a standing because of it with my friends.

I went to an independent private girls' school. It was unashamedly academic, so they say in the prospectus, and quite privileged and rich. I had an assisted place and we were one of the poorest families there. Everyone else had swish houses and swish cars. I found that more difficult than being different because of my parents' sexuality. Of course, the other girls all had straight parents, but I didn't envy them that! I was very happy with my family. I'd always been in good communication with

138

my mother particularly, and I haven't resented my father that much. So I never had anything to envy. In fact my friends were envious of the open communication I had with my parents and the fact that I could be what I wanted. I certainly didn't prefer my friends' families over my own. They seemed so repressed, didn't seem to talk to each other. I don't know if that's normal, or if I had particularly uptight friends. My friends say how difficult it is when they know their parents are making love. What a hideous thought! I suppose mine must have done at some point. But you don't like to think about it. Whereas it doesn't bother me to think of my parents having sex with people of the same sex.

Other families like mine
I don't know anyone else with gay parents, but I didn't feel that I needed support because of it. I had my close friends and I would go and have a bitch to them when I needed to. They listened and that was OK. A disproportionate number of my friends are gay, so although their parents aren't, I found them supportive, especially when they said how fabulous it must be to grow up in that free environment.

It might have been nice to know others in the same circumstances, but it wasn't essential. Maybe it would have helped to have had a friend who could actually understand. When I didn't get on with my Mum's first two girlfriends and I'd complain to friends about it, they didn't understand at all. In that sense, it would have been useful to know someone from a similar family. But it was never that much of an issue for me.

Having children
I would like to have children, but I'm not sure in what context. I wouldn't want to do what my parents have done, because I couldn't cope with having three small children on my own. Naturally enough I don't believe in marriage. Marriages split up. I don't believe people ought to stay together because of the children. Particularly with the kind of indistinct sexuality that I have, I wouldn't want to commit myself to sharing my life with anyone, particularly not with a man.

I'm very independent and a free spirit. Last year I went to India and Nepal by myself. I can't wait to do it again. Although I'm close to my sister and her two children, I still can't comprehend what it must be like not to have that sort of freedom. You obviously can't do that with kids. I feel very young and I'm just starting out being my own person.

Pros and cons

The obvious disadvantage in both my parents being gay is that they are therefore not together. It must be useful to have a mother and a father living together, supporting you together, and taking equal responsibility. I'm sure that's a bit of a dream anyway. I don't know many men who do that. Maybe there's something in the theory that children need a father-figure, but I don't see that I've suffered too much from not having my father around when I was little. So I don't see why anyone else should. Even a stable relationship is not necessary for children's development – my parents weren't in one and I haven't had a replacement father-figure. I think that as long as the parents are happy, it doesn't really matter whether they're living together or with anybody else, or who they're sleeping with. I don't see what that's got to do with their ability as a parent.

I have never encountered serious homophobia, so it's strange for me to think that anybody really does mind about people being homosexual. I can't see what the problem is. I have had a sheltered life, because the majority of people are prejudiced and I've never come across them. I've been taught that society is a bit twisted and that the opinions of ignorant people don't count for much. I do believe that. I wouldn't have a friend who was homophobic, not just because I'm bisexual myself, but because anybody that's prejudiced isn't really worth knowing.

What the media says about gay families isn't about real life. I think lesbians and gay men with children need to press society's buttons and show that they're here and that it's absolutely fine. People are afraid of what they don't know. A happy family is rare enough these days, with marriages breaking up all the time. How much more traumatic for a child to go through a messy divorce than to have homosexual parents!

The advantage of gay parents is that I have parents who are well integrated, are doing what's right for them and are happy. Therefore they've been able to give more to us. If your parents are happy, then obviously they're going to be better parents. My Mum's been very good to me, and I can't fault her. Since my Dad's come out, he's been happier in himself and has been a much better father to us. I'm lucky that I've been brought up in the way that I have and that I get on with my parents so well, that I'm a sorted and well-rounded person. So their sexuality has not been a problem for me.

SIXTEEN

Stephen Harwood

Stephen was born and brought up in Shrewsbury, a small market town in Shropshire. He lived with his parents, and his brother and sister, who are both younger than him. His background is working class. When he was sixteen, he started spending a lot of time with a gay couple, Peter and Geoff. Eventually he moved in and lived with them for three and a half years. He sees himself as having two families – his gay family and his birth family. Stephen is twenty-three now and lives with his boyfriend, Colin, in the East End of London.

A gay teenager

I knew I was gay from the time I was eleven or twelve, but at that time I had no language to use to identify myself. I didn't know any other gay people. There was nothing very much I could do about being gay while I was still a teenager. At first that felt all right. I knew I just had to wait until I left school.

I have always been an arty sort of person. When I was about fourteen, I discovered clothes, began to dye my hair and started listening to bizarre music. But it was OK for me to look slightly odd and behave in an eccentric way, because I was respected in school for my artistic talents. I was able to be different yet still be accepted, because I could slot into the arty role. Looking back, I see how important it was for me to be able to act out my difference in this way.

Most of my friends in secondary school were the children of ex-hippies who had moved out from London to live in the Shropshire countryside. Their parents were broad-minded and had no problem about gay people. I could talk about being gay with some of my friends. To the outside world, they were girlfriends, but we never had a sexual relationship. We were close mates. It wasn't a big shock to tell them when I fancied a boy.

Relationship with my parents

All throughout this period, my relationship with my parents was terrible. We had screaming rows, bordering on violence. I was resentful and angry towards them. They couldn't see who I was and I felt that there was an immense gulf between us. The problem was that I couldn't talk to them about being gay. I was scared of how they would react and what would happen to me if they didn't want to see me again. Perhaps I wasn't ready then, as I didn't feel strong enough in myself. I wished they could help me be strong. Considering my relationship with my parents now, I can't imagine how I ever felt that way, but it was real to me at the time.

At this point, I had no relationship at all with my brother and sister. My brother is two years younger and my sister about six years younger than me. As far as I knew, they were just two people who lived in Mum and Dad's house. I had a relationship when we were very much younger, but all throughout my teenage years there was nothing at all between us.

Coming out

I came out as gay when I was fifteen. The man who eventually became my gay parent played an important part in this process. There were three steps. The first was a public meeting about Clause 28 which I went to with friends. It was unusual for a place like Shrewsbury and very inspiring to me. One of the speakers was Geoff Hardy. He used to live in London and had been an activist in the Gay Liberation Front, but had since moved to Shrewsbury.

A few days later, I took my second step. My mother had gone out shopping and I was alone and feeling desperate. I phoned the only place I could think of that might be able to help – a wholefood shop in Shrewsbury called Crabapple. In country towns, places like that are more than shops – they're centres for anything alternative. I asked for the number of a gay switchboard, but was invited to speak to Geoff Hardy instead. He was working one day a week at the wholefood shop and happened to be there the day I phoned. One of the first things Geoff asked me was how I felt about being gay. Although I'd known it for such a long time, it struck me as a sudden realization that yes, I was gay. I was worried that he might think that I was being gay in order to be trendy. Somehow, being gay was mixed up in my mind with fashion and music and my painting and being an alternative sort of person. I was frightened that he might not believe that I was genuine if I reached out in this way. In any case, he did, and invited me for dinner with him and his partner, Peter.

The third step was actually meeting Geoff and Peter. I had been walking by their house every night for the past ten days, debating whether or not to go. I had seen a small, thin, slightly gaunt man with high cheek-bones outside the house and had wondered if that could be Peter, which it turned out to be. On the night of the dinner, I went to a friend's house and sat with her on her doorstep. I was completely terrified and started crying. I didn't know what to expect. I didn't know any other gay person who was out and certainly not one who was more than twice my age. I felt vulnerable and I was putting myself in a vulnerable position. My friend put her arm around me and encouraged me saying, 'You owe it to yourself to go.' So I went, before I could think about it any more. I knocked on Geoff's door and Geoff pulled the door back. He's an outward person, quite loud, with long hair, very much a queen. His exact words were, 'You've just walked into a household of gay men. Come on in.' The door opened straight into the living room. There was nowhere I could go to prepare for the shock of entering a room full of six gay men. I was shy and conscious of being very young. In the end they all went off to a gay social night in a local wholefood café so Geoff and I were left on our own. We spent the evening talking about being gay, artists and school. I found I could talk with him, which I couldn't do with my parents. That was an important night for me.

Over the next couple of months, I wavered about being out. I kept coming out and owning it and then not owning it. Twice I saw Geoff in the street and turned the corner so he wouldn't see me. When I did see him, he would give me a big kiss right there in the street. He almost forced me to be out. That's why I sometimes pretended I hadn't seen him. We started to build a close friendship. I was pleased that there was no sexual relationship. I had been afraid that somebody would try and get me to do things that I didn't want to do. I found that I could be myself with Peter and Geoff, which I couldn't be with my parents. I began spending more and more time with Peter and Geoff, staying at their house at night and telling my parents I was staying with a friend.

About six months after I met them, Peter and Geoff moved to a larger house on the other side of town. Just before they moved, I came out to my parents. I had a heated argument with my Dad one night in the car as he was dropping me off at a friend's house. I told him that I couldn't talk to him. He asked what was wrong and said, 'Look, you can talk to us. You can tell us anything. We love you. We're your parents. Talk to us. Try us.' I shouted at the top of my voice, 'Dad, I'm gay.' His reply was, 'Oh, shit.' I got out of the car and went into my friend's house in floods of tears, completely out of control. My friend held me and tried to calm me down. I didn't see my parents for a couple of days after that.

Moving in with my gay family

During the summer I was sixteen, I stayed with Geoff and Peter so often that it was unusual for me to be at my parents' house. One weekend I had to go back to my parents' house for a night when Geoff and Peter took a weekend break in a hotel not many miles away. My parents and I got into a furious argument. In the middle of the shouting, Geoff phoned up to see if everything was all right. Mum answered the phone and was short with him. I suppose she was confused and jealous that I was able to go to them and not to her or my Dad. I was crying over the phone and Geoff and Peter drove over and picked me up.

Shortly after this, my parents went on holiday and gave their blessing for me to stay with Peter and Geoff for the two weeks they were away. It was a sensible decision. They realized I was better off with Peter and Geoff. My parents' attitude at this point was that there was nothing they could do with me. They didn't understand how I could be gay. They admitted that they didn't know the right things to say or the right way to act. We all knew it was unworkable for me to live at my parents' house. In my darkest moments, I felt as if there was no way out. But throughout all of this, I was always sure it would be OK between us one day.

Those two weeks were glorious. I began coming out of myself, became more open as a person, started growing up and finding out who I was. I read interesting books, grew my hair long, wore cravats and suits through the streets of Shrewsbury under the inspiration of Quentin Crisp. Peter and Geoff introduced me to gay politics, which helped me form a sense of gay pride.

After eighteen months of staying with Peter and Geoff most of the time, they asked if I wanted to move in with them. There was plenty of space in their new house. I introduced the idea to my parents calmly.

They weren't at all surprised. They said that I may as well move as I practically lived there anyway. A lot of my clothes and stuff were there already. When I took the rest of my furniture from my parents' house to theirs, I felt that it really was my home and that I had two families.

Relations with my birth family

My relationship with my parents improved noticeably the moment I moved out of their house. I only went over when I really wanted to see them, and because of that we had enjoyable times. I'd go over, we'd spend the evening together, then Dad would give me a lift back to Peter and Geoff's. Because I wanted to see them and they felt the same way, we were able to begin building a good relationship again. Before I moved out, I had been cruel to them because they didn't understand me. I'm sure I said some awful things to them in the heat of the moment. Once I'd started living with Peter and Geoff, I became centred, calm and happy and my relationship with my parents was much better. It was very loving of Mum and Dad to be able to say, 'Yes, we love you but there's nothing we can do at the moment. Even though it hurts us, we're going to have to hand you over to someone else.' I didn't see that as rejection.

Having two families

Peter and Geoff didn't become my family only for a specific phase of my life. It's a lifelong thing. I have a strong sense that I'll know these people and love them until we die. We have a history together. I enjoy going back there and I talk to them every week. We try and get up and see them whenever we can, or Peter and Geoff come down to us and stay.

I can't imagine how it would have been if I hadn't met Peter and Geoff. Would I even have a relationship with my parents now? One of my cousins ran away from home and no one in my family ever spoke of why he ran away. It's obvious to me, because he was the campest teenager I've ever met. He's not been in touch with his parents since. Recently my mother mentioned him and said to me, 'I'd hate it if you had done that.' I did want to run, but I was too sensible to get on a train and go. I stayed because I always knew it had to get better sometime. It was only a matter of waiting.

I have a very good relationship with both my families. I'm open and relaxed with my parents and have a marvellous relationship with them now. My sister is fabulous. She's a wonderful creation. She's like a female version of myself when I was sixteen. I like her a lot. I still don't have a good relationship with my brother. He hasn't said how he feels about me being gay. His girlfriend has been helping him to open up, so there's hope yet.

My parents and Peter and Geoff have a wonderful relationship now. They get on really well, are even good friends. It was the last thing I ever expected to happen. They actually knew each other long before I met Geoff. My Dad works with cars and he had done their car for them. They don't spend a lot of time together. It would be nice to have a long day out with them all. But maybe they like the sense of being separate.

I've been fortunate in having two families. Family is very important to me. It provides me with a still centre, a refuge that I can go to if things go wrong, a place where there's an enormous feeling of love and acceptance of who I am. The problem for me is where do I go – both families feel equal. Christmas and birthdays are really difficult.

Geoff and Peter

I don't call Peter and Geoff Dad or anything in particular. They're just Peter and Geoff. They call themselves my aunties. Their story is that they had me and gave me over to these nice heterosexuals (my birth parents) to raise until I was sixteen and then they took me back. They don't describe themselves as my parents, because we all know who my parents really are. But Peter and Geoff have a parental relationship to me. My relationship with Peter is different than my relationship to Geoff, just as my relationship to my Mum is different than my relationship with my Dad. I argue with Geoff sometimes. Because he was the first one who helped me, I've always been closer to Geoff than to Peter. But I can say almost anything in the world to Peter and it will be OK, and I know that he loves me.

Geoff and Peter are very different, but they also fit together perfectly. Geoff can be like a steamroller. He's a powerful personality, terribly garrulous, dives in with people – very much an instant sort of person. Peter is a calm person, also camp but dry and more reserved than Geoff. Peter's influence on the household is like the traditional idea of the breadwinner. He's the head of the household. Things are proper when he's around. As a double act, they're really interesting and work very well together.

Geoff is a nest builder. It's his nature to bring people together, perhaps because his own family background was really difficult. He took Matthew (another gay boy) in when Matthew was fifteen. Matthew met Geoff in exactly the same way I did. He had gone into Crabapple and asked for the number of gay switchboard and Geoff was there. When I was still living with Peter and Geoff, Matthew and I described ourselves as brothers, which Geoff wanted us to do.

A good upbringing

Geoff and Peter have had a major influence on me in several ways. One is that I don't think about being gay any more. It's not something I question. Maybe that's due to them. I can see that they influenced my relationship with my boyfriend, Colin. Geoff and Peter have been together for fifteen years. When I was much younger, they instilled in me a sense of how positive, loving and long-lasting gay relationships can be. I saw how they talked to each other, how they were in a room together. I observed their freedom with each other and their extraordinary awareness of each other. I remember them quoting from Kahlil Gibran, saying the 'pillars of the temple stand apart'. I could see that they were happily married. I think Colin and I have that now. I feel married to Colin. We have a lot of love for each other.

Geoff helped me build my painting career. He brought me down to London for a little while when I was sixteen and introduced me to various people. I started selling my work and had a feature in *Square Peg* and *Gay Times*. At that point, my paintings were clearly coming-out paintings – anger working itself out.

My boyfriend

I'm with somebody who I love very much. Colin and I have a very rewarding relationship and we've been through a lot together. I can't imagine living without him. We're looking forward to the future. We want to build a home together and make our own family. We're interested in different things, but we have similar values. We are thinking of getting married. We want to have a ceremony, with a public declaration saying we love each other and want to be together. We're not sure yet how to do it. We're both very spiritual people, in the sense of the spirit. We're not sure what the ceremony will be.

Gay men as parents

In my experience, gay men make very good parents. I haven't seen any disadvantages to having a gay parent. Colin thinks about being a parent in the future. He loves children. I think he would be an excellent father. He would really want his child. I'm sure it can be very hard work in practical terms and in terms of other people's attitudes, especially in a place like Shrewsbury. It's probably different being a gay father in London. If a gay man is in a position to foster a gay teenager, it can be very rewarding watching somebody change and grow and develop. It was a life-saver for me. Colin and I look forward to being able to help when we're older.

SEVENTEEN

Zoe Georgia

Zoe is twenty-four and was brought up in north-west London by her mother after her parents separated when she was one. For most of her life, she has lived in a communal house with lesbians, knowing and accepting that her mother was a lesbian. She's in her third year at university in Birmingham doing cultural studies.

My mother and father married at the beginning of 1970 and I was born at the end. In 1972, my Dad went off and my Mum had a few affairs with blokes. When I was six, Angela moved into our house. At the time, I thought she was just a friend of my Mum's, but when I was twelve, my mother told me that they had been lovers. Angela had a daughter about the same age as me, which was nice. Her daughter lived with me in my room.

We moved into a big house when I was ten and I lived there until I came to university. It was a woman's house. I grew up assuming and accepting that being lesbian was perfectly normal and natural. I can't remember when my Mum first used the word 'lesbian' with me. I just gathered that she was. My Mum never actually sat me down and told me.

At school

I can't really remember Mum's lesbianism being an issue at primary school. Maybe I didn't know then whether my Mum was a lesbian, or I didn't know how to verbalize it. It seemed most important to me when I was at secondary school. I went to a liberal school which was as interested in being 'right-on' as it was in education. Even in such a groovy school, I knew that being lesbian wasn't completely acceptable. Although I didn't find it odd myself, I knew there were people who would think it was abnormal.

My Mum wears a lesbian necklace and I remember saying to her, 'You've got to hide your necklace when you come in to school.' My Dad was a headteacher in London and I was concerned that someone was going to see it and tell him. My Mum always respected the fact that I might not want my friends at school to know – that it was my choice not hers. A friend of hers refused to hide the fact that she was lesbian when she went to her kids' school. I thought that was unfair, because this woman wouldn't have to go through the daily traumas of thinking, 'Oh my God, what are people thinking? Someone's going to say something to me.'

I always felt awkward about asking Mum to hide signs of her lesbianism. She used to tease me about it. I think she knew that it was fair enough. But we weren't always completely clear about what were the issues of her life and what were mine. I eventually decided that I love my mother, but she has her own life and I have mine. What she does is separate from what I do, even though she has influenced me in so many ways.

Telling people

I usually try to tell people that my Mum's a lesbian after they've already met her. I don't think I've ever told anyone and they've said, 'Oh no!' It's always been, 'So! That's really exciting.' I told a couple of good friends in a science lesson in the first year of secondary school, when I was twelve. They just said, 'So?' It was no big thing to them.

When I was a teenager, I would try to make sure that there weren't any lesbian leaflets or books lying around when my friends came to visit. But I wasn't always successful. I made two good friends at a theatre group when I was fourteen. I didn't tell them that my Mum was a lesbian for a while. Eventually I had a long heart-to-heart with each of them separately. After I'd told them, they said to me that when they left my home the first time they came round, they had said to each other, 'Did you see all the books on her mum's bookshelf?' It gave the game away.

I find that it's a much bigger deal working up to telling people than actually telling them. If I get into a relationship or am becoming good friends with someone, it's important to me that I tell them, because it's such a big part of my life. And even though I don't want to make a big deal out of it, I do feel it's something that they should know.

Now that I'm at university, a lot of my friends are lesbians and it's almost like I've got some 'street cred'. A couple of months ago some friends made some comment about my sexuality because I'd used the word 'dyke'. I was trying to explain that my mother was a lesbian, without actually spelling it out. It's difficult, because you wouldn't go up to someone and say, 'Hello. My name's so-and-so. My Mum's heterosexual.' You just don't do that. The next thing I knew, someone came into the room and said, 'And Zoe's mum's a lesbian.' And they all turned around and went, 'Oh, right!' It kind of explained why I'd used the word dyke.

I've got to a point now where I'm not sure which people know and which don't. It doesn't seem to matter to me any more, especially as a lot of my friends are lesbians. Also I'm older and I don't live at home. There's not any worry about custody. In some ways I think it's really important that people know, because telling helps make it more accepted. But then on the other hand, why should people know? I'm not going to sit down to dinner with people and say, 'Oh by the way, did you know this? My Mum's new lover is a woman.' My Mum's made it quite clear that it's her private business who she's having a relationship with. I completely respect that. There is no reason for me or her to tell people if she doesn't want to.

Children of lesbians

At school, there was one kid whose mother was bisexual. His mum knew my Mum, and he and I had a peculiar kind of bond, though we didn't ever speak about it. I can't think of anyone else at school with a lesbian mother.

When I was fourteen, I met a woman who had a lesbian mother. I don't know how we got put in touch with each other, but we decided to try and set up a support group for other children of lesbians. We called the group DOLs for Daughters of Lesbians. I had a positive experience having a lesbian mother, but I think she might have had a harder time. The idea of a support group came about through discussions about not wanting it to be talked about at school and feeling funny about telling people. I think it's really important to let other people know that you can cope with it at school. I wanted to let people know that it's not completely strange to go through those things. At the end of the day I came out of it feeling positive about my Mum's sexuality and wanted to pass on my positivity to other people.

Unfortunately, the support group didn't ever get off the ground. It was difficult getting younger people to come over on their own. We wanted to do it without their parents' knowledge in case they were having problems with their parents. The dilemma is that the only people who hear about these kind of groups are people whose parents tell them, and their parents tell them because they get on well with their children. It's hard to find children of lesbians who are having difficulties with their mothers' lesbianism, though they're the ones who most need a support group.

Who counts as family?

My family is my Mum and my Dad, my Mum's mum and my step-grandfather and my Dad's mum. Also in my family is Diane, who is like an auntie and lived in our house most of the time that I was growing up. Hazel was also like an auntie. She lived in our house too, but she died of cancer in 1989.

My grandparents don't know about Mum being a lesbian even now. I wouldn't mind if they did know. I think my Mum's mum sort of knows without actually using the word 'lesbian'. She's quite liberal. Once when my Mum split up with a lover, she said to my Mum, 'There's plenty more fish in the sea.' You can ignore things if you don't want to know about them.

Relationship with Dad

I don't remember seeing my Dad until I was about five, though I'm sure I did see him every now and then. From the time I was five until I was eighteen, I saw him once a week and stayed with him one weekend of every month. Then when I was older and doing my own things, I still went out with him once a week for dinner. It was really nice 'quality time'.

He supposedly didn't know that Mum was lesbian until I was about sixteen. I suppose keeping it a secret from my Dad must have affected my relationship with him to a certain extent. I didn't want him to know until I was old enough to stand up in court and speak for myself. Even though I was pretty sure my Dad wouldn't try to take me away from my Mum, I couldn't be one hundred per cent certain. If he had tried anything, I would have said, 'I don't want to see you ever again.' My Mum was involved in lesbian custody campaigns. I was aware of a friend from Sheffield who was going through hell with her custody case.

One night, when I was sixteen, I went out to have a meal with my Dad and we started talking about relationships. I'd been thinking about telling him for ages and ages. I'd built it up to be a major thing. When I did tell him, he said that he already knew. It was no big thing to him. I said, 'How could you put me through this all my life?' Thinking that he didn't know was a big stress on me. Apparently he was told by a friend who had met my Mum at a party. My Mum had mentioned to this friend that she was going on holiday with her partner. But my Dad might have known anyway from things that I'd let slip.

It's hard to talk to my Dad about Mum being a lesbian. I don't know whether he'd tell me if it was a problem for him or not. I think he might, because we do talk to each other quite a lot. It's difficult, because it's about my Mum's private life, which is her own business. They've got completely separate lives and there's no reason my Dad should know what's going on in my Mum's life or my Mum should know what's going on in my Dad's life.

Relationship with Mum

I've always been close to my Mum. We're quite similar in a lot of ways. We used to get the same haircut and wear the same clothes. She's very easy-going and fun. She likes to talk about things and draw diagrams when I don't understand something. She's supportive of me. I tease her about women she might fancy, more so now than when I was younger. Then it wasn't the kind of thing you're supposed to joke about with your mother.

We do lots of nice things together. A couple of years ago I taught in Spain for a month. My Mum flew out and we went cycling in northern Spain, just me and her. I don't go down to London that much now, but we try to go out to the cinema or for a meal when I do. I use it as an excuse for getting tasty meals! She came up here last week to do some work and we went out and had a meal together – good quality time.

Being an only child has made my relationship with my Mum stronger. When I see people who get on well with their brothers or sisters, I wish I could have had one. It would have taken the pressure off being an only child. On the other hand, I don't think I would have been as close to either of my parents if I'd had siblings. My parents are two of my closest friends. There have been times when I've felt protective of my Mum. It's partly because we're so close, but especially now that I'm older, I feel that I have to look after her more. I want to be sure that nobody is going to do anything horrible to her, like a mother would feel towards a daughter. But that's about being good friends more than about being my mother.

My Mum and I share a lot of values in common. But she's more prudish than I am – she doesn't really talk about sex. I think it would be a bit odd to talk to my mother about sex anyway. Now that I'm at college, she's into talking about intellectual academic things, which I was never able to talk to her about before because I didn't know enough. Now we can talk on a more equal level.

My Mum was always active in lesbian and feminist politics. I was aware of what was going on. I did some things with her, like going to Greenham Common when I was thirteen. I suppose she went on many demonstrations without me. She used to call herself a separatist. I'm not sure that she would any more. When she'd meet my male friends, she'd say, 'Well they're very nice, Zoe.' Most of my male friends have been nice and interesting and my Mum can hold conversations with them about real things.

Mum's lovers

Two of the women who lived in our house were my Mum's lovers. I didn't get on with one of them until after she moved out, when she and I sat in the kitchen for ages and had a long chat. I got on really well with Mum's other live-in lover. It must have been odd for them, because my Mum and I are quite close. It would have been difficult for someone else to move into our territory. Apart from those two, none of her other lovers lived in our house. I got on with most of Mum's lovers. There have been other women who have been really important to me who haven't been my Mum's lovers.

I don't think I ever consciously felt jealous of any of Mum's lovers. My Mum made a real effort to stay close with me. There's one famous family story, when I went out with some friends and was late home. I was fifteen then. I lied to my mother about where I'd been. My Mum was just getting together with a new woman for the first time. Instead she had to phone up all my friends to find out where I was and was up half the night worrying. When I finally got home, she kept saying, 'It's because you didn't want me to be with her, wasn't it?' I said, 'No. Honestly. It wasn't.' But she still doesn't believe me. I was only vaguely aware of the fact that she was with this woman. That was one of the two times I got grounded for being out late.

I've always known who her lovers are. It's been quite important to me that I've met them. Now that I've left home, it feels peculiar knowing that she's having a relationship with someone and I haven't met her. None of her lovers ever became a parent to me.

My sexuality

A year or two before I started going out with my first boyfriend, I said to my Mum, 'If I do get involved with a boy, can I have him to stay the night?' She's very liberal, probably more so than a lot of parents. She agreed and ever since has said, 'This is a woman's house, but my daughter has male friends who might come and stay every now and again.' Sometimes this caused problems in our house. It's a woman-oriented house. None of the women who live there have men staying the night. One woman said that she felt she had moved into a woman's house and that meant she didn't want blokes coming round. When it was my boyfriend, Julian's, birthday, I asked whether he could stay an extra night as it was a special occasion. This woman said, 'No. We've agreed that he can only stay two nights a week.' I thought that was taking it just a bit too far. I was upset, but there was nothing I could do because that was the agreement that had been made. Even though my Mum owns the house, it's a communal house and she wants everyone to feel that it's their home too.

Until very recently I was in a relationship with a bloke named Toby, so I considered myself heterosexual. I just became involved with a woman called Sam. It is new and exciting, as is any new relationship, but it was also sad leaving Toby. He was, and is now again, a very good friend of mine. I did not get involved with Sam because she is a woman but because she is who she is. I've started questioning what it means to label yourself. If I were really thinking seriously about it, I'd call myself bisexual. There are problems with the bisexual label. It's an ambiguous term. Nobody likes it. Although labels remain problematic for me, this is where I'm at now.

I used to think that if people knew about my Mum being lesbian, they would assume that I was a lesbian as well. It took me a long time to realize that that's about my Mum, and it's nothing to do with me. It's ridiculous the way people go on about how you're more likely to be a lesbian if you're brought up by a lesbian. Among all my lesbian friends up here, of which I have many, I only know one whose mother is a lesbian. The rest of them have straight parents. Having a lesbian mother gives you more choices. I still maintain that my mother being a lesbian has not actively encouraged me to be a lesbian myself. It has simply meant that I feel comfortable being sexually involved with a woman.

I feel I've been more influenced by the fact that a lot of my friends in Birmingham were lesbians and that heterosexuality was not the accepted norm. I have seen the stress that some of my friends, both male and female, have gone through when questioning their sexuality and having to decide about telling their parents. Some of them were lucky enough to have parents as supportive and understanding as mine.

Advantages and disadvantages

I don't think there have been any disadvantages to having a lesbian mother. It's been a major issue for me only because people can be funny about it. I've always got on really well with my Mum. I'm lucky, because I don't know that many people who have the sort of relationship that I have with my Mum. Having a lesbian mother has made me see things in a broader way. I suppose I've questioned things more about myself and about other people. I've been forced to think about things I might not have thought about otherwise, which I think is good. I think too many people just don't question anything.

EIGHTEEN

Nicolas Rea

Nicolas is sixty-six, happily married and the father of four grown-up sons and two teenage daughters. A retired GP, he is currently carrying out research and is active in health-promoting organizations. He has been a peer in the House of Lords since 1982. In the 1930s, his family life changed when his parents separated and his mother began living with a lesbian companion, Nan Youngman. He continued to see his father and they were all on amicable terms. Nicolas has had relatively little continuous time living with his mother and Nan as a family unit, because he was sent away to boarding schools and to the USA for much of his childhood.

My mother was Betty Bevan, the daughter of a fashionable private family doctor in London. She was the eldest of three children and did not get on with her father. He was an angry, forceful, tyrannical character with a difficult temperament. My mother had a strong sense of self and independent radical views. She had artistic talent and went to the Royal College of Art, where she trained as a sculptor.

While at the Royal College, she met my father, James Rea. She fell for him, as he was rather dashing and had a moustache. He was a gentle man, very different from her father. In those days it wasn't the done thing for a married woman to continue as a student, so she left after only two years. Both of them wanted to leave home. He also had difficult relationships with his parents. He'd just come down from Cambridge, where he got what was called a Special (in other words, a Fail). He had squandered a lot of money through drink and had had to be bailed out by his father. He then 'ate his dinners at the Bar' and became a barrister. He got jobs as a legal adviser. Unfortunately, he was very unreliable. Twice in his life he went bankrupt. On both of those occasions, he was living with my mother.

Once married, my parents moved to a very pretty little square off

Kensington High Street in London. This is where I was born in 1928. I was the first child. My brother, Julian, was born three years later, by which time we had moved to a bigger house the next square along. My parents were not getting on with each other, though overtly they managed it incredibly well. I didn't witness any quarrels, but I'm sure I sensed the tension. I remember some nasty nightmares and an uneasy relationship with my mother. She wasn't always as available as I would have liked.

When I was six, we moved out, this time to a spacious fourth-floor flat in Notting Hill Gate, west London. I remember that there were a lot of steps to climb to get up to it. My father helped us move and then he wasn't there any more. Eventually, the announcement was made that they were going to live separately. I think my father had had a financial disaster which precipitated the break-up. He had continued to drink. This was really why my mother became disillusioned with him and with the male sex in general. The separation came as a surprise to me, but I was an accepting sort of person. I internally shrugged and thought, 'Well, that's what they want to do.'

My mother was thirty when she decided to take stock of her life and strike out into new fields. She got rid of her husband, who wasn't much use to her. She made a big change in her orientation and began having affairs with both men and women. She had a whirlwind affair with a well-known left-wing professor of crystallography. Then she started to prefer the company of women. She developed a powerful relationship with a woman gynaecologist, who got cancer and died soon after. My mother was comforted by a friend named Nan, who was wonderfully sympathetic and brought her flowers. Nan had fallen in love with my mother while she was still with the gynaecologist. Eventually my mother noticed Nan and in 1936 they got together. They became lifelong partners. My mother died quite young, at the age of sixty, from a cerebral haemorrhage. She was still living with Nan at the time she died.

In the 1930s, my mother was part of a group who were avant-garde in many ways. She was the secretary of the Artists' International Association, a left-wing group of painters and sculptors, strongly identified with the Republican cause in Spain. In that particular group, it wasn't unusual to experiment with many sexual partners. In those days, lesbian relationships weren't known about or talked about in the same way as they are today. Same-sex pairs could go together without comment, because most people didn't have any concept of it. There were some people who did know and who were not judgemental. Of course, it was all regarded as beyond the pale by people like my mother's father. In fact, he was so disgusted by the fact that she'd joined the Communist Party and had gone on public marches that he cut her out of his will. When he died, my mother didn't get a penny.

My mother was always interested in women's issues and was very anti-establishment. She would be quite a strong feminist if she were alive today. But in those days there wasn't such an opportunity, except through radical political organizations. In the 1930s she became very active in the popular-front campaign for the Republican cause in Spain, and during World War II with the movement for the Second Front. She went to Russia in the 1930s and arrived back very excited. She decided not to hear what was going on in the show trials in the 1930s. After the Second World War she joined the peace movement, which was partly a Stalinist propaganda ploy. By the time of Hungary, she finally saw the light and resigned in 1956. She realized she'd been conned by the Communists. But she remained very much on the left wing politically.

My first encounter with my mother's politics was at the time of the Silver Jubilee of King George V. This was 1935, shortly after we moved into the flat in Notting Hill Gate. Everyone was hanging flags out their windows. At the age of six and a half, I thought it was lovely and asked my mother if we could put out some flags too. She was a member of the Communist Party by then and categorically refused to help. I pleaded with her, but her only compromise was to allow me to ring up my father and ask him. So I did just that. He came round and fixed the flags so they were facing onto the road. There we were – a republican flat displaying monarchist tendencies.

When I was eight and my brother five, we were sent to a boarding school so my mother could sort out her emotional life. We both hated it. After our summer holidays, I went to a different boarding school, Dartington Hall, a progressive co-ed school in Devon. I stayed there from the ages of eight to twelve and I was very happy. The attitude at the school towards children was permissive but with a degree of discipline. But even so, it didn't have quite enough rules for me. I found it quite agonizing to get any work done when it all depended on me.

In 1940 when I was twelve, my brother and I were evacuated to the United States to escape what my mother thought was the imminent invasion of Britain by Hitler. We risked attack by Nazi U-boats by sailing in a single fast liner, the *Duchess of Atholl*, across the Atlantic. I spent two enjoyable years with a generous and supportive American family just outside Boston in Massachusetts. They were friends of Nan's and had offered to have us when it looked as though Britain were going under. I went sailing and skiing, played ice hockey and became a keen baseball fan. I got a scholarship to a prestigious private school in New Hampshire. But I never took it up, because I decided to return to Britain in 1942. I was only fourteen, but I thought it was wrong that I should be outside the country when there was no longer any danger of a German invasion.

We came back from America in a convoy of fifty ships, zigzagging across the Atlantic with destroyers around us to guard us against the U-boats. When we arrived in London, we were put up in a bed and breakfast place near King's Cross. I remember the English breakfast as being the best breakfast I'd ever had. My father finally got to hear of us and he was the one who greeted us. That was really nice. Then we went to Huntingdon, where my mother and Nan had a house ready for us.

When Julian and I arrived home, my mother and Nan were firmly established as a couple and had been for six years or so. Nan was an art teacher whose school had been evacuated to Huntingdon. They'd been living in a caravan while we were in America, and then found a house to rent just outside Huntingdon from 1942 onwards. I went out to do my bit for the war effort, which actually meant picking up potatoes from a field and being grossly exploited by the local farmers.

I was then sent to a boys' boarding school in Wiltshire until I was eighteen. I really wanted to go to the local grammar school and stay at home with my mother and Nan. But for some reason the headmaster persuaded my mother to send us to a boarding school. It was not a particularly progressive school, but they got me my O and A levels and an entrance to Cambridge. I only had a family life in the school holidays when I came home to be with my mother and Nan. They came to visit me at school. The school seemed to be quite tolerant of their relationship if they even knew or bothered to think about it very much.

I accepted Nan completely as a member of the family. We had a very full and happy life together, partly because of Nan's personality. She was very witty, educated, intelligent and fun. She was good for my mother. They had a loving relationship, though it must have been difficult at times. My mother was a manic depressive, and I think that's one reason Nan went off and had an affair with another woman in Wales.

Nan and my mother were never outwardly affectionate within the sight of me and Julian. They were friendly towards each other and would touch each other. They slept in the same bed, but there was never anything that would remotely suggest a sexual relationship. In fact, until I was eighteen, I couldn't envisage what really went on in that bed. I just thought they were very good friends and maybe had a cuddle together. I regarded it as companionship. My brother was a bit more worldly-wise than I was, even though he was three years younger! There was a definite division of roles between the two. Nan had short hair and she normally wore trousers but not necessarily 'the trousers'. Figuratively speaking my mother wore the trousers, though she was more often wearing a skirt.

Julian and I were always respected as individuals and our opinion was sought about arrangements. As teenagers, we were very much equal members of the household, as much as we could be. I don't think that's got anything to do with the fact that our parents were both women. I think it could equally well have happened if my mother and father had been living together, because his attitude was not dissimilar. Although he tried to be a little more of a disciplinarian, it didn't work. Since I've been a parent, I've also tried to relate to children as people and not as objects to be pushed about.

When my parents separated, my father had said he'd see a lot of us, and he did. I met him in the school holidays three or more times a year. Sometimes he came down to visit me at school in the term time, alone or with his new wife. My father always respected Nan. He was extremely civil to her and tolerant. He never caused any bother at all.

Nan just died at the age of eighty-nine. I had been visiting her quite often and keeping in touch by phone. My brother had a closer, more special relationship with Nan because he spent more time with her as a child. He had whooping cough and had to stay at home for a long period. He also lived with them at home between the ages of five and eight when I was away at Dartington. Nan told me that the years she lived with us were the happiest years of her life. At one point before she met my mother, she had had an attempt at a heterosexual relationship, but she decided very early on that she was lesbian in orientation. Knowing she was lesbian, she hadn't thought she would ever have children, so moving in with my mother and two boys was a wonderful opportunity for her. She wrote us into her will on an equal basis with her nephew and niece. She saw me and Julian as her children.

I think that having a lesbian mother probably made me more tolerant of homosexuality. But among boys who have been to British public schools, there is an underlying tolerance of homosexuality, however much they may outwardly condemn it and publicly pillory people for being in homosexual relationships. There is far greater understanding of homosexuality among the British upper crust than they'd ever admit. I'm thinking about those people who have been to public schools as boarders – those monastic single-sex institutions. They are very prominent in the older Tory party (though not so much the modern Thatcherite one) and among senior civil servants and Foreign Office types.

I have a heterosexual orientation. I've never wanted to have an emotional relationship with another man. In fact, when I was younger and certain advances were made to me, I've rejected them. I haven't had any recently. When I was twenty-two and rather too young, I got married. There was no real need for me to get married. My wife wanted to do it to get out of where she was, and I went along with it. Although it lasted a long time, my first marriage was not a success. We had some good times together and produced four boys, all of whom are grown up now and a great success in the world. But our personalities weren't right for each other. She was much too controlling. I remember falling out of love with her before I even put the ring on her finger, but not having the courage to call it off when it had all been arranged. I don't ever remember it as a loving relationship. I doubt whether that's got anything to do with the fact that I was brought up from the age of six by two women. I married again three years ago and am very happy in my second marriage.

I became a GP after trying out zoology, paediatrics and epidemiological [public health] research. I've always enjoyed patient contact and visiting people in their homes. I was in general practice for twenty-five years until I retired. But I've subsequently gone back to doing a little epidemiology based on general practice. My research is into the effect of socio-economic factors on the use of health services.

I'm a Labour peer in the House of Lords, which is a very strange institution. It's ever so seductive, but completely anachronistic in this day and age. The title of Baron Rea of Eskdale was created for my grandfather, Walter Russell Rea, in the 1930s. He was the Liberal Chief Whip, who'd lost his seat in the Commons and thus got booted upstairs. When he died, the title was inherited by my uncle, my father's older brother. The title passed to me upon his death, as I was the next surviving male in the chain of inheritance (my father had died in 1951).

The first time I said anything in the House of Lords about my upbringing was during the debate on Clause 28. This was to stop 'the promotion of homosexuality' by local authorities, and there was much discussion of 'the pretended family'. I was very cross about this, because the so-called 'pretended family' that I had from the age of six was to me a very real family. I would have liked to have spent more time with that family. I objected to the use of the phrase 'pretended family' and I said in the House of Lords debate that lesbians can make a very satisfactory loving environment for the bringing up of children. I said it didn't really matter if one partner is the same sex as the other, providing that the children had the support and stimulus and nourishment in all senses that they needed. People seemed to like what I said. The more traditional types were a bit surprised. There is one lovely remark from Lord Moyne, who said, 'May I suggest the noble Lord, while rambling over many curious and peculiar arrangements which I did not understand, none the less was at times confusing friendship with homosexuality?' I replied, 'Definitely not. Although I wouldn't want to reveal any details, I am quite certain it was a lesbian relationship.' I didn't say then, 'Because they told me so.' But I virtually said, 'What do you expect me to have done, gone into the bedroom and seen what was going on?' What I said seemed to have put him in his place.

There have been other occasions since then when the question of fostering by same-sex couples has been raised. The point I've made several times is that there is a shortage of good foster homes and that by excluding gay and lesbian couples, the government is losing out on a very considerable resource. However, I do know that a number of social services departments around the country are happy to have lesbians and gay men on their books.

PART II

The Issues and the Evidence

NINETEEN

Living with Prejudice

'I'd say the downside of having lesbian parents is other people's attitudes towards lesbians. . . . I feel very strongly about gay rights. It makes me furious when anybody says anything against gays.' (Alice, fifteen)

'The only disadvantage to having a gay dad are those people who can't accept it. It hurts me when people are homophobic, because I think how much I love my Dad and [his boyfriends] and all those people I know who are gay.' (Fiona, nineteen)

Concern that children will be stigmatized as a result of their parents' homosexuality is given as a reason to remove them from their parents' care and to deny lesbians and gay men the opportunity to adopt and foster children. But such concern is a false reason for protecting children. Fear of stigma is merely a defence of prejudice, ignorance and hatred, an implicit acceptance that society is, and should be, ruled by bigotry. It cannot be in the best interests of children to teach them to value conformity, to fear difference, to be ashamed and frightened of homosexuality and to live their lives according to the standards of people who hate.

This chapter explores the nature of prejudice against homosexuality as it relates to children who have lesbian or gay parents, shows some of the ways the children experience it, what strategies they use to deal with it and how they can best be supported.

Prejudice against homosexuality and children

Homosexuality is vilified as being unnatural, wrong, sinful, morally degenerate, deviant, perverted, a threat to society, a disease. Prejudice against homosexuality is widespread in society, its expression ranging from unintentional neglect through to violent assault. Whether it operates by privileging heterosexuality or by outright gay-bashing, prejudice is a powerful force in the lives not only of lesbians and gay men but of their children.

Anti-gay prejudice touches every member of a family where there is a lesbian or gay parent, because of the apparent incompatibility between homosexuality, children and families. Homosexuality may just about be tolerated if it remains among consenting adults in private, but when children are involved, the tolerance is often stretched past its limits. The confusing and deceptive argument of 'naturalness' is frequently evoked. Homosexuality is branded as unnatural because homosexual sex does not lead to reproduction. Few heterosexual people in late twentieth-century Britain conduct their lives according to 'natural' law. Like lesbians and gay men, they separate sex from reproduction, using birth control methods when they want sex without reproduction and technologies such as in vitro fertilization and donor insemination when they want reproduction without sex.

Nevertheless, the attitude persists that heterosexual sex is the 'natural' way to have children and that the family, the institution where children are raised, is the domain of heterosexuality and indeed of all intimate relationships. Lesbians and gay men are excluded from the legal and social conventions that legitimate intimacy. Only heterosexual people can marry and have their partnerships recognized in law. When lesbians and gay men announce their sexuality, prejudice demands that they renounce their membership in the family and in any intimate relationships. The stereotype portrays them as solitary, lonely, deviant people who are not sons, daughters, mothers, fathers, brothers, sisters, cousins, aunts, uncles and grandparents. Excluded and stigmatized, prejudice thus establishes homosexuals as a threat to children. The rationale is that people who break with the norm of sexuality may violate other sexual conventions regarding children. Thus many people regard homosexuals as child molesters, contaminating children's 'naturally' heterosexual identity with a despised sexuality.

Where does this prejudice come from? People who express anti-gay views often cannot articulate why they despise homosexuality, beyond saying that it is wrong or unnatural. Ignorance fuelled by uncritical acceptance of others' views is the most likely source of prejudice. If based on ignorance, prejudice is potentially amenable to evidence and logic. People who confront prejudice by telling others about their parents' sexuality are assuming that this is the case. Fear of their own unexplored sexuality is another likely explanation. The term 'homophobia' has been introduced to reflect this fear and to explain the intensity of the hatred against homosexuality. Blaming it all on individual pathology does not completely explain anti-gay prejudice, though it is a convenient term to use. Another basis for prejudice against homosexuality is disagreement about values. Davina Cooper (1994, p. 162) explains that many on the political right perceive lesbians and gay men as representing progressive values of self-determination and choice that those on the right dislike and disagree with.

Whether the basis for prejudice is fear, ignorance or disagreement, few people are consistent in their views, often believing contradictory ideas at the same time. People can and do change apparently fundamental attitudes, especially if it concerns someone they love or know personally.

How children of lesbians and gay men experience homophobia

It is prejudice, rather than the homosexuality itself, that represents the source of difficulty for the children of lesbians and gay men. There are many ways in which children experience homophobia. Based on the interviews I conducted, I illustrate just a few here.

In the courts, custody disputes often result in children being removed from lesbian and gay parents because of the parent's homosexuality. Judges may be swayed by their own prejudice, clouding their judgement as to what is in the best interests of the child. Decisions in favour of lesbian mothers have been slowly increasing in Britain, but homophobia still dominates the outcome in cases involving gay fathers, particularly where the father is HIV-positive.

'My parents had a custody battle from the time I was three until I was about seven. They went to court and my Dad got care, custody and control. . . . [Mum] applied for custody immediately after she moved out . . . She was out as a lesbian and never hid the fact that she was gay. I guess the judge didn't think lesbians should be mothers. What I find horrific is that the judge . . . must have thought that [my brother and I] were better off with someone who was abusing us than with someone who was gay [Ed.: the children were on the social services at-risk register because of abuse by their father's new partner]. . . . It's very frustrating how much the system failed us.' (Rachel, nineteen)

'When I was living with Dad, [my mother] tried to get a court order to stop [my brother and sister] seeing Dad. It was horrible, because it would have stopped them seeing me as well. In court, the sheriff testified that they shouldn't see Dad because of Dad's gay lifestyle. Dad appealed and won, and then they were allowed to see us.' (Fiona, nineteen)

Prejudice may emerge within the extended family. Relatives who cannot accept homosexuality may ostracize the children along with the lesbian or gay parent. Grandparents may try to sustain a relationship with their grandchildren, while ignoring or censuring their own child. They may undermine the parents' relationship with their children and may even go to court to gain custody. The Children Act 1989 provides the right for grandparents and other adults with an interest in the children to apply for residence or contact orders.

'My Nan [her mother's mother] loves me very much, but she was naive and said some painful things to me, threatening to call me a lesbian if I mentioned Mum's lesbianism. Hearing that as a ten-year-old child from my Nan was really scary. I thought she was saying there was something wrong with my Mum. It alienated me from her.' (Mandy, twenty-four)

'My Gran, Dad's mum, has only come to Edinburgh once to visit my Dad since he has been living here, and then only for an hour. . . . My Gran came with my aunt and they sat in the kitchen with their coats on. . . . It doesn't upset me that I don't see Gran, but it upsets me that Dad's relations ignore him. In my Dad's family, none of my aunties and uncles like my Dad since he's come out. . . . One cousin has had a violent reaction. She's spiteful and ignores him. If they're eating dinner together and he asks her to pass the butter, she pretends she hasn't heard. He used to try and give her a hug or touch her. He would deliberately talk to her and look her in the eye. She just looked away.' (Fiona, twenty)

Where a lesbian or gay couple are raising children, relatives may refuse to accept the children as part of their family if there is no biological connection, and may not accept the parental status of the non-biological parent. A sign of anti-gay prejudice is when grandparents send birthday cards or presents only to those grandchildren they are biologically related to.

Children of primary-school age may act as powerful agents of prejudice even when they do not have a clear understanding of sexuality. When my daughter was seven, the boys in her class were expressing their contempt for lesbians in the way seven-year-old boys do. When my daughter asked what they thought a lesbian was, they asserted in all seriousness that a lesbian is half girl and half boy, the halves being the right and the left. At her primary school, Gretel, eleven, hears children ridiculing homosexuality, 'making up silly rhymes about gays'. Mandy's experience was more extreme. In 1980, when Mandy was ten, she and her mother appeared on a TV programme about lesbian mothers. As a direct result, she lost all her friends at school and was harassed by her classmates.

It is at secondary school, however, that peer pressure is greatest. Lesbian and gay teenagers are often the victims of verbal and physical harassment from their peers (see Chapter 22). Having a lesbian or gay parent can also put heterosexual teenagers at risk. Katrina, seventeen, found herself in a potentially dangerous situation from one of her brother's friends, who had discovered her mother's sexual identity during a visit to her home. He told teenagers attending the youth centre that Katrina's mother was lesbian and pestered Katrina to admit it:

'He was a malicious, conniving little git and would do anything to hurt people. . . . I don't know what I expected to happen – the house fire-bombed, bombs posted through the letter-box. . . . I denied it . . . and after a while, he got fed up with asking me about it.'

Adults as well as children can be overtly cruel. Kieron, fifteen, mentioned a woman helper at his secondary school who knew his mother was a lesbian. She 'was horrible to me. . . . She made fun of me, saying things [about lesbians] like, "Actually they are disgusting." I just hated her. I did complain about her to the headmistress, but nothing was done.'

Not all children of lesbians and gay men encounter direct anti-gay intolerance, but all experience the insidious prejudice of invisibility. There are few, if any, obvious signs of recognition of the existence of lesbian and gay parents in the media or in schools. Images of families on TV and in the movies never show lesbian or gay parents with their children. It is rare for a library to stock the children's books that are available (see Appendix B) and almost unheard of for teachers to read them to children at school. When teaching about families, few schools dare to educate their pupils about the diversity of family types or to validate the families of those children with lesbian or gay parents.

> 'I think all the teachers knew I'd got two mothers. And they were fine about it. But they didn't talk about lesbians or have any positive images of lesbians. They didn't talk about different kinds of families or about how babies are made.' (Kieron, fifteen)

> 'We could never turn on the TV and see somebody with parents like ours. . . . When you're asking for equal acknowledgement, it's not just for gay people themselves but for all the people around them, their families, children, parents and friends. If you don't acknowledge gay people, you're denying a lot of other people as well.' (Rikki, thirty-four)

Education authorities that wish to promote positive images of lesbians and gay men in schools risk extreme reactions, and may find it impossible to do so publicly. Davina Cooper (1994) describes the story of Haringey Council's unsuccessful attempt in the late 1980s to implement an anti-discrimination policy in the local secondary schools. Those opposed to the council's policy used scare tactics that must have been puzzling and frightening to children with lesbian or gay parents. The Parents Rights Group publicly burned copies of an innocuous book for young children called *Jenny Lives with Eric and Martin*. The book showed five-year-old Jenny at home with her gay father and his boyfriend. A local Baptist minister went on hunger strike, vowing to fast until death unless the council took back its policy. Ultimately such tactics made homosexuality more visible, but did not portray it in the favourable light needed by lesbian and gay students, teachers, parents and their children.

Central government has also made it its business to pass legislation designed to keep homosexuality invisible and maligned. In 1988, the

Local Government Act was passed containing a section (s. 28) which prohibits the promotion of homosexuality by local authorities. The section denies the families lesbian and gay men create, labelling them as 'pretend' family units:

> '[During the debate about Clause 28 of the Local Government Bill,] I said to my Mum, "Look, they're trying to say that we have a pretend family relationship. How outrageous!" We both felt that it was a real infringement upon our lives.' (Mark, twenty-nine)

Strategies for dealing with homophobia

Children are acutely aware of anti-gay prejudice and develop their own strategies for dealing with the prejudice they experience or anticipate. Like their parents, it is rarely a choice of whether or not to use a strategy but of which strategy to use in which situation. Some children persevere with one strategy, consistently taking measures either to avoid or to confront prejudice. But most have an eclectic and pragmatic approach, using whatever tactics they feel safe with at the time.

Children of lesbians and gay men have the option to disclose or not to disclose their parents' sexual identity. Motivations for keeping quiet may include shame and embarrassment about homosexuality, but are more likely to arise out of the desire for self-protection and to avoid the unpleasantness caused by others' prejudice:

> 'No one can tell that I've been brought up by a gay man unless I let them know. To the outside world, I'm just another person.' (Mary, twenty)

> 'I don't go around shouting about my parents' sexuality wherever I am. Not everyone can take on board the fact that I have two gay parents. Initially I thought it was going to put people off me, so I used to not say anything until I had to.' (Kate, twenty-four)

> 'I've always got upset when people make jokes about gays and I'd say, "I don't want you to talk about it in front of me." . . . Sometimes I get upset and feel like I've betrayed my Dad if I don't say something to challenge homophobia. But I can't go round being a crusader all the time.' (Fiona, nineteen)

Some children take the view that a parent's sexuality is not for public disclosure, that it is a personal and private matter. Most people with heterosexual parents do not routinely talk about their parents' sexual identity with friends:

'In some ways I think it's really important that people know, because telling helps make it more accepted. But then on the other hand, why should people know? . . . My Mum's made it quite clear that it's her private business who she's having a relationship with. I completely respect that. There is no reason for me or her to tell people if she doesn't want to.' (Zoe, twenty-four)

'Mum's sexuality doesn't come up with close friends very often. It's only when a friend confides in me something that's relevant that I would share something about Mum back. I've talked to my partner and other close family, but generally I don't drop it into the conversation. I got the feeling from Mum that it wasn't something that she wanted known about.' (Claire, thirty-three)

As children reach adolescence, they become more concerned about being different and are under intense pressure to conform. They are developing their own personal and sexual identity, differentiating themselves from their parents. In addition to fear of harassment, they may well fear that others will think that they are homosexual if they reveal their parent's sexuality:

'Lesbianism is so taboo. As I was growing up, I would hotly deny it if my Mum was accused of being a lesbian. None of my friends ever knew, apart from [a friend who also had a lesbian mother] and a girl who was like a second daughter to Mum. Mum was aware that I didn't want everyone to know, because it wouldn't have been acceptable in the circles I moved in. My Mum never jeopardized anything for me.' (Katrina, seventeen)

'When you're a child, all you want is to be the same as everyone else. It's only when you're an adult that you revel in being different. Many aspects of Mum's lifestyle that weren't anything to do with her sexuality made our family different from the norm. If I'd known she was a lesbian when I was a child, it would have been one more thing that made us different. I probably would have found it a burden knowing she was lesbian. I was already uncomfortable that my packed lunches were radically different from all my friends!' (Claire, thirty-three)

Keeping a parent's sexual identity secret means that children have to control their parents' behaviour as well as their own. Frederick Bozett (1987) describes the strategies that children of gay fathers use when setting boundaries on the expression of a father's homosexuality. The same strategies may be used by children of lesbians. Control over a parent's behaviour usually involves asking the parents to be discreet in public. Some children may control their own behaviour by refusing to be seen in public with an obviously gay father or lesbian mother.

'For about three years after the custody case, we had a rule that my Mum and her lover didn't hold hands or make any display of their relationship when we went out or were near my friends. I loved her lover at the time. We were all very close, a great family. But I needed boundaries and rules to protect me when I started secondary school. I was not ashamed of Mum's lesbianism. It was purely about my fear of being rejected. My Mum supported that. I was never angry with my Mum, just frightened of reactions after her sexuality came out into the open.' (Mandy, twenty-four)

There may be times when the child decides that non-disclosure is the best strategy but the parent is convinced that a strategy of openness is necessary for their psychic survival. Many lesbian and gay adults have been through a long process of coming out and have no desire to go back in the closet. Negotiation may lead to conflict when it is difficult to find a balance between the different needs of the children and parents:

'My Mum wears a lesbian necklace and I remember saying to her, "You've got to hide your necklace when you come in to school." . . . My Mum always respected the fact that I might not want my friends at school to know – that it was my choice not hers. . . .
'I always felt awkward about asking Mum to hide signs of her lesbianism. . . . I think she knew that it was fair enough. But we weren't always completely clear about what were the issues of her life and what were mine. I eventually decided that I love my mother, but she has her own life and I have mine. What she does is separate

from what I do, even though she has influenced me in so many ways.' (Zoe, twenty-four)

In families where the parents are not open about their sexuality, children are expected to maintain the secrecy. The family may perceive the dangers of disclosure as a greater burden than keeping a secret:

'my Dad had a generalized anxiety that I would be taken away if someone official discovered he was gay. He was worried about what I might say at school and what would happen if a teacher got hold of the information. I don't know if my Dad told me to keep quiet about it or if I just picked the message up.' (Mary, twenty)

Children become adept at assessing the intensity of anti-gay prejudice and knowing whom to trust and when to tell. Even young children are able to discern the social acceptability of homosexuality and to determine whether it is safe to come out. Gretel, eleven, tells children at school that her mother's partner, Amanda, is 'just sharing a house with us'. She says Amanda's daughter is her sister, 'except at school [where] I just call her a sort of sister, because people there don't understand'. Other interviewees displayed a similar caution:

'I only mentioned it to one person at the schools I went to in Gloucestershire. They're all very small-minded there and had no understanding at all. No one at my school even knew anyone who was gay. They used to joke about gays. They saw gays as people out there somewhere – as other. So to tell anyone would have been impossible. . . . It wasn't until I'd moved into cities where people are more liberal that it became easier.' (Kate, twenty-four)

'When I was just twelve and starting at secondary school, I felt nervous about revealing my secret. I was worried that people would hold it against me. I chose a few apparently trustworthy people to tell. . . . Although I was so careful about who I told, when I left school five years later, I discovered that the entire school already knew. My 'best friend' had made it her business to gossip about me to everyone.' (Mary, twenty)

'I don't tell most people. You have to work out who you can trust. . . . Boys get hit more often. I have to be more cautious.' (Lawrence, fourteen)

Keeping a secret about something as important as a parent's homosexuality is difficult. Any taboo topic can affect friendships. Relationships are much deeper and more relaxed without such a burden. Kieron, fifteen, felt encouraged by the positive responses he had from the friends he decided to tell and finds that he 'feels better with the friends that I've told'. Kate, twenty-four, also discovered that 'the burden has got lighter as I've grown up and talked about it more. I told my last two boyfriends on the first night – just got it over and done with. They were shocked for about five minutes and then that was it. . . . My boyfriends are interested in me, not in my parents.'

One purpose of public disclosure is to change people's attitudes. Presenting themselves as an example, children of lesbians and gay men take on the responsibility of educating others. As Lawrence, fourteen, said, 'We always have to be training people.'

'I've never had any stick at school about my Mum being lesbian. When people say to me, "Is your mum gay?", I say, "Yeah". That's it. I'm not ashamed about it, and if they want to make a big thing out of it, they can. I'm not interested in their opinions about it. It helps other people change their attitudes about gay people when they look at me and think, "It's not such a weird thing, is it? Her mum is a lesbian and had children. She's a human being."' (Rachel, nineteen)

'In my religious education class, they didn't know anything about lesbian mothers until about three months ago, when I said, "You're speaking complete garbage because you've never met any lesbian mothers. And actually why shouldn't lesbians be mothers? I have three who are my mothers."' (Alice, fifteen)

'I didn't make a big thing about it. I just let people know naturally. When friends came to the house, I'd say, "That's Daddy and Andrew's room." I'd talk about Dad and Andrew living together, about going places with them. I let people work it out for themselves. I thought of it as pretty normal, so I talked about it as if it were normal.' (Fiona, nineteen)

Choosing friends who share similar values is necessary to pursue a strategy of openness as well as a reflection of the child's own values. In certain situations, such a revelation will enhance their standing with peers:

'At school, I chose friends like myself, people who are very open. Some of my closest friends identify as lesbian now. They find it incredibly refreshing to come to my home and see my parents as role models. . . . I wouldn't have a friend who was homophobic, not just because I'm bisexual myself, but because anybody that's prejudiced isn't really worth knowing.' (Rosie, twenty)

'I went to Birmingham to go to university, where I met Brian who became my best friend. He is gay and I went to gay pubs with him and his gay friends. They thought having two gay parents was cool and trendy. Whenever Brian introduced me, he'd say admiringly, "Kate's parents are gay. She's great."' (Kate, twenty-four)

Children are best able to adopt a strategy of openness and to challenge homophobia when they perceive it as a problem belonging to other people and can put it into a broader perspective. Families are different for many reasons, and the sexuality of parents is not necessarily the only significant one:

'There are only disadvantages [to having a lesbian mother] if you care what other people think. Children are affected by what people say, it can't be denied, but it's impossible to go through your childhood and not have anybody say anything bad about you or your parents. Kids will always find something. My family was completely different from the other families we knew in many ways. There was only one black family where we lived, which made us very different. . . . As I grew older, I came to realize that I had an unconventional family, but we didn't worry about what other people said about us.' (Rikki, thirty-four)

'I have never encountered serious homophobia, so it's strange for me to think that anybody really does mind about people being homosexual. I can't see what the problem is. . . . I've been taught that society is a bit twisted and that the opinions of ignorant people don't count for much.' (Rosie, twenty)

Support from parents

Parents are not responsible for the distress caused to their children by bigotry, but they do have some responsibility for their children's emotional and moral development. A parent's job is not to give children a good time, to keep them entertained or to see that they are always happy. It is to help them live their lives with strength and humanity, and to be individuals who can stand up and think for themselves.

Prejudice is hurtful and parents do not seek it out. While they can try to protect their children from the most damaging consequences and aim to change intolerant attitudes, ultimately prejudice against homosexuality is a fact of life. Sometimes, the best a parent can do is help the child learn something positive from a bad experience. The issue is not whether lesbians and gay men have a right to have children in the face of universal condemnation of homosexuality but how they can best make use of these opportunities for the development of strength of character and positive moral values. In her book *Reinventing the Family* (1994), Laura Benkov asks:

> How do children flourish and grow amid bigotry? How do parents face the pain of this question and help their children with this task? How and when do parents try to shield their children from pain, to actively advocate for them, to hold back and let them find their own way of dealing, to be present and bear witness to their suffering? (p. 190)

The answer is that parents teach these values by the way they live their lives. If they are comfortable with their sexuality, they model pride and self-acceptance. If they know a variety of people and types of families, they teach children to value diversity and to understand that there are many routes to happiness and self-fulfilment. If they act according to their own standards of right and wrong and challenge injustice and prejudice, they teach that 'people of integrity do not shrink from bigots' (quotation from judge in custody case, taken from Benkov, 1994). Most of all, they teach reality – a better preparation for life than myths about how the world should be.

Community support

> The greatest single problem for daughters and sons of lesbian and gay parents is our isolation. When kids from similar families just get together, regardless of what we do or say, it is a positive experience we can't underestimate. (COLAGE Guide)

Children are more susceptible to the prevailing prejudice against homosexuality when they are isolated and do not know any other children who have lesbian or gay parents. Many lesbian mothers place great importance on building a sense of community. Wherever possible, they form support networks and organize groups for lesbians and their children. They maintain friendships with other lesbian mothers so that their children can get to know other children from similar families. They move to areas where lesbian mothers live and send their children to schools attended by other children with lesbian mothers. The need for such contact is appreciated by the children:

> 'Every month we go to a lesbian parents' group. It's a bit boring. The adults just go and talk and I sit downstairs playing darts. . . . There are lots of other children, but I'm the oldest. I would like a group for kids my age who have lesbian mothers. I don't know what kind of things we'd talk about – the same things we talk about anyway – but at least I would feel safe. In case of a slip of the tongue – saying something about lesbians – it wouldn't matter.' (Josh, twelve)

> 'What was missing for my mother and for us was a sense that there was a community of people like us. It would have helped us to feel normal. One of my mother's girlfriends had children and they lived with us for about two years. So we knew that there were other lesbians with children.' (Rikki, thirty-four)

The children of gay men often lack this sense of community. Men, whether gay or heterosexual, are not the primary carers of children, so it is not surprising that the gay male community is largely childless and often unsympathetic towards gay parenthood. The few gay men raising children tend not to be visible as gay fathers. It seems to be much harder for gay men to integrate the two separate identities of gay man and parent than it is for lesbians. Consequently, their children do not grow up knowing other children of gay men:

> 'Being a father isn't great for my Dad's image. Dad likes to look good. . . . He thinks men won't look at him if they know he's got a daughter, that they won't think he's gay.' (Fiona, nineteen)

> 'When I was growing up, my Dad identified himself more as a single parent than as a gay father.' (Mary, twenty)

There are many support groups established by and for lesbian mothers in Britain and a few for gay fathers. As I write, Stonewall is just forming a group for both lesbian and gay parents. But as yet, there do not seem to be any that are run by and for the children of lesbians and gay men. As a teenager, Zoe, twenty-four, tried to set up one for children of lesbians:

> 'At the end of the day I came out of it feeling positive about my Mum's sexuality and wanted to pass on my positivity to other people.
> 'Unfortunately, the support group didn't ever get off the ground. . . . It's hard to find children of lesbians who are having difficulties with their mothers' lesbianism, though they're the ones who most need a support group.'

(See Appendix B for details of COLAGE, an American support group run by children of lesbians and gay men.)

Conclusion

Prejudice against homosexuality is real and pervasive and affects the children of lesbians and gay men as much as it affects their parents. People with lesbian and gay parents have developed various strategies for dealing with prejudice, and learn to assess what strategy to use in different situations. The following quote comes from a 1979 decision by an American court in which the judge argued that the lesbian mother should keep custody of her two daughters:

> It is just as reasonable to expect that they will emerge better equipped to search out their own standards of right and wrong, better able to perceive that the majority is not always correct in its moral judgments and better able to understand the importance of conforming their beliefs to the requirements of reason and tested knowledge, not the constraints of currently popular sentiment or prejudice.

If they were to be removed, the judge predicted,

> instead of forbearance and feelings of protectiveness, it will foster in them a sense of shame for their mother. Instead of courage and

the precept that people of integrity do not shrink from bigots, it counsels the easy option of shirking difficult problems and following the course of expedience. Lastly, it diminishes their regard for the rule of human behaviour, everywhere accepted, that we do not forsake those to whom we are indebted for love and nurture merely because they are held in low esteem by others. (Quoted in Benkov, 1994)

References

Benkov, L. (1994) *Reinventing the Family: The Emerging Story of Lesbian and Gay Parents*. New York: Crown Publishers.

Bozett, F.W. (1987) 'Children of gay fathers', in F.W. Bozett (ed.), *Gay and Lesbian Parents*. London: Praeger.

Cooper, D. (1994) 'With God's help and common sense', in D. Cooper, *Sexing the City: Lesbian and Gay Politics within the Activist State*. London: Rivers Oram Press.

TWENTY

Psychological Development – What Do Children Need from Their Parents?

'What's important is how much the child is loved and how well the parents look after their child. There are so many parents out there that are not doing a decent job of bringing up their children, while my Dad, without exception, has done a good job for me. I am really proud of him for being what he is.'   (Mary, twenty, daughter of gay father)

In this chapter, I discuss the relevance of the research done on the development of children raised by lesbian mothers or gay fathers. From the research and from my sample, I extract five lessons about what children need for their psychological development:

1. Children do not need their parents to be heterosexual.
2. Children do not need one parent to be male.
3. Children need their parents to be happy.
4. Children are happier when their parents have an equal relationship.
5. Children learn positive moral values from lesbian and gay parents.

The research

There exists a good-sized body of research into the psychological and social development of children raised by lesbian mothers and gay fathers. Most studies have been done in the USA, with the notable exception of the work of Susan Golombok and her colleagues in Britain. Nearly all research is on white children whose parents volunteered to participate. Most were financially well off, and apart from a few studies, the lesbian and gay parents had their children when they were in heterosexual relationships. Some studies have looked at adult offspring but most have focused on young children and teenagers. (See the review articles by Patterson, 1992, 1995b; Golombok and Tasker, 1994.)

Much of this research has been designed to answer a narrow set of questions. These are the questions raised by judges in custody cases and policy-makers when formulating rulings about adoption and fostering. They want to gauge the psychological effect on children of being raised by lesbian or gay parents. Will the children develop normally? Will they be confused about whether they are male or female? Will they behave in sex-stereotyped ways? Will they be lesbian or gay? Will they feel bad about themselves? Will they have behaviour problems and psychiatric disorders? Will they be able to make friends with other children? Will they suffer from the stigma against homosexuality?

Because of the meanings our society attaches to homosexuality and to sexuality, the focus of these questions is inevitably rather negative. They come from the political agenda that says homosexual people are substantially different from heterosexual people and substantially similar to other homosexual people – that people with lesbian and gay identities have enough parenting qualities and circumstances in common that generalizations can be made about them as parents. The research has focused on the structure of the family (the number, gender and sexual identity of parents) rather than on the process of parenting (the quality of the relationships in the family).

Nevertheless, within the narrow scope of the questions asked, the results from numerous studies are consistent, if not one hundred per cent conclusive. They all point to the conclusion that, compared to heterosexual parents, lesbians and gay men are just as capable of raising children who conform to the norms of gender and sexuality and who are not psychologically damaged. This evidence poses a challenge to the meanings given to homosexuality in relation to parenting and to psychological theories about child development. If children raised by lesbians and gay men are no different from children raised by heterosexual parents, then it would appear that children do not need the unique input of a heterosexual parent of each gender for healthy personal and social development.

Lesson one: children do not need their parents to be heterosexual

'Having a lesbian mother has enabled me to have a head start on everybody else emotionally, psychologically, intellectually – in every way. I wouldn't know the things that I know, wouldn't be the person I am now, and I wouldn't be as assertive as I am now if I hadn't been brought up by a lesbian mother. My Mum has drilled it into me since I was small that you stand up for yourself, you say what you want and you don't let any man tell you what to say or do.' (Katrina, seventeen)

While Katrina sees advantages to being raised by a lesbian mother, the research has done no more than confirm that there are no disadvantages for children's development. Researchers have investigated many aspects of children's personal development, including their self-esteem, their gender identity (whether they feel themselves to be male or female), their gender-role behaviour (how well they conform to expected masculine and feminine behaviour), their intellectual and emotional development, whether they are more likely to suffer from a psychiatric disorder, and their attainment of typical developmental tasks. Studies have also been done on aspects of social development – how well they form relationships with their peers and with adults (see the References at the end of this chapter).

While each study has its biases and limitations, taken together the results are clear and consistent. The studies show no meaningful or significant differences between the children of homosexual and heterosexual parents. It is not possible to predict how a child will develop from knowing the parents' sexual identity. To the people I interviewed, as well as to lesbian and gay parents, this is common-sense. Sexuality is just one aspect of an individual's identity and one that is not relevant to the person's skill as a parent. Just as some heterosexual people are bad parents, so are some lesbian and gay people. Neither are lesbian and gay people as a group any better at these aspects of parenting than heterosexual people.

Lesson two: children do not need one parent to be male

'Children need a male and a female. . . . Men and women think differently and bring up children differently. . . . My husband demonstrates to my son how to use strength gently. . . . Imagine a boy living with two female parents. . . . There's no male role model. How's that boy going to find his way in the world?' (Studio audience discussion on *Esther*, BBC, 21 February 1995)

Children will not be conceived if there is no contribution from both a male and a female, but they do not need to be raised by both a male and a female for healthy psychological development. This lesson is based on research carried out on the children of lesbians. The majority of gay fathers do not have custody of their children and there are apparently no studies on the gender development of children who have only been raised by gay fathers (Golombok and Tasker, 1994).

Male role models

The claim that every child needs a father to model maleness seems to suggest that any model of maleness is preferable to none, that the presence of a male is more important than the quality of the father's parenting. Yet fathers are individuals, and not all present positive role models of their gender. A father may be physically present yet emotionally absent. He may be abusive, manipulative, uncaring, bad-tempered, indecisive or any number of undesirable versions of a male role model. He may demonstrate strength with brutality, or he may not demonstrate any strength at all.

How can the typical gender-role behaviour of the children of lesbians and of single heterosexual women be explained? The cognitive development theory, widely accepted among psychologists, says that parents are not the only influences on their children's gender-role development (Golombok and Tasker, 1994, 1996). According to this theory, rather than passively modelling themselves on the sex-stereotyped toys, games, TV programmes and bedroom furnishings they are given, children are more likely to be active participants in their own development. Once children learn that gender is constant (about age five or six), they look for models of both genders, emulating models of their own gender and observing models of the other gender. These models include their parents but are not limited to them. All children have some contact with the world beyond their immediate family, even if it is only by watching TV. In lesbian families where there has never been a father, the children have the opportunity to observe men at school, in their community, in the media or in their mothers' extended family. It would be difficult for children to be shielded from all male influence.

In fact, the children of lesbian mothers are more likely to have contact with their fathers and other adult men than the children of heterosexual divorced mothers (DiLapi, 1989; Patterson, 1992; Golombok and Tasker, 1994.) In several studies comparing divorced lesbian and heterosexual mothers (Patterson, 1992), the lesbian mothers made more efforts to include male relatives and male friends in their children's lives and to maintain frequent contact between the children and their fathers than did heterosexual mothers. In one study (Golombok, Spencer and Rutter, 1983), twelve of the thirty-seven children with lesbian mothers saw their fathers at least once a week, compared with two of the thirty-eight children of heterosexual mothers.

Sons and daughters may have different needs for male role models. It may be that for some sons in lesbian-mother households, the contact they have with men is not enough for them:

'[Having a lesbian mother is] more a problem for boys growing up without a man in the house to explain things. My Mum never could. She bought me books and tried to show me. I guess you can always find someone else to talk to. I talked to my Dad and my uncle about growing up. But I was never that open with them. I kept quiet, which was fine with me.' (Lawrence, fourteen)

One advantage of lesbian mothers is that they do protect their children from the worst aspects of masculine behaviour, both in the home and in the lessons they teach their children about relating to men:

'Other girls my age aren't able to hold their own, because they've been brought up by dominating fathers. They can't stand up to boyfriends that bully them. My Mum is assertive and strong. She just won't be pushed around. I've learned that from her. . . . I've got confidence in myself. I'd say I'm more emotionally stable than many of my friends who are living with both their mum and dad.' (Katrina, seventeen)

The claim that every child needs a father because of the difference fathers bring to their children ignores the fact that lesbians are also individuals. No two women care for their children in exactly the same way. They each bring different skills and perspectives to their parenting. They have gender in common, but gender is not necessarily the most meaningful attribute of an individual. Lesbian couples inevitably differ in personality, interests and abilities and may well differ in class, age, education, race and ethnic background. The same applies to gay fathers.

Divorce and the absent father

> 'A happy family is rare enough these days, with marriages breaking up all the time. How much more traumatic for a child to go through a messy divorce than to have homosexual parents!' (Rosie, twenty, daughter of lesbian mother and gay father)

When parents get divorced, children often suffer (Amato, 1993). On average, they have more problems with behaviour, self-esteem, relationships with other people and achievement at school than children who have not experienced divorce. These problems continue into adulthood. Children of divorced lesbian mothers may also suffer as a result of divorce, but they do not have more problems than the children of divorced heterosexual mothers (Golombok and Tasker, 1994).

Why do children suffer as a result of divorce? Is it because a family with both a mother and a father is necessarily a better environment for children than a single-parent family or a lesbian family? Since not all children of divorced parents do suffer negative consequences, could there be something else associated with divorce that causes children to have problems? Paul Amato (1993) tried to account for the differences in children's adjustment to divorce by analysing the results of 180 studies on divorce. He looked at five possible theories and the weight of evidence supporting each theory. These were: the loss of one parent; the well-being of the parent still caring for the child; the amount of conflict between parents, both before and after divorce; the economic hardship for children living with mothers after divorce; the number of stressful life events the children experience. The theory concerning the role of conflict between the parents is supported by more evidence than any of the others, but no single theory on its own tells the whole story.

Thus, it is not the absence of a father which harms children's development but the way the divorce is handled. Acrimonious divorce after bitter fighting, followed by continuing conflict, causes more problems for children than amicable separation followed by cooperative co-parenting. For some children, divorce improves their well-being if the parents get along better after they separate. Claire's parents divorced when she was eight:

> 'My Mum had day-to-day care of us, but she was happy for Dad to see us. We had a lot of contact with him. For our sakes, they always

managed to get on and be friendly. . . . It's very easy for parents with different views to use their children as pawns in their own battles, but I think both my parents did a brilliant job of avoiding that sort of situation. . . . I've always had a relationship with my Dad and it's been important for me . . .' (Claire, thirty-three)

Children who have never had a father

Some children of lesbians grow up without a father, either because their mothers conceived by donor insemination using an anonymous donor or because the fathers were never involved with them (Saffron, 1994). Lesbians who conceive by donor insemination have to be committed to parenting by virtue of the greater level of planning involved. There are no accidental pregnancies for lesbians who get pregnant by this method. Their children have not experienced the loss of a father through divorce or death, nor suffered tension and conflict between unhappily married parents. There is much less research on planned lesbian families than on children of divorced lesbians. The few studies that have been done are of young children. They do not reveal any problems (McCandish, 1987; Steckel, 1987; Patterson, 1992, 1995a, 1995b; Golombok and Tasker, 1994; Flaks, 1995).

One of these studies was conducted by David Flaks and his colleagues. They studied the children of fifteen lesbian couples who conceived by donor insemination and fifteen heterosexual couples. The children were between the ages of three and nine years, with equal numbers of boys and girls. Using standard methods of assessment, they examined the children's intellectual development, behaviour and social competency. The two groups displayed many similarities, but the children of lesbians were better adjusted in seventeen of the twenty-four comparisons made. Both groups were well adjusted in comparison to population norms.

Lesson three: children need their parents to be happy

'[My mother has] always been strong and independent. She had to be ever since [her second husband] died and she found herself on her own raising three children. But since coming out, she's that much stronger. She's calmer as well, at peace with herself almost. She's got herself sorted out. A lot of women still think they need a man for fulfilment in life, but she doesn't. She's been so happy since she came out. For the first time in her life, she's had two very good, steady relationships.' (Kate, twenty-four, daughter of lesbian mother and gay father)

'The advantage of gay parents is that I have parents who are well integrated, are doing what's right for them and are happy. Therefore they've been able to give more to us. If your parents are happy, then obviously they're going to be better parents. My Mum's been very good to me, and I can't fault her. Since my Dad's come out, he's been happier in himself and has been a much better father to us.' (Rosie, twenty, daughter of lesbian mother and gay father)

It is the experience of many lesbians and gay men that openness about their sexual identity leads to greater psychological well-being, while hiding their sexuality is damaging (Strommen, 1990). Not disclosing something as fundamental as sexuality causes anxiety about being discovered, guilt over misleading people and results in distant and false relationships which would otherwise be more intimate. Though the research is limited, most writing on coming out to children asserts that telling children tends to improve the relationship with the lesbian and gay parent even if the child does not accept the parent's homosexuality (Bozett, 1987). The earlier children learn of their parents' sexual identity, the easier they find it to accept and the better for them. In one study of children of lesbians, teenage daughters who had been told of their mothers' lesbianism as young children had higher self-esteem than those who were adolescent when they were first told (Huggins, 1989).

Frederick Bozett (1987) described the process by which gay fathers gradually reformulate their sexual identity from one of married father with clandestine gay sexual encounters to that of an openly gay father. He noted that as they progress from denial to acceptance of their homosexuality, their sense of well-being increases. This is despite the homophobia they experience once they come out. Gay men who keep their sexuality hidden and remain married spend less quality time with their children compared to openly gay fathers who have better relationships with their children.

Studies on heterosexual mothers quoted in the review by Charlotte Patterson (1992) confirm the observation that a happy parent is a good parent. Patterson referred to one study which found that the psychological well-being of lesbian mothers was linked with their openness about their sexuality. Those mothers who were more open about being lesbian at home as well as at work and with their extended family were more likely to score high on well-being.

Lesson four: children are happier when their parents have an equal relationship

Charlotte Patterson (1995a) studied twenty-six lesbian couples in California who had at least one child between the ages of four and nine years. The parents were questioned about what and how much childcare and housework they did and about their perceptions of their children's behaviour. Children were also asked for their views, but were not assessed by an independent observer.

The study found that in those families where both the biological and non-biological mothers shared the childcare responsibilities equitably, the children had a greater sense of well-being. This was also true in cases where the non-biological mothers declared themselves satisfied with their involvement with the children, and was confirmed by reports from the biological mothers that the children had fewer behavioural problems. Likewise, non-biological mothers described how the children had fewer behavioural problems when the biological mothers were able to share the childcare responsibilities.

Biological mothers spent more time on childcare and housework and less time in paid employment than non-biological mothers. But the differences were minor compared to the differences between husbands and wives in heterosexual couples. Both the biological and non-biological mothers in the lesbian couples expected to have an egalitarian relationship, and most were satisfied with the way it had worked out for them since they had children. In contrast, heterosexual mothers often express dissatisfaction with the amount of childcare and housework their husbands do after they have children. Patterson believes that parents who divide the household labour equally benefit their children's social development by modelling fairness and participation in family decision-making. They may also be modelling happiness, which will have a positive effect on the children.

Lesson five: children learn positive moral values from lesbian and gay parents

'Mum's lesbianism and her strength of character have given me many choices in my life and so much freedom. My Mum brought me up so that I can take care of myself and so I'm confident enough to be myself. She taught me about being female in this society, about loving your body in a positive way, but being aware of the need to protect yourself from abuse by men. She made me aware of racism and other important issues at a very young age.' (Mandy, twenty-four, daughter of lesbian mother)

'Everything about having a gay father is an advantage. . . . I wonder how many people with straight parents have as much love as I do and are as happy as I am with my Dad. I've always been broad-minded, but having a gay father has made me even more broad-minded. I can accept people for what they are. I don't worry about people's sexuality. . . . Having a gay dad has made me realize that love can manifest itself in so many different ways. I vaguely felt all this before, but the reality of having a gay father has undoubtedly shaped my views.' (Fiona, nineteen, daughter of gay father)

Because the research on lesbian and gay parenting has focused on children's adjustment and their gender development, it has missed some of the potential advantages to children's development which could arise from having a lesbian or gay parent. These are the moral and social values modelled by parents who are different from the norm. Whether they teach by example or by explanation, having a lesbian or gay parent is a lesson in acceptance of diversity. Children are growing up in a changing society, where there are few certainties and no blueprints for living. In this society, at this time in history, there is a wealth of sexual identities, cultures, lifestyles, types of families and values. The most important lesson for our children is to teach them to value diversity, to be empathic with people who are oppressed and not to be afraid of difference. They need to learn to determine for themselves what they value and how they are going to live their lives.

The goal of parenting should be broader than the mere socialization of children into prescribed gender roles and one acceptable sexual identity. Dr Haim Ginott, a child psychologist, phrased the question in the following way:

> What is our major goal as parents? It seems to me that our large goal is to find the ways to help our children become humane and strong. For what does it profit us if we have a neat, polite, charming youngster who could watch people suffer and not be moved to take action? And do we really want children so well-adjusted that they adjust to an unjust situation? If we use methods that are humane, then we've shown the child how to be a person – a *mensch*, a human being who can conduct his life with strength and dignity. (Faber and Mazlish, 1990, p. 15 – *mensch* is a Yiddish word, meaning a person with dignity and self-respect)

Conclusion

The research on the children of lesbian and gay parents has consistently shown that a heterosexual mother and father is not essential for children's psychological development. So what do they need? They need their parents to provide plenty of positive resources, such as love and the ability to express love, emotional support, moral guidance, the skills to help them become happy and self-respecting people and an adequate level of financial resources. They need their parents to protect them from too many stressful events, such as destructive relationships with partners, loss of a parent, extreme poverty, violence, or mental and physical abuse:

> 'It sounds like a cliché, but it's more important to be loved by your parents than who or what they are. And to be taught common-sense by your parents is more important than to be taught to behave in an acceptable way.' (Rikki, thirty-four, son of lesbian mother)

References

Amato, P. (1993) 'Children's adjustment to divorce: theories, hypotheses and empirical support', *Journal of Marriage and the Family*, 55, February, 23–38.

Bozett, F.W. (1987) 'Gay fathers', in F.W. Bozett (ed.), *Gay and Lesbian Parents*. London: Praeger.

DiLapi, E.M. (1989) 'Lesbian mothers and the motherhood hierarchy', in F.W. Bozett (ed.), *Homosexuality and the Family*. New York/London: Harrington Park Press.

Faber, A. and Mazlish, E. (1990) *Liberated Parents, Liberated Children: Your Guide to a Happier Family*. New York: Avon Books.

Flaks, D.K., Ficher, I., Masterpasqua, F. and Joseph, G. (1995) 'Lesbians choosing motherhood: a comparative study of lesbian and heterosexual parents and their children', *Developmental Psychology*, 31 (1), 105–14.

Golombok, S., Spencer, A. and Rutter, M. (1983) 'Children in lesbian and single-parent households: psychosexual and psychiatric appraisal', *Journal of Child Psychology and Psychiatry*, 24, 551–72.

Golombok, S. and Tasker, F. (1994) 'Children in lesbian and gay families: theories and evidence', *Annual Review of Sex Research*, 4, 73–100.

Golombok, S. and Tasker, F. (1996) 'Do parents influence the sexual orientation of their children? Findings from a longitudinal study of lesbian families', *Developmental Psychology*, 32 (1), 1–9.

Huggins, S.L. (1989) 'Comparative study of self-esteem of adolescent children of divorced lesbian mothers and divorced heterosexual mothers', in F.W. Bozett (ed.), *Homosexuality and the Family*. New York/London: Harrington Park Press.

McCandish, B. (1987) 'Lesbian mother family dynamics', in F.W. Bozett (ed.), *Gay and Lesbian Parents*. London: Praeger.

Patterson, C.J. (1992) 'Children of lesbian and gay parents', *Child Development*, 63, 1025–42.

Patterson, C.J. (1995a) 'Families of the lesbian baby boom: parents' division of labor and children's adjustment', *Developmental Psychology*, 31 (1), 115–23.

Patterson, C.J. (1995b) 'Sexual orientation and human development: an overview', *Developmental Psychology*, 31, (1), special issue 3–11.

Saffron, L. (1994) *Challenging Conceptions: Planning a Family by Self-insemination*. London: Cassell.

Steckel, A. (1987) 'Psychosocial development of children of lesbian mothers', in F.W. Bozett (ed.), *Gay and Lesbian Parents*. London: Praeger.

Strommen, E. (1990) 'Hidden branches and growing pains: homosexuality and the family tree', in F.W. Bozett and M. Sussman (eds), *Homosexuality and Family Relations*. New York/London: Harrington Park Press.

TWENTY-ONE

Influences on Sexuality

'I used to think that if people knew about my Mum being lesbian, they would assume that I was a lesbian as well. It took me a long time to realize that that's about my Mum, and it's nothing to do with me. . . . Among all my lesbian friends up here, of which I have many, I only know one whose mother is a lesbian. . . . Having a lesbian mother gives you more choices. . . . It has simply meant that I feel comfortable being sexually involved with a woman.'   (Zoe, twenty-four, bisexual)

This chapter addresses the following questions. Does having a lesbian or gay parent influence attitudes towards sexuality? Does having a lesbian or gay parent influence attitudes towards homosexuality? What attitudes do lesbian or gay parents take towards their heterosexual children's sexuality and sexual partners? Are the children of lesbian and gay parents more likely to be gay or lesbian than the children of heterosexual parents?

Attitudes towards sexuality

'As I grew up and learned that there are different kinds of sexuality, I began to put two and two together. The way I felt about it was, "All right, so [my Dad] does it that way rather than this way." It wasn't a big deal for me.' (Mary, twenty)

Parents who are comfortable with their homosexual identity are likely to impart a liberal understanding of sexuality to their children. The people I interviewed believed that there is more than one acceptable sexual identity. Some expressed uneasiness with labels and the limits they impose on people's understanding of each other. Many spoke of their willingness to question their own sexuality.

Sexual identity or sexuality is a broad term which is generally defined by psychologists (Patterson, 1992; Golombok and Tasker, 1994) as a person's sexual orientation, their gender identity and their gender-role behaviour. Sexual orientation is about sexual attraction to partners of the same or other sex, regardless of whether the feelings and fantasies are acted on or not. Gender identity is whether people see themselves as male or female. Gender-role behaviour is whether they behave in ways defined as masculine or feminine by their culture.

Any sexual identity is just one aspect of an individual's total identity. But it has different meanings for different sexualities. For heterosexual people, heterosexuality is usually an unquestioned given, something perceived as normal and natural, not requiring explanation or justification. Few heterosexual people are subjected to intense questioning about the origins of their sexual identity. Claiming a homosexual identity has a very different meaning in our society. Due to negative stereotypes and the stigma associated with homosexuality, not everyone who is sexually attracted to people of the same sex wants to identify with such a label. They may deny their feelings or explain them as a phase they will grow out of. When people claim a homosexual identity, it is done in the context of the broader political battle for recognition and acceptance of sexual diversity. It is not just about sexual activity and sexual orientation but about lifestyle and the right to belong.

Asking about sexual identity assumes, often unfairly, that there are clear categories into which people can slot themselves. Based on extensive research carried out in the 1940s and 1950s into the sexual behaviour of Americans, Alfred Kinsey proposed a description of sexuality as a continuum rather than as two mutually exclusive categories. To this end, he developed a seven-point scale to place people along the continuum (Kinsey and Gebhard, 1948; Kinsey et al., 1953). However, the language in popular use does not reflect this way of thinking. There are still only two, or possibly three, labels to choose from – heterosexual, homosexual and bisexual – and these are still considered as categories that are fixed for life.

When asked how they defined their sexuality, some of the people I interviewed had a ready answer, while others could not categorize themselves so easily. The answers they gave were couched in terms of sexual orientation. Nobody expressed confusion about their gender identity. One woman whose mother had died when she was five referred to earlier anxiety about her femininity, but no one else had been concerned about their gender-role behaviour. Of the fourteen people over the age of eighteen, seven identified themselves as heterosexual, one as lesbian, three men as gay, two as bisexual and one uncertain. The lesbian and gay adults in my sample were sure of their sexuality before they were eighteen, but the six people I interviewed who were under eighteen were not ready to claim a sexual identity. Reactions ranged from discomfort to proud proclamation to casual acknowledgement:

'I understood I was gay before I recognized that my mother was. . . . When you're young, you instinctively don't like the idea of being labelled. I still don't like labels. They're very limiting. I hated the idea of being what people said I was. . . . We all use these labels. I'm as bad as everyone else. But it's a scary thing to take on the label, especially at seventeen when you know that the world hates gay people.' (Rikki, thirty-four)

'I define myself as a dyke. If Mum were forced to classify herself, she would say she is a lesbian or that she is gay. But given the choice, she would prefer not to label herself. That's a cop-out to me, but I can't judge her for it. I'd rather that she call herself lesbian, because it's important for me to have that identity.' (Emily, twenty-one)

'I have a heterosexual orientation. I've never wanted to have an emotional relationship with another man. In fact, when I was younger and certain advances were made to me, I've rejected them. I haven't had any recently.' (Nicolas, sixty-six)

'[My father's] homosexuality influenced me to question my sexuality more than I might have done. Until recently, I would have said I was straight, but I'm not sure at the moment.' (Mary, twenty)

'Until very recently I was in a relationship with a bloke . . ., so I considered myself heterosexual. I just became involved with a woman . . . [not] because she is a woman but because she is who she is. I've started questioning what it means to label yourself. If I were really thinking seriously about it, I'd call myself bisexual. But there are problems with the bisexual label. It's an ambiguous term. Nobody likes it. Although labels remain problematic for me, this is where I'm at now.' (Zoe, twenty-four)

No individual can pinpoint all the influences on their beliefs and attitudes about sexuality. Perhaps a group of twenty sons and daughters of heterosexual parents would have the same open-mindedness about sexuality as this sample. However, I suspect that having a lesbian or gay parent has been an important influence on attitudes about sexuality.

Attitudes towards homosexuality

According to a 1994 survey (Wellings *et al.*, 1994), a distressingly large percentage of the British population – two-thirds of men and over half of women – believe that homosexual sex is wrong. It seems reasonable to expect that the sons and daughters of lesbian or gay parents will not be among the homophobic majority. Their parents aspire to influence them, by explanation or by example, to be accepting of homosexuality. Without exception, this was true of the people I interviewed, regardless of the family situations they were raised in. Their attitudes can be summed up by Mary, twenty:

> 'On the whole, it's a straight world, with heterosexuality pushed on you from every direction. Like everyone else, I've been influenced by that. But because my Dad's gay, I've also had the added benefit of a positive experience of homosexuality. His homosexuality influenced me to question my sexuality more than I might have done.'

Kate, twenty-four, who has a lesbian mother and a gay father, expressed a similar view:

> 'The main thing having gay parents has done is help me understand gay society and changed my view of gay people. There isn't that much to understand, because they're normal people. It's just that they experience a lot of prejudice. If I hadn't had gay parents, I would have been carrying on like the rest of society, thinking they're in gay clubs and I'm not, and if it crosses my path then so be it. I wouldn't really have understood. My parents have given me hands-on experience, so to speak.'

Their progressive attitude was undoubtedly one reason for agreeing to the interview. There may be just as many people who feel ashamed of their parents' homosexuality or find it awkward to talk about sexuality in general who wouldn't volunteer to be interviewed. It would be difficult to locate them, and even harder to get them to express their views.

Everyone in my sample was sympathetic towards homosexuality. For some, acceptance and understanding was part of their everyday reality but not the issue they chose to do public battle over. Others actively championed homosexuality despite their non-homosexual identity. Several had appeared on TV or radio shows with their parents to show support for lesbian and gay families. Lord Rea used his position as a peer in the House of Lords to speak against a bill which would have restricted the rights of lesbians and gay men to adopt and foster children. Many showed their solidarity by going on the annual Gay Pride march.

Some parents actively promoted homosexuality to their children, while others kept a low profile. Some made sure their children knew about their homosexuality from a young age, while others were not told until they were in their teens. Regardless of their circumstances and initial reactions, the children of lesbians and gay men I interviewed expressed positive attitudes towards homosexuality. The lesson may be that good relationships with parents who feel happy about their own sexual identity is more important than any particular conscious technique the parent might adopt to teach their children about acceptance and diversity.

Josh and Rachel's parents energetically fostered acceptance of homosexuality. At the age of twelve, Josh boasted that he had only missed two Gay Pride marches in his life. He spoke enthusiastically about meeting lesbian and gay friends on the marches and how much he enjoys the festival atmosphere. Josh was conceived by self-insemination and lives with his mother and her woman partner. His mother makes sure he 'knows about all these sex things', as he puts it. Not surprisingly, he has an easy acceptance of homosexuality and a knowledge about sexuality that is not often found in a twelve-year-old.

At nineteen, Rachel has always known that her mother is lesbian. Her mother was outspoken about her lesbianism, taking Rachel on gay rights marches and lesbian events and introducing her to her partners. Rachel grew up regarding her mother's sexuality as unremarkable, as just one other fact about her. Rachel says she can't imagine what it would be like for either her father, who is heterosexual, or her mother to have anything but women partners.

Some of the interviewees grew up in environments where homosexuality was not part of the fabric of their everyday life. Until

Fiona was eleven, she lived in an isolated Scottish village where her father was a minister in a strict fundamentalist church. Homosexuality was never preached against in church, but neither was it mentioned in a favourable light, if at all. Fiona's family had no TV and no opportunity to see positive images of homosexuality. It was not until Fiona was thirteen that she and her brother and sister were told that their father was gay. Fiona recalls:

> 'Somehow I understood deep inside me that he was gay and I totally accepted it, right from the start. Even though I was brought up so religiously, I've always had my own views about things. . . . Because I love my Dad so much and have always been close to him, it's been no problem for me.'

At the age of nineteen, Fiona is heterosexual, but says she 'wouldn't be particularly bothered' if she fell in love with a woman.

When Claire was eight, her parents divorced. Claire didn't know until she was sixteen that the reason for the divorce was her mother's attraction to women. Both parents felt that it was in the best interests of their four children not to know, as they lived in a small Sussex village not renowned for its open-mindedness. Even though her mother's girlfriends often shared the family home, they were described as lodgers and the lesbian nature of their relationship was kept secret. Claire appreciates the secrecy, as it was difficult enough being different over less shocking issues, such as the kind of food their mother served. Claire is thirty-three with four children of her own and does not see any problems with lesbian mothers.

Not all the external influences on children push them in the direction of negative attitudes towards homosexuality. Nicolas acknowledged the influence of his lesbian mother on his tolerance of homosexuality but wondered if his experience at single-sex public schools was even more influential. He observed that boys who have been to British public schools have an 'underlying tolerance of homosexuality, however much they may outwardly condemn it and publicly pillory people for being in homosexual relationships'.

Experiences of heterosexual sons and daughters

It is a rare parent who can be impartial about how their children turn out and who has no unrealistic expectations of them. It would not be surprising to find some lesbian and gay parents who want their children to be the same sexuality as themselves, just as most heterosexual parents aspire for heterosexuality for their children. Among the heterosexual people in my sample, most felt that their parents had shown them an acceptable alternative to heterosexuality. The parents demonstrated by their example that heterosexuality is not the only way. Some parents achieved this without disparaging heterosexuality, while other parents did tease and urge their children to consider same-sex partners. None of the heterosexual people I interviewed described blatant disapproval or active hostility towards their choice of sexual partner.

Mandy, twenty-four, and Rachel, nineteen, perceived their lesbian mothers as encouraging and supportive of their adolescent sexual relationships with boys. While a teenager, Mandy became involved with a man she describes as 'the typical down-at-the-pub-with-his-pint kind of bloke', someone she would not consider now that she is older and more experienced. Mandy knew that her mother worried about the effect such a relationship could have on her independence and self-respect. But Mandy feels that her mother's non-interfering but understanding approach allowed her to emerge several years later, without having been pregnant or married and with her independence intact.

Rachel's lesbian mother encouraged her daughter to have relationships, without expressing a preference that it be with boys or girls. Rachel began dating boys at the age of thirteen. She wishes now that her mother had not been quite so tolerant of her youthful sexual activity. If either of her parents had tried to counter the peer and media pressure to be sexually active during adolescence, Rachel imagines she would not have had a baby at the age of nineteen.

Both Katrina, seventeen, and Kate, twenty-four, have lesbian mothers with clear preferences for their daughters' sexual orientation. Katrina says her mother would love it if she brought home a girlfriend instead of the boyfriends she has introduced her to over the last four years. Her mother teases her, saying, 'Oh I don't like that one, Katrina. Why don't you bring a girl home?' Katrina says she does not mind the joking, because she knows that when she is ready, she will discover her true sexuality. Kate has no doubt about her heterosexuality and finds it amusing when her mother suggests she try women whenever she is between boyfriends.

Mary, twenty, has been heterosexual and finds that she and her gay father have a common interest in men. She feels she can talk with him on a more equal level and that he understands her better than a heterosexual father would.

Development of sexuality – can you catch it from your parents?

'The fact is that I am gay. I don't care why. Whether it's nature or nurture is irrelevant.' (Mark, twenty-nine)

Unfortunately, the question of what influence parents have on children's sexuality is highly relevant to those who regard homosexuality as undesirable and wrong. Some people may be motivated by scientific curiosity about the human condition, but most people want to know in order to find a way to prevent the generation of more homosexuality. Would it matter what causes an individual's sexuality if sexual diversity were as acceptable as diversity in musical ability or eye colour?

Heterosexual parents are among those who think the question is relevant. Parents blame themselves, or are blamed, when their best efforts at socialization do not yield the desired results. When my daughter was a toddler, I made the mistake of attending a workshop advertising support for single parents. I was the only lesbian mother. When I referred to my sexuality, the sympathetic atmosphere turned nasty, eye contact suddenly vanished and the previously supportive single mothers bombarded me with questions about my upbringing: 'Are your parents heterosexual? Are they real heterosexuals? Are you sure they weren't closet gays? Did your parents have a good relationship? Do you want your daughter to be one?'

Child welfare professionals such as judges, social workers and solicitors are among those who consider the question to be relevant. During the custody case between her parents, Emily's lesbian mother was accused of brainwashing her daughter. The welfare officer wrote that Emily idolized her mother and imitated her. The report recommended that Emily be removed from her mother's influence, so that she would no longer be a lesbian and a risk to her younger sisters.

Policy-makers and legislators believe it is relevant. They make it difficult for lesbians to be accepted as patients at donor insemination and infertility clinics, and they do not welcome lesbians and gay men as adoptive and foster parents.

The studies done so far indicate that lesbian and gay parents are *not* likely to produce more lesbian and gay children than heterosexual parents. (For a good review of the studies, see Patterson, 1992; Golombok and Tasker, 1994.) The largest study was undertaken by Michael Bailey (1995) and his colleagues, and involved eighty-two sons of gay fathers in the USA. This study found that 9 per cent of the sons were gay, as indicated by their fathers. This 9 per cent is not significantly different from the 6 per cent who identify themselves as primarily homosexual in a recent large survey of Americans quoted by Diana Baumrind (1995).

However, the conclusion from these studies is still uncertain and cannot be generalized to those children brought up by openly lesbian or gay parents from birth in a society where lesbian and gay identities are much more accepted. Another interpretation of Michael Bailey's study is that the percentage of sons of gay fathers who are gay may actually be greater than the percentage of the population who are gay. Perhaps the true figure is not 9 per cent but nearer 16 per cent. (The 9 per cent is really plus or minus 6 per cent – by statistical tests there is a 95 per cent certainty that the figure is between 3 and 16 per cent.) In any case, Bailey's conclusions cannot be applied to the daughters of gay men or to the sons and daughters of lesbians. The other studies are based on even smaller samples than Bailey's. All use unrepresentative samples and include children who had at least one heterosexual parent for part of their lives. In some of the studies, the children were too young to have a defined sexual identity. No studies of sexual orientation have yet been done on children brought up exclusively by openly lesbian and gay parents from birth.

There is considerable debate about the origins of sexual identity. According to Charlotte Patterson's 1995 review of research into sexual orientation, there has been very little analysis of how people develop a homosexual identity. The debate is best summed up by Diana Baumrind (1995) who put the question in this way: 'Do people develop a permanent sexual orientation or identity early in life and then discover what they are, as the essentialist believes, or is their sexual identity and even their preferred object of erotic attraction socially created, bestowed, and maintained, as the constructionist believes?' Various theories have been put forward to explain how people might develop a sexual orientation. Each theory is only a partial explanation, and some theories have been discredited altogether. After studying what has been published on the subject, Susan Golombok and Fiona Tasker (1996) presented the current thinking. They found that though no consensus exists, most believe that there are a number of influences acting on individuals to shape their sexual development. It seems most likely that people follow different developmental pathways: some individuals are perhaps more influenced by genes, while others are affected more by socialization; some may be more responsive to parents, while others prove to be more susceptible to cultural influences.

Sexuality as social construction
This is not so much a theory about the development of sexuality as a different way of looking at the issue (Baumrind, 1995; Weeks, 1995). Jeffrey Weeks argues that sexuality is about choice and the debate should be about what, how and why we choose what we do. Instead of viewing sexuality as a fixed and fundamental characteristic of an individual, social constructionist theorists view it as a creation of the particular culture and historical moment in which we are living. Sexual identities have whatever meanings our culture gives them at this time. Lesbian and gay identities have not meant the same thing in the past and in different societies as they do to us now in late twentieth-century Britain. As identities, they have not always existed, though there undoubtedly have been people having sex with members of the same sex throughout history. That sexual identities are important to us is obvious from the intensity of the debate about the role of parents. But a social constructionist approach is not concerned with the mechanics of how individuals develop a sexual identity. What matters is the meanings homosexuality has for individuals in their private and social lives and how those meanings affect their moral values and the choices they make.

Social learning theory
'[When I was living with my father as a teenager,] he never allowed me to have friends, either girls or boys, in my bedroom. I had to entertain them in the living room with him sitting there behind the newspaper. He told me recently, "With a mother like yours, what did

you expect?" . . . He couldn't trust me alone in my bedroom with a woman, because I might end up the same way as my [lesbian] mother.' (Claire, thirty-three)

At the age of twelve, Mandy met her father whom she had not seen during most of her childhood:

'He'd bought me an expensive gold chain, which terrified me. He let me open the box and he took it out and put it on me. It was as if he were buying me. I have never liked that kind of thing anyway. Give me a skateboard and I'd be fine. He was scared that because my mother was a lesbian, she would corrupt my life and I would become a lesbian. I knew he was thinking, "My girl's going to be a little girl. She's going to be feminine."' (Mandy, twenty-four)

Clearly, both fathers believed that children learn their sexuality from their parents. The social learning theory (Golombok and Tasker, 1994; 1996) says that children use their parents as role models of gender-role behaviour and that gender-role behaviour is linked to later sexual orientation. Thus, by encouraging stereotypical gender-role behaviour when children are very young, parents should be able to mould their children into heterosexuality. Dressing boys in pink and giving tool sets to girls should point them in the direction of homosexuality.

When described so simplistically, the social learning theory is not supported by the evidence. The overwhelming majority of lesbian and gay people have heterosexual parents who are 'real' heterosexuals by any definition, who act as role models for heterosexuality and who encourage stereotypical gender-role behaviour. The research on the children of lesbians and gay men shows that they do not differ from the children of heterosexuals in their gender role behaviour. It is a controversial point whether there is even a link between young children's gender-role behaviour and their later sexuality (Baumrind, 1995; Golombok and Tasker, 1996). Most lesbians and gay men behave in culturally accepted gender roles as children.

However, it is unfair to discredit the theory entirely. It may be that most children are susceptible to such socialization and respond as expected, but that some are not and are less readily influenced by their parents. Or it could be that active discouragement of non-stereotypical gender-role behaviour or of homosexuality is more successful than active encouragement. As discussed above in the sections on attitudes, children do learn more liberal attitudes towards sexuality from growing up in a family atmosphere of openness and acceptance of homosexuality. Those children may learn to be more open to having same-sex sexual relationships themselves. Susan Golombok and Fiona Tasker (1996) found this to be the case in their long-term follow-up study, where they compared the children of lesbian mothers with children of single heterosexual mothers. They found that the adult sons and daughters of lesbians were more likely to have considered and to have had same-sex sexual relationships when teenagers than the sons and daughters of the heterosexual mothers. However, nearly all claimed a heterosexual identity as adults. There was no difference between the two groups in terms of sexual identity.

Cognitive development theory

Stephen, twenty-two, knew he was gay from the time he was eleven or twelve, but knew no other gay people at that time. The need for contact with gay culture grew over the next few years until it became a matter of urgent necessity. Living in a small market town with heterosexual parents, he phoned the only place he could think of that might help – a wholefood shop. Fortunately for him, one of the workers at the shop was a gay man who offered to talk to Stephen, and he subsequently became an important role model.

The cognitive development theory (Golombok and Tasker, 1994; 1996) sees children as actively participating in their own development. They seek out role models and information from the wider society that fit with their own emerging sexuality and gender behaviour. Parents may be one influence but not the most important. The family can make it easier or harder for the young person to find the models they want to identify with. Having a lesbian and gay parent will provide role models for children developing a lesbian or gay identity and will often mean that the children have access to a wider lesbian and gay culture. For children developing a heterosexual identity, the role models are, in any case, hard to escape.

Psychoanalytic theory

Psychoanalytic theory has largely been discredited as an explanation for the development of homosexuality. Based on their observations of gay men with psychological problems, psychoanalysts proposed that particular types of unhealthy relationships with parents were responsible for homosexuality. But large studies of gay and heterosexual men who were not patients of psychoanalysts did not confirm this (Golombok and Tasker, 1994, 1996; Bailey, 1995).

Biological transmission
Other theories of parental transmission are biological – that parents pass on their sexuality through the effects of sex hormones on the foetus during pregnancy. However, there is not enough evidence to establish what part, if any, sex hormones play (Reinisch, 1992; Golombok and Tasker, 1996).

Genetic transmission

The mother of Katrina, seventeen, told her that 'if you are homosexual, then you're born with a gene for it'. Jane, twenty-five, says, 'After my Mum told me she was lesbian, I wondered if I was too. My mother's brother is gay as well. I did think that it could be hereditary and maybe I was going to be like them.' Kate's mother is lesbian and her father is gay, while she and her sister are heterosexual. Kate, twenty-four, questioned her mother about it, asking '"my genes are made up of you two, and you two are gay, so why aren't [my sister] and I like you two?"'

The theory that genes play a part in influencing the development of homosexuality is based on evidence from biological research (Burr, 1993; LeVay, 1993; Bailey *et al.*, 1995; Patterson, 1995; Golombok and Tasker, 1996). This research claims to explain part of the origins of homosexuality, while still leaving open the explanation for the rest. Simon LeVay (1993) concludes that there is a 'strong but not total genetic influence on sexual orientation in men and a substantial but weaker genetic influence in women'.

The evidence about the role of genes comes from studies of male and female twins. There are a few studies of twins separated at birth, but most are of twins raised together in the same family, where they are presumably subject to similar influences from their parents. When siblings have no genes in common because one or both have been adopted, they are no more likely to be homosexual than any two people from different families. However, the twin sisters and brothers of lesbians and gay men are much more likely to be lesbian or gay as well. If the twins are identical, it is even more likely for both to be homosexual than for non-identical twins. For both males and females, the chance that the other identical twin will also be lesbian or gay is more than 50 per cent. For non-identical male twins, the chance of his twin brother also being gay is 25 to 30 per cent, higher than for unrelated people but not as high as for identical twins. For non-identical girl twins, the chance is about 16 per cent, about the same as if they were not genetically related. This kind of evidence leads researchers to believe that genes partially explain the origins of sexual orientation. Since roughly half of identical twins differ in a characteristic as fundamental as sexual orientation, genes clearly do not fully explain sexual diversity. The rest of the explanation is environmental, which is where the other theories come in.

Conclusion

Those lesbian and gay parents who are proud of their sexual identity inevitably communicate a positive attitude towards homosexuality. The sons and daughters I interviewed were accepting of homosexuality, open-minded about sexual diversity and often questioning of their own sexual identity. As children grow up, they make their own choices about who they have sex with, what sexual identity they claim, and what values they live by. While there are many significant influences on these choices besides parents, having a lesbian or gay parent must have some bearing on the meaning they give to sexuality.

References

Bailey, J.M., Bobrow, D., Wolfe, M. and Mikach, S. (1995) 'Sexual orientation of adult sons of gay fathers', *Developmental Psychology*, **31** (1), 124–9.

Baumrind, D. (1995) 'Commentary on sexual orientation: research and social policy implications', *Developmental Psychology*, **31** (1), 130–6.

Burr, C. (1993) 'Homosexuality and biology', *The Atlantic Monthly*, March 1993, pp. 47–65.

Golombok, S. and Tasker, F. (1994) 'Children in lesbian and gay families: theories and evidence', *Annual Review of Sex Research*, **4**, 73–100.

Golombok, S. and Tasker, F. (1996) 'Do parents influence the sexual orientation of their children? Findings from a longitudinal study of lesbian families', *Developmental Psychology*, **32** (1), 1–9.

Kinsey, A., Pomeroy, W.B. and Martin, C.E. (1948) *Sexual Behavior in the Human Male*. Philadelphia: W.B. Saunders.

Kinsey, A., Pomeroy, W B., Martin, C.E. and Gebhard, P.H. (1953) *Sexual Behavior in the Human Female*. Philadelphia: W.B. Saunders.

LeVay, S. (1993) *The Sexual Brain*. London: Bradford Books/MIT Press.

Patterson, C.J. (1992) 'Children of lesbian and gay parents', *Child Development*, **63**, 1025–42.

Patterson, C.J. (1995) 'Sexual orientation and human development: an overview', *Developmental Psychology*, **31** (1), 3–11.

Reinisch, J.M. (1992) 'Did prenatal hormones make her gay?' Text on Compuserve Human Sexuality Forum, United Feature Syndicate.

Weeks, J. (1995) *Invented Moralities: Sexual Values in an Age of Uncertainty*. Cambridge: Polity Press.

Wellings, K., Field, J., Johnson, A.M. and Wadsworth, J. (1994) *Sexual Behaviour in Britain: The National Survey of Sexual Attitudes and Lifestyles*. Harmondsworth:Penguin.

TWENTY-TWO

Lesbian, Gay and Bisexual
Daughters and Sons

We're Here! We're Queer!! And so are Mum and/or Dad!!!
(Banner carried at Stonewall Parade, New York, 1995)

Adolescence can be a particularly difficult time for lesbian, gay and bisexual teenagers. The problems arise not only from outright persecution but from the denial of their emerging sexuality and lack of support from their family and peers. Taken together, these problems can have a major effect on their mental health. Is it any easier for such teenagers when they have a lesbian or gay parent?

Emerging sexuality and positive role models

Most lesbian, gay and bisexual teenagers are not supported or encouraged to develop a homosexual identity. Indeed, they are actively pressured to develop a heterosexual identity. Most have no homosexual adult role models during the formative years of their sexual development and may not know any lesbian or gay people their own age. They know they are different and are painfully aware of the stigma attached to their difference. Stephen, twenty-two, has heterosexual parents. He moved in with a gay couple at the age of sixteen. 'I knew I was gay from the time I was eleven or twelve, but at that time I had no language to use to identify myself. I didn't know any other gay people. . . . The problem was that I couldn't talk to [my parents] about being gay.'

Parents, teachers and agony aunts may try to reassure teenagers that they are merely going through a phase or that it is a normal stage in the inevitable development of heterosexuality. Some argue that there is no such thing as a lesbian or gay adolescent, that only if sexual identity persists into adulthood can the person claim to be gay or lesbian. These explanations deny the reality of many teenagers and are more likely to cause stress and anxiety rather than reassurance. Instead of describing same-sex attraction as a phase, Ritch Savin-Williams (1990), who has studied lesbian and gay teenagers, claims that during adolescence, sexual identity is not firmly linked to sexual behaviour. While lesbian and gay teenagers may be sexually active with people of the same sex, many may not be sexually active at all; others are heterosexually active; and even some heterosexual adolescents are homosexually active:

'I was not out at school. I was terrified of anyone guessing my sexuality and covered up as much as I could. . . . I was so worried about discovery that I made sure one girlfriend called herself by a different name every time she rang. I was also extremely heterosexually promiscuous. That was the way I coped at the time. . . . I'd much rather have been brave enough to come out, but I couldn't have done at the time.' (Emily, twenty-one)

Inasmuch as they accept their sexuality and are open about it to their children, lesbian and gay parents act as a positive role model. Theoretically this openness should make it easier for their gay and lesbian children to accept themselves and adapt to a homosexual identity than it is for those teenagers without such positive role models. The lesbian, gay and bisexual people I interviewed did perceive this as an advantage:

'That my parents were gay made it a lot easier for me to come out and to see that there could be a physical dimension to my friendships with girls. . . . [I] was encouraged to be what [I] wanted to be. I have experimented sexually, and my parents have created a supportive environment for that.' (Rosie, twenty, bisexual, daughter of lesbian mother and gay father)

'Having a lesbian mother has made it easier, because there's an acceptable role model for me. Mum has always been my ally. . . . For quite a while, she was the only out lesbian that I knew.' (Emily, twenty-one, lesbian)

A potential disadvantage of having a lesbian or gay parent is the assumption that the teenagers are imitating their parents and that they are lesbian or gay merely because their parents are. Emily, Mark and

Rikki were at pains to point out that they were aware of their own sexuality before they knew of their mothers' lesbianism. Especially in the context of a society which denies adolescent homosexual identity, lesbian and gay teenagers feel it is important that their sexual identity be accepted as their own.

> 'Because of the way lesbianism was dealt with in the custody case, I needed to prove to myself that my sexuality was my own, that it wasn't to do with Mum. In the welfare officer's report, Mum was accused of influencing me. I was told that it was just a phase, that it wasn't my decision. It's been important for me to realize that I was attracted to women before I even knew about Mum. . . . It really helped me accept my sexuality. . . . I don't feel I've got anything to prove any more.' (Emily, twenty-one)

> 'I'm not gay because my Mum is a lesbian. I was gay first. I had no idea my Mum had slept with women when I was having sex with boys. People say, "Oh you picked up on that." They also say, "You had two horrible fathers." So what! The fact is that I am gay. I don't care why.' (Mark, twenty-nine)

> 'One thing people often say is that if you've got gay parents, you will be gay yourself. I suppose that can be said of me but it's not true of my brother and sister. I don't really think it affected us at all. Not everything we do is due to her influence. Anyway, I understood I was gay before I recognized that my mother was and possibly before she even realized she was.' (Rikki, thirty-four)

The advantage of positive role models for gay teenagers is illustrated in Stephen's story. While a teenager, Stephen was befriended by a gay couple, Geoff and Peter. They became his unofficial foster parents when his relationship with his parents deteriorated, largely due to Stephen's crisis over his emerging gay sexuality. Stephen moved in with Geoff and Peter and they offered him valuable support during his adolescence:

> 'Geoff and Peter have had a major influence on me in several ways. One is that I don't think about being gay any more. It's not something I question. . . . I can see that they influenced my relationship with my boyfriend. . . . Geoff and Peter have been together for fifteen years. When I was much younger, they instilled in

me a sense of how positive, loving and long-lasting gay relationships can be. . . . I could see that they were happily married. I think [my boyfriend] and I have that now.' (Stephen, twenty-two)

(See the information about the Albert Kennedy Trust in Appendix B.)

Coming out

Positive role models of parents or other adults certainly help teenagers develop their lesbian and gay identity, but even the most positive models don't alter the reality that homosexuality is not considered acceptable in society. As Mark, twenty-nine, says, 'Coming out is one of the biggest things in your life. . . . It's a mixture of being proud to be gay at the same time as thinking I'm a disgusting pervert. I'd had fifteen years of indoctrination by straight society to overcome.'

Lesbian and gay people with heterosexual parents risk rejection by their families when they come out or when their sexuality is discovered. The rejection may be mild and temporary as Stephen, twenty-two, experienced when he finally told his father: 'He asked what was wrong and said, "Look, you can . . . tell us anything. We love you. We're your parents." . . . I shouted at the top of my voice, "Dad, I'm gay." His reply was, "Oh, shit."' Or the rejection may be more extreme, resulting in physical abuse or the young person being forced out of their home and onto the street.

Erik Strommen (1990) summarized the reactions heterosexual families tend to have. Not all are negative, but it is rare for a coming-out announcement to be greeted with joy. The most negative, rejecting reactions occur in religious families, in families with traditional stereotyped gender roles, and in conventional families who are more concerned with their standing in the community than with loyalty to individual members of the family. Fathers tend to have stronger negative reactions than mothers and often find it harder to accept gay sons than lesbian daughters. Parents usually feel guilty, often believing that they are responsible for their child's homosexuality, a popular view held by many (see Chapter 21). Teenagers may be frightened to talk to their parents, unsure whether their disclosure will be received with love or denial. Many heterosexual parents do come to accept a lesbian daughter or a gay son in time. To do so, they go through a process of adjustment which often requires them to redefine their own values and come to a more realistic understanding of homosexuality.

How different is the process of coming out when a parent is lesbian or gay? Among the people I interviewed, two gay sons and one lesbian daughter came out to their lesbian mothers when they were teenagers. There were no gay fathers with lesbian or gay children in my sample. While Emily's lesbian mother was generally happy about Emily's lesbianism, she had difficulty accepting her desire to become a lesbian mother, citing the easier time she had as a heterosexual mother than as a lesbian mother. When Rikki came out to his mother at the age of seventeen, he knew that being lesbian herself she wasn't going to 'throw him out of the house, murder him or drag him off to be exorcized'. Nevertheless, being lesbian didn't guarantee a positive response either:

> 'People often say to me that it must be so cool to have a gay mother, that she would be much more understanding. But in the end your mother is your mother, and you . . . just don't want to talk to your mother about sex when you're sixteen.
> 'She didn't disapprove of me being gay. But telling her wasn't particularly easy. . . . Now she'd be terrific about it.' (Rikki, thirty-four)

When Mark's lesbian mother was told, she went quiet and then began crying. Finally she told Mark how proud she was of him for being different but how worried she was that he 'was in for a hard life'.

Clearly, from these experiences, coming out to a lesbian mother is not as risky as coming out to a heterosexual parent, but it also shows that the declaration will not necessarily be greeted with delight and celebration.

Persecution

Persecution because of one's homosexuality, known as gay-bashing, is a common experience of lesbian and gay teenagers. Scott Hershberger and Anthony D'Augelli (1995) questioned more than 220 lesbian, gay and bisexual teenagers about their experience of victimization. The teenagers attended gay community groups in large American cities. The percentage of these young people who reported persecution was disturbingly high: verbal insults 80 per cent; threats of attack 44 per cent; objects thrown

33 per cent; being chased or followed 30 per cent; property damage 23 per cent; sexual assault 22 per cent; physical assault 17 per cent; being spat on 13 per cent; and assault with a weapon 10 per cent. Whether this level of victimization is typical of the experience of most American or British teenagers is not certain. The young people in this study were attending a gay-identified centre and probably displayed their sexual identity more openly than many lesbian and gay teenagers. As a result, they could have been more obvious targets of attack. The study does not truly reflect the experience of teenage girls, since only a quarter of the sample were girls. It is likely that many lesbian and gay teenagers have a smoother ride through adolescence.

Sadly, however, the bleak reality portrayed by this study was confirmed by the people I interviewed. And the persecution may be worse for some teenagers than for others. Gay youths undoubtedly experience more physical abuse than lesbians. Black lesbian and gay teenagers are affected by more than one prejudice and undoubtedly have a harder time of it than white lesbian and gay teenagers:

'There were . . . kids in the neighbourhood who gave me lots of trouble for being gay. Starting when I was ten or eleven, I was bullied often. . . . My family has had trouble from white people putting fireworks through the letter-box, because we lived in a National Front area. As a black person you expect to be treated badly. . . . And as a gay person you learn that as well. Luckily my mother and I haven't had any abuse because of being gay.' (Rikki, thirty-four)

Mental health and family support

Gay-bashing is a fact of life and there is a limit to what a lesbian or gay parent can do to protect their children from it, especially as the adults are subject to the same persecution. Whether or not the persecution and stigmatization lead to mental health problems depends on the teenager's personality and self-esteem, which in turn depends on the extent of family and peer support the young person has.

The studies of lesbian and gay teenagers with heterosexual parents (Savin-Williams, 1989, 1990; Baumrind, 1995; Hershberger and D'Augelli, 1995; Patterson, 1995) reveal a higher than normal risk of depression, suicide, attempted suicide, thoughts of suicide, substance abuse, feelings of isolation and alienation, stress, high-risk sexual behaviour, acting-out behaviour, and feelings of self-doubt and vulnerability compared to non-gay teenagers. One American study quoted by Hershberger and D'Augelli (1995) estimated that 30 per cent of all youth suicides were committed by lesbian and gay teenagers. Estimates of lesbian and gay attempted suicide rates range from 21 to 35 per cent depending on the study, compared to a suicide attempt rate of below 13 per cent for high school students. I know of no similar studies in Britain, nor whether the situation in the USA is the same as in Britain.

One of the people I interviewed described how she endured a particularly difficult four-year period when she left school:

'I've been to places in my head where I felt like I was on the edge. . . . I was very lonely, made suicide attempts, ended up on different medications and had to go and see a shrink at the hospital. I used to self-mutilate. . . . It was a coping mechanism. . . .

'Most of it was to do with different forms of abuse that I've experienced. I wouldn't say that any of it was to do with my Mum being a lesbian. But some of it was to do with internalized homophobia. I was really angry that my sexuality had caused so many problems socially. . . . I didn't have any other outlet for that anger.' (Emily, twenty-one)

Family support is crucial to self-esteem. Hershberger and D'Augelli (1995) found in their study that those teenagers who accepted their sexuality and felt good about themselves were less likely to suffer mental health problems. And those who felt good about themselves were more likely to have good relationships with their parents. Diana Baumrind (1995) made an interesting observation about the suicide rate of American lesbian and gay teenagers compared with that of African-American teenagers. Both groups are persecuted for who they are, but the suicide rate of black teenagers is much lower than that of lesbian and gay teenagers. The explanation she puts forward is that young black people are not routinely rejected by their family and peers, while lesbian and gay youth are.

Rikki, thirty-four, is an example of a black gay teenager whose self-esteem was high despite the persecution he experienced. Coming from a strong family, Rikki was able to maintain his place among his friends and to handle the peer pressure to conform to social expectations of masculinity. He explained that in his family, 'There's no chance that somebody could be disowned. . . . We do communicate and we know each other well. We know every emotion. As a result, our family is strong.' This stood him in good stead for the anti-gay persecution he experienced:

'I got a bit of teasing when I was very young [for being gay], and as I grew older, I got tons of it. But I was never pushed outside of my group of friends. All my friends were tough street kids, the kind who run around causing trouble. But all of them accepted me, because I was very creative, had lots of ideas and I led a lot of activities. So my friends excused me for not being as masculine as you're supposed to be. I had a vigorous personality and that got me by.'

Conclusion

Lesbian or gay parents who are open about their own sexual identity model pride and self-acceptance and provide crucial support to their lesbian and gay teenage children during the difficult adolescent years. However, there are limits to the protection and encouragement a parent can provide in the face of a homophobic culture.

References

Baumrind, D. (1995) 'Commentary on sexual orientation: research and social policy implications', *Developmental Psychology*, **31** (1), 130–6.

Hershberger, S.L. and D'Augelli, A.R. (1995) 'The impact of victimization on the mental health and suicidality of lesbian, gay and bisexual youths', *Developmental Psychology*, **31** (1), 65–74.

Patterson, C.J. (1995) 'Sexual orientation and human development: an overview', *Developmental Psychology*, **31** (1), 3–11.

Savin-Williams, R.C. (1989) 'Coming out to parents and self-esteem among gay and lesbian youths', in F.W. Bozett (ed.), *Homosexuality and the Family*. New York/London: Harrington Park Press.

Savin-Williams, R.C. (1990) 'Gay and lesbian adolescents', in F.W. Bozett and M. Sussman (eds), *Homosexuality and Family Relations*. New York/London: Harrington Park Press.

Strommen, E. (1990) 'Hidden branches and growing pains: homosexuality and the family tree', in F.W. Bozett and M. Sussman (eds), *Homosexuality and Family Relations*. New York/London: Harrington Park Press.

TWENTY-THREE

Family-Making
– Who Counts as Family?

Many lesbians and gay men have adopted the idea of family to describe the circle of meaningful people in their lives. They do it partly as a defiant gesture to a society which refuses to recognize the value of lesbian and gay relationships. It is also a positive reclaiming of an institution from which lesbians and gay men have traditionally been excluded (Weston, 1991; Benkov, 1994). While this is a significant political and psychological step for lesbians and gay men, the perspectives of their children may well be different. I asked the people I interviewed who they counted as family, what family meant to them and what the circumstances were of their particular families.

When I asked Mark, twenty-nine, about his family, he answered that he counts his boyfriend, his lesbian mother, his mother's first woman partner and several friends:

> 'We're a family and we're part of other families as well. I use the word 'family' on my own terms, not the way heterosexuals use it. Close support or community doesn't give it the oomph that I'm trying to convey, so I say family. Family doesn't necessarily have to mean biological relationships, but it can involve them. It's a family of our own choosing, which is important.'

A lesbian or gay parent is itself a challenge to conventional ideas of family where parents are meant to be heterosexual. But people brought up by lesbians or gay men questioned an even more fundamental concept of family – the absolute and necessary link between biological kinship and family relationship. Time and again, the people I interviewed counted people with no biological connection as family and excluded others with a biological bond. Family membership was earned by the quality of the relationship rather than by the mere sharing of genes.

Biological ties

Everyone I interviewed counted some biological kin as family, both in their immediate and their extended families. However, biological kinship did not automatically guarantee a place. Fraught or distant relationships were the most common reasons why some people excluded biological kin. Several of the people in my sample described circumstances where bonds based on genes alone withered through lack of interest or were actively severed. Katrina, seventeen, is well aware that she shares half of her genes with her father, yet she is under no illusions about his relationship to her. She was not impressed when he appeared on her doorstep after an absence of four years. Nor was she pleased with the 'Happy Sixteenth' card he sent on her fifteenth birthday. She says, 'I may have wished for a father-figure in my life, but that was a dream really. I never had one. A dad is the word for the person that is the other half of my genetic make-up, but he's not my parent.' On the other hand, biological connection to her mother and her mother's extended family has created solid social bonds: 'I have my family who are blood-related, and we are all colours of the rainbow. There is a very strong bond there because of our biological connections.'

Emily, twenty-one, includes her lesbian mother, her mother's partner and her three younger sisters as her immediate family. She reluctantly counts her father as family, explaining that she does not feel close to him. She has no hesitation in discounting her father's new wife as family.

Lawrence's lesbian mother wanted to have a child by herself and got pregnant by a friend who was not involved with Lawrence as a social father. Lawrence, fourteen, struggles to find words that reflect his reality: 'I don't call my father Dad, but I consider him my father.' He definitely regards both sets of grandparents as family, 'because they are my biological family'.

Fiona, nineteen, counts her immediate family as her father, her brother and her sister. She does not count her biological mother and relatives as family, feeling angry at the way they treated her and her gay father after her father came out: he is scarcely tolerated since revealing his sexual identity to his family. His mother has visited him once for only an hour, his brothers and sisters ignore him and one cousin makes her rejection painfully explicit.

When Alice, fifteen, was five, her biological mother's sister was granted custody of her. She was raised by three lesbians, only one of whom has a biological connection to her. Alice did not see her biological mother for nearly ten years, but met her when she was fifteen and decided to count her as a fourth mother. At the same age, she met her biological father for the first time, but decided she had 'enough family' by that time and does not count him. She regards the biological extended families of her three mothers as family.

Lesbian couples who co-parent

One way that a child acquires an extra lesbian mother is through the woman's relationship to a partner who conceives by donor insemination. The non-biological mother relationship is created by the commitment she makes during the planning, by the bond she forms with the baby and by her parenting role as the child grows up. It would be surprising if a child born and raised in this family would count her as anything less than a mother. That does not mean that children in this type of family have the same relationship with each of their mothers or that the children do not know which woman gave birth to them. Besides personality differences, there may be differences in the significance the mothers attach to the biological tie and in the amount of time they spend with the child. Some children have a more intense and confrontational relationship with their biological mothers and a more distant but smoother one with the mother who does not have a biological connection; there may be any number of types of relationships.

If the parents separate, the parental relationship between the non-biological mother and the child does not necessarily end, any more than with a divorced heterosexual parent. When Kieron, fifteen, was born, his two mothers were living together. They separated when he was four but continued to share the parenting equally. Kieron and his brother move between the two households during the week. Kieron considers both to be his mothers.

There have been a few studies of families created this way which suggest that lesbian co-parents divide the childcare fairly equally and have good relationships with their children. One study by Charlotte Patterson (1995, also discussed on page 191) revealed that non-biological mothers spend more time caring for their children than heterosexual fathers who live with their wives. Another study by David Flaks (1995) and his colleagues (also discussed on page 189) compared fifteen lesbian couples who had children by donor insemination with fifteen heterosexual couples. The study did not look at the quality of the parent-child relationships but at their parenting skills. The lesbian couples were more aware of the skills needed for effective parenting than the heterosexual couples. They were better able to recognize problems in parenting and to envisage solutions for them. The heterosexual couples did less well in this comparison, because the fathers performed poorly in the test. All the mothers, whether lesbian or heterosexual, were aware of good parenting skills.

Gay men becoming fathers

Most people with gay fathers have fathers who were once married or lived with a woman. Some gay fathers remain married because they feel there is no alternative, afraid that contact with their children would be denied if they were open about their sexuality. The majority do not remain in a heterosexual relationship once they accept their sexual identity. But when gay men leave, the mother is more likely to be awarded custody. It is more common for lesbian mothers to be living with their children than for gay fathers. Mary, however, was raised by her gay father. Her mother died when she was five, but her parents had already separated when she was two and she had remained with her father after the separation. Fiona's parents divorced when her father told his wife that he was gay. Initially, Fiona and her brother and sister lived with their mother, but Fiona and her mother did not get on well and eventually Fiona left to live with her father.

Gay fathers may find it more difficult to tell their children they are gay than do lesbian mothers. Mostly the children react with understanding and acceptance, but researchers have found that gay fathers experience more negative reactions than lesbian mothers. It is harder for gay fathers to integrate their parenting identity and their sexual identity than it is for lesbian mothers. (Bozett, 1987, 1989)

Surrogacy is one way for a gay man to become both a biological and a social father. Surrogacy involves an arrangement with a woman to conceive by donor insemination, carry the baby to term and give birth, but not to function as a social mother. Commercial surrogacy is illegal in Britain and though it is possible to make informal arrangements, it is not often done. In many states of the USA, commercial surrogacy is legal and gay men have become fathers through this route as well as through informal arrangements, sometimes with lesbians acting as the surrogate (Benkov, 1994; Martin, 1994). Other ways in which gay men become fathers include donor insemination and adoption and fostering.

Donors and fathers

One way that lesbians separate biological parenthood from social parenthood is by the use of donor insemination. This is a relatively simple process by which a man donates his sperm. When performed at a clinic, the donor is always anonymous, but lesbians often make informal arrangements with men for 'self-insemination'. In these situations, the social relationship between the donor and the child is negotiated in advance between the mother or mothers-to-be and the donor. Children sometimes redefine these relationships as they become older. Where the donor's identity is known, children can initiate contact if they choose (Weston, 1991; Benkov, 1994; Martin, 1994; Saffron, 1994;).

Some donors arrange to be co-parents, so that they are fathers in both the biological and social sense of the word. Many lesbians, however, prefer the donor to remain anonymous and not become a father (Saffron, 1994). Kieron's mother conceived by self-insemination using an anonymous donor and when asked about his father, Kieron, fifteen, simply says he does not have a father. Other lesbian mothers want the child to know the donor's identity but to have no contact. Some want the donor to have some kind of contact with the child but not a parental relationship. Josh's mother conceived by self insemination using a gay friend as donor. Josh, twelve, wanted to get to know the donor when he was six and began seeing him on a weekly basis until he and his mother moved to another city. Josh calls the donor his father, but he has not had any contact for several years.

Adoption and fostering

When a lesbian or gay couple adopt or foster children together, neither partner has any biological connection to the children. They are beginning their family on a potentially equal basis with no reason for either parent to have a deeper or stronger bond with the children than the other. As soon as the adoption is finalized, however, only one parent has legal status, creating the potential for inequality in their relationships. British law does not allow lesbian or gay couples to adopt children. Single people can adopt, and one partner in the lesbian and gay couple is normally approved as the legal parent. The other partner can apply to a court for a residence order granting parental responsibility. Although the Children Act 1989 says that 'no group should be arbitrarily excluded for consideration as carers' (Children Act 1989, Regulation and Guidance), many local authorities and voluntary organizations working with children do not consider lesbian and gay applicants for fostering or adoption. (See Appendix A for details about the Lesbian and Gay Fostering and Adoptive Parents' Group.)

Stephen, twenty-three, was fostered informally by a gay couple when he was a teenager. He describes himself as having two families – his birth family and his gay family. While his birth family donated his genes and raised him until the age of sixteen, both families provide love, acceptance, a refuge in times of trouble, a shared history and a lifelong commitment. Being fostered by a gay couple can be a life-saver for a gay teenager. Stephen recalls, 'Once I'd started living with Peter and Geoff, I became centred, calm and happy and my relationship with my parents was much better.' Stephen and his boyfriend hope to foster or adopt a gay teenager when they are older. (See Appendix A for information about the Albert Kennedy Trust and fostering lesbian and gay teenagers.)

When friends become family

Friendships can be transformed into family relationships by conscious acknowledgement and sometimes difficult negotiations; however, not every close friend becomes part of the family. Alice, fifteen, counts three women as her mothers. They live in two separate households and Alice moves between the two. None of the three mothers is her biological mother. Alice's family has applied to court under the Children Act for a joint residency order for all three. She says, 'It would be a precedent-setting case, because not only is it women sharing the wardship it would be three women. What we really want is to get recognition for all three being my parents, and there is no history of anything like that.'

Alice's definition of her family is expansive, including close friends and people who once shared a household as well as biological relations of her non-biological mothers and a woman partner of one of her mothers. Alice says of this last woman, 'She's not a mother. . . . She'd hate me to think that she was another mother. She's not into all this family business. She's her own person. But she's definitely family. I've claimed her. She's mine.' But Alice differentiates close friends from family. She described a friendship as so close that she almost counted the girl as her sister, but accepted that she is really a best friend.

Mary, twenty, was raised by her gay father in a communal household which consisted of several adults and children. Sylvia had been living in the household for most of Mary's life. In her teens, Mary negotiated with Sylvia to establish a mother-daughter relationship. It was hard work due to the history of complex feelings Mary had about the death of her mother when she was five and about Sylvia's relationship to her foster daughter who also lived in the household. For most of her childhood, Mary did not want a replacement for her mother and pushed away anybody who tried to mother her. Eventually, Mary realized that her relationship with Sylvia was deteriorating. She made the decision to be honest both with herself and with Sylvia, and during a heart-to-heart talk told Sylvia that she considered her part of her family and wanted her to be her mother. The honesty paid off and their relationship improved.

Step-families – partners who become parents

Children can acquire lesbian or gay parents when their biological parent starts a relationship with a new partner (Baptiste, 1987). Both partners may have children, so that each child has both a biological and a non-biological parent and new siblings. These types of family are essentially step-families, in many ways no different from the families created when heterosexual people divorce and remarry. The step-family associations of the USA and Britain (Robinson and Smith, 1993; Gerlach, 1995) were established to provide support and to challenge misguided expectations and myths about step-families. Despite obvious similarities between lesbian and gay families and the step-families they describe, there is no mention of lesbians or gay men in any of the literature published by these associations. However, there are many similarities between lesbian and gay step-families and heterosexual step-families. To begin with, neither a heterosexual step-parent nor a lesbian or gay step-parent has any legal status as a parent to their partner's children unless they acquire it by court order (see 'Legal ties' below). Moreover, compared to biological parents, step-parents do not have a clear role to play. The cultural expectations of biological parents are probably impossible to meet. They may be even more difficult for step-parents. Children expect unconditional love from their biological parents, but it is not clear what they should expect from a step-parent and how long it should take for a parent-child relationship to form, if it ever does. Children may not be willing to accept the authority of a step-parent and may not cooperate with the discipline or rules they set.

Children may be confused by the lack of recognition of the step-parent. Outside the immediate family, other people may discount the step-parent's position either openly or more covertly. Ex-partners and relatives may be hostile or dismissive. Lesbian, gay and even heterosexual step-parents often comment on how invisible they feel.

The bond between the child and the step-parent is never going to be the same and is unlikely to be as strong as the bond between the child and a biological parent, who have had years of shared experience. The children may be expected to love and accept the step-parent and the step-parent's children, but may instead be rejecting or indifferent. Children may also compete with the step-parent for the attention and affection of the biological parent.

If the parent starts a live-in relationship after years of functioning as a one-parent household, the change can be very stressful for the child. An only child can develop an emotionally intense relationship with their single parent, and they may have had more involvement in family decision-making and household responsibility than a child with two parents. The child may have to accept a less important role in the family when there are two adults. The child has to share the parent with the new partner and accept a different kind of relationship with their biological parent, all of which can be difficult.

The step-family associations warn that it takes at least five years, and often more, for the heterosexual step-family to form a new family identity and sense of belonging. This is likely to be true for lesbian and gay step-families as well.

Despite these similarities, lesbian and gay step-families have unique concerns that distinguish them from heterosexual step-families. Most significantly, lesbian and gay families have to contend with prejudice against homosexuality. Heterosexual step-families are still struggling for recognition as a valid type of family, but they have greater social legitimacy than lesbian and gay families. The lesbian and gay step-parent is more often than not invisible as a parent. There are no public rituals confirming their membership in the new family. If the couple are keeping their homosexuality secret, children, neighbours, relatives and friends may not treat them as a couple and may not expect the step-parent to behave like a parent.

All parents are under pressure to conform to the myths of the perfect family, especially the one which says that the perfect family has no troubles and that a family consists of heterosexual male and female parents. But different myths are driving heterosexual and lesbian/gay step-families. Heterosexual step-parents have to contend with contradictory myths about the wickedness of stepmothers and the monstrosity of mothers who don't feel instant and unconditional love for their children. Lesbian and gay step-parents have to combat the belief that homosexuality and the nurturing of children are incompatible.

On the positive side, lesbians and gay men fall outside any expectations of being the perfect parent. There are no set roles to model themselves on, no restrictions on how to parent. They have the space to create the roles that suit their individual and joint styles. Unlike heterosexual couples who have generations of gender conditioning to contend with, lesbian and gay couples have the potential for equality in parenting. Children raised by two parents with equal power have a unique opportunity to learn about equality in relationships.

Children may react differently to a lesbian or gay step-parent than to a heterosexual step-parent. From her experience as a psychotherapist with children of lesbians in California, Saralie Pennington (1987) concluded that children don't take the relationship with their mother's partner as seriously as they would if it were with a male partner. But this was not the conclusion of Fiona Tasker's and Susan Golombok's study (1995), comparing adult children of divorced lesbian mothers with adult children of divorced heterosexual mothers. They found that the children of lesbians had closer relationships with their lesbian step-parents than the children of heterosexual mothers had with their stepfathers.

The people I interviewed recalled many experiences with lesbian stepmothers. Lawrence, fourteen, defines his immediate family as the people he lives with. When his biological mother's partner lived with them, he 'didn't think of her as a stepmother exactly, but as another mother. Calling her a stepmother implies it's in place of my mother, and it wasn't. [She's] not my family now that she's moved out. But I still think of her son . . . as family.'

'When my Mum got into a relationship with Susy, I was a teenager and knew what was what. I understood that it was a sexual relationship. Susy was a big kid, and she was great with kids. We did things together all the time. She was into the music I liked. She accepted me, which made me accept her. I loved her so much.' (Mandy, twenty-four)

'Until my mother had a long-term, stable relationship, I was the second parent in my family, being the oldest and a take-charge type of person. Together with my mother, I helped bring up my brother and sister. When I was seventeen, my mother started living with Susan, who was the same age as me. I felt relieved, because my mother was very unhappy unless she was in a proper relationship. . . . I didn't want to be at home with responsibility for my brother and sister. Susan took on the role of mother with my brother and sister and brought them up. They grew up with a sense of having two mothers. . . . Susan didn't bring me up, because she was the same age as me. I saw her as a member of my family, but more like a sister than a mother.' (Rikki, thirty-four)

From the age of six, Nicolas Rea lived with his lesbian mother and her partner, Nan: 'I accepted Nan completely as a member of the family. We had a very full and happy life together, partly because of Nan's personality.' Attempts to dismiss lesbian and gay relationships as 'pretended families' made him very cross, because the 'so-called "pretended family" that I had from the age of six was to me a very real family'.

Legal ties

The law is used to legitimate family bonds that are not based on biological ties. Legal bonds are created by marriage, child support and adoption laws, and are dissolved by divorce laws; they are reinforced by laws and rulings covering inheritance, insurance, state benefits, immigration, housing and many other aspects of life. Unfortunately, most family law does not accept the social bonds created by lesbians and gay men. Here are two examples that emerged from my interviews.

Kieron, fifteen, was conceived by self-insemination. His family includes two mothers but not the donor. Under the Child Support Act 1992, the donor is considered to be Kieron's social father, and is liable for financial support should Kieron's biological mother ever claim state benefits.

If Gretel's mothers were to apply for state benefits, they would not be classified as partners but as two single mothers sharing a home together. The agency of the state which manages state benefits defines a partner as a 'person you live with as if you are married to them' (see Benefits Agency, 1995) Although they do all the same things married couples do, they are not considered partners, since the law does not allow two women to marry. Legalizing marriage for lesbian and gay couples would legitimize certain lesbian and gay relationships at the expense of others: not everyone chooses to be in a couple.

One promising exception is the Children Act 1989 (described in Saffron, 1994), which makes it possible for non-biological parents to acquire parental responsibility by applying for a court order under Section 8 of the Act. Under this section, any adult with a significant interest in the child can be granted the right to share parental responsibility with the biological mother. There have been several cases where the parental status of non-biological lesbian mothers was recognized legally (Dyer, 1994; Skinner, 1995).

Conclusion

The children of lesbians and gay men whom I interviewed are redefining family to incorporate those relationships that are significant to them. This is happening regardless of the legal invisibility of non-biological family relationships. From their experience it is clear that no single definition could encompass all the different types of families. In any case, few families fit the conventional definition of a family as a group of people united by biological or legal bonds with heterosexual parents living together in the same household with their biological children. A more expansive definition of family might include any group of people (and pets) that meets the needs of its members for growth and personal development, love and intimacy, caring and support, identity and sense of belonging without restriction on the number, age, sexuality or gender of those people or whether they live in the same household. As Katrina, seventeen, says, 'When I say family I use it as a broad term. . . . A family includes anyone who's going to love and care for you unconditionally. That doesn't necessarily have to be your biological mother and father.'

References

Baptiste, D.A. (1987) 'The gay and lesbian step-parent family', in F.W. Bozett (ed.), *Gay and Lesbian Parents*. London: Praeger.

Benefits Agency (1995) *A1 Notes*, Income Support booklet, UK Department of Social Security, p. 4.

Benkov, L. (1994) *Reinventing the Family: The Emerging Story of Lesbian and Gay Parents*. New York: Crown Publishers.

Bozett, F.W. (1987) 'Gay fathers' and 'Children of gay fathers', in F.W. Bozett (ed.), *Gay and Lesbian Parents*. London: Praeger.

Bozett, F.W. (1989) 'Gay fathers: a review of the literature', in F.W. Bozett (ed.), *Homosexuality and the Family*. New York/London: Harrington Park Press.

Dyer, C. (1994) 'Court makes lesbian pair joint parents', *Guardian*, 30 June and 'More lesbian parents win', *Guardian*, 6 July.

Flaks, D., Ficher, I., Masterpasqua, F. and Joseph, G. (1995) 'Lesbians choosing motherhood: a comparative study of lesbian and heterosexual parents and their children', *Developmental Psychology*, 31 (1), 105–14.

Gerlach, P.K. (1995) 'What's "normal" in a step-family? Turning myths into realistic expectations', text on Compuserve Human Sexuality Forum, by Peter K. Gerlach, Co-founder of the Step-family Association of Illinois.

Martin, A. (1994) *The Guide to Lesbian and Gay Parenting*. London: Pandora.

Patterson, C.J. (1995) 'Families of the lesbian baby boom: parents' division of labor and children's adjustment', *Developmental Psychology*, 31 (1), 115–23.

Pennington, S.B. (1987) 'Children of lesbian mothers', in F.W. Bozett (ed.), *Gay and Lesbian Parents*. London: Praeger.

Robinson, M. and Smith, D. (1993) *Step by Step: Focus on Step-families*. London: Harvester Wheatsheaf.

Saffron, L. (1994) *Challenging Conceptions: Planning a Family by Self-insemination*. London: Cassell.

Skinner, K. (1995) 'Lesbian couple in joint custody first', *Pink Paper*, 13 October.

Tasker, F. and Golombok, S. (1995) 'Adults raised as children in lesbian families', *American Journal of Orthopsychiatry*, 65, 203–12.

Weston, K. (1991) *Families We Choose: Lesbian, Gay, Kinship*. New York: Columbia University Press.

Further Reading: Books and Articles on Lesbian and Gay Families

Turan Ali, *We Are Family: Testimonies of Lesbian and Gay Parents*, Cassell, London, 1996.

Harriet Alpert (ed.), *We Are Everywhere: Writings by and about Lesbian Parents*, The Crossing Press, Freedom, CA, 1988.

Katherine Arnup (ed.), *Lesbian Parenting – Living with Pride and Prejudice*, Gynergy Books, Canada, 1995.

Laura Benkov, *Reinventing the Family: The Emerging Story of Lesbian and Gay Parents*, Crown Publishers, New York, 1994.

Frederick W. Bozett (ed.), *Gay and Lesbian Parents*, Praeger, London, 1987.

Frederick W. Bozett (ed.), *Homosexuality and the Family*, Harrington Park Press, New York and London, 1989.

Frederick W. Bozett and Marvin Sussman, *Homosexuality and Family Relations*, Harrington Park Press, New York and London, 1990.

D. Merilee Clunis and G. Dorsey Green, *The Lesbian Parenting Book: A Guide to Creating Families and Raising Children*, Seal Press, Seattle, 1995.

Susan Golombok and Fiona Tasker: 'Do parents influence the sexual orientation of their children? Findings from a longitudinal study of lesbian families', *Developmental Psychology*, 1996, **32** (1), 1–9.

Susan Golombok and Fiona Tasker, 'Children in lesbian and gay families: theories and evidence', *Annual Review of Sex Research*, 1994, **4**, 73–100.

Lesbian Information Service, *Lesbians Who Are Mothers – Resource List*, LIS, PO Box 8, Todmorden, Lancashire OL14 5TZ, Tel. 01706–817–235. Send £2.

Geoff Manasse, (photographer) and Jean Swallow, *Making Love Visible – In Celebration of Gay and Lesbian Families*, The Crossing Press, Freedom, CA, 1995.

Laura Markowitz (editor-in-chief), *In the Family*, quarterly magazine about lesbian and gay families, PO Box 5387, Takoma Park, MD 20913. Subscription $22 per year.

April Martin, *The Guide to Lesbian and Gay Parenting*, Pandora, London, 1994.

Charlotte J. Patterson (ed.), 'Sexual orientation and human development', *Developmental Psychology*, 1995, **31** (1), special issue.

Charlotte J. Patterson, 'Children of lesbian and gay parents', *Child Development*, 1992, **63**, 1025–42.

Cheri Pies, *Considering Parenthood*, Spinsters Book Company, San Francisco, 2nd edition, 1988.

Sandra Pollack and Jeanne Vaughn (eds), *Politics of the Heart: A Lesbian Parenting Anthology*, Firebrand Books, Ithaca, NY, 1987.

Louise Rafkin (ed.), *Different Mothers: Sons and Daughters of Lesbians Talk about Their Lives*, Cleis Press, Pittsburgh, 1990.

Lisa Saffron, *Challenging Conceptions: Planning a Family by Self-insemination*, Cassell, London, 1994.

Fiona Tasker and Susan Golombok, *Growing up in a Lesbian Family*, Guilford Press, New York, 1997, in press.

Kath Weston, *Families We Choose: Lesbians, Gay, Kinship*, Columbia University Press, New York, 1991.

Resources and Organizations

The Albert Kennedy Trust,
23 New Mount Street, Manchester M4 4DE
Tel. 0161–953–5049
The Albert Kennedy Trust is a charity set up to help lesbian, gay and
bisexual teenagers. It arranges for homeless teenagers to live with
lesbian or gay carers, who help them with any problems they might
face as well as providing them with a home. It also supports teenagers
who live on their own. The goal is to improve attitudes and promote
greater understanding of lesbian and gay young people and to help
them become independent and proud of their sexuality. The Trust
currently works in London and Manchester, but hopes to expand to
other cities.

COLAGE (Children of Lesbians and Gays Everywhere),
2300 Market St #165, San Francisco, CA 94114
Tel. (001) 415–861–5437, fax (001) 415–255–8345,
e-mail KidsOfGays@aol.com
A lively support group that is run by children of lesbians and gay men
and was formed in the USA in 1990. COLAGE aims to 'foster the
growth of daughters and sons of lesbian, gay, bisexual and trans-
gendered parents of all racial, ethnic and class backgrounds by
providing education, support and community on local and
international levels, to advocate for our rights and those of our families
and to promote acceptance and awareness in society that love makes a
family'. COLAGE has over 1,000 members and a range of
programmes and resources to support its mission, including a
newsletter, conferences, workshops, pen-pal connection, booklets,
videos, T-shirts, Kids Club, plays and local groups. No British chapters
exist at the moment, but COLAGE produces a guide for starting and
running a group.

Gay and Lesbian Parents Coalition International,
PO Box 43206, Montclair NJ, 07043, USA

Lesbian Information Service,
PO Box 8, Todmorden, Lancashire OL14 5TZ
Tel. 01706–817–235
Produces *Lesbians Who Are Mothers – Resource List* for £2.

Lesbian and Gay Fostering and Adoptive Parents' Group,
c/o BM Friend, London WC1N 3XX
A support group for lesbians and gay men who are considering, or are
in the process of, adopting or fostering children.

Lesbian Custody Project, Rights of Women,
52 Featherstone St, London EC1Y 8RT
Tel. 0171–251–6577

London Lesbian Parenting Group
Contact: Ann on 0171–249–9951

Stonewall Parenting Group,
c/o Stonewall, 16 Clerkenwell Close, London EC14 0AA
Tel. 0171–336–8860
e-mail: mark@stonewall.org.uk

Books for Children and Teenagers Featuring Lesbian and Gay Parents and Role Models

Books for children under eight

Anna Day and the O-Ring, by Elaine Wickens. Alyson Wonderland: Boston, 1994.

Asha's Mums, by Rosamund Elwin and Michele Paulse, illustrated by Dawn Lee. Women's Press: Toronto, 1990.
  Asha, a black girl with two mothers, successfully deals with homophobia in her classroom. Good for beginner readers.

A Boy's Best Friend, by Joan Alden, photographs by Catherine Hopkins. Alyson: Boston, 1992.

The Daddy Machine, by Johnny Valentine, illustrated by Lynette Schmidt. Alyson: Boston, 1992.

Daddy's Roommate, by Michael Willhoite. Alyson: Boston, 1990.

The Entertainer, by Michael Willhoite. Alyson: Boston, 1992.

Families: A Coloring Book, by Michael Willhoite. Alyson: Boston, 1991.

The Generous Jefferson Bartleby Jones, by Forman Brown, illustrated by Leslie Trawin. Alyson: Boston, 1991.

Gloria Goes to Gay Pride, by Leslea Newman, illustrated by Russell Crocker. Alyson Wonderland: Boston, 1991.

Heather Has Two Mommies, by Leslea Newman, illustrated by Diana Souza, In Other Words Publishing: Northampton, MA, 1989.

> Three-year-old Heather lives in the lesbian version of the ideal nuclear family. Comments by my daughter Dena (aged ten): 'It is a good book. Everyone is very open and happy. It shows a happy family without many problems about being lesbian. Nice that it has a cat and a dog in it with such good names. Very clear about how Mama Jane got pregnant. I like the illustrations.'

Jenny Lives with Eric and Martin, by Susanne Bosche, photographs by Andreas Hansen. Gay Men's Press: London, 1983.

One Dad, Two Dads, Brown Dad, Blue Dads, by Johnny Valentine, illustrated by Melody Sarecky. Alyson Wonderland: Boston, 1994.

Saturday is Pattyday, by Leslea Newman and Annette Hegel. Women's Press: Toronto, 1993.

Two Moms, the Zark, and Me, by Johnny Valentine, illustrated by Angelo Lopez. Alyson Wonderland: Boston, 1993.

Books for children age seven to twelve

Beach Party with Alexis, by Sarita Johnson-Calvo. Alyson: Boston, 1993.

Belinda's Bouquet, by Leslea Newman, illustrated by Michael Willhoite. Alyson: Boston, 1991.

The Day They Put a Tax on Rainbows and Other Stories, by Johnny Valentine, illustrated by Lynette Schmidt. Alyson: Boston, 1992.

The Duke Who Outlawed Jelly Beans and Other Stories, by Johnny Valentine, illustrated by Lynette Schmidt. Alyson Wonderland: Boston, 1991.

> This is a series of fascinating fairy tales with superb illustrations. All the children have lesbian mothers or gay fathers, but this is put across so naturally that it doesn't detract from the story line.

Families: A Celebration of Diversity, Commitment, and Love, by Aylette Jenness. Houghton Mifflin: Boston, 1990.

First-person accounts from children and teenagers describing their families, with photos of each family. Includes child adopted by gay male couple and child of lesbian couple. No family structure is presented as the norm.

How Babies and Families Are Made (There Is More than One Way!), by Patricia Schaffer, illustrated by Suzanne Corbett. Tabor Sarah Books: Berkeley, CA, 1988.

An illustrated account of family-making which has clear explanations of heterosexual sex, donor insemination, pregnancy, birth and adoption and includes problems such as miscarriage, prematurity and Caesarean birth. It shows a variety of types of families and, while it does not explicitly mention lesbians or gay men, one illustration is of two women with a baby. The illustrations are rather off-putting.

How Would You Feel If Your Dad Was Gay?, by Ann Heron and Meredith Maran, illustrated by Kris Kovick. Alyson: Boston, 1991.

Comments by Dena Saffron, ten: 'The book was about a little girl called Jasmine and her brother Michael who are bullied when Jasmine tells her class they have gay fathers. I respect Michael for not wanting to tell everyone about his family, but I also respect Jasmine for not wanting to keep secrets about her family. The fathers handled it very well by telling the headteacher, and the head handled it rather well by getting an expert in to explain to the children about families. It was a very good book but too short. I would have liked to know more about their family and to get to know the characters better. I would have liked to see a chapter about Jasmine and Michael at Brownies and Cub Scouts, at school, going to Gay Pride. Good for children under the age of ten.'

A Kid's First Book about Sex, by Joani Blank, illustrated by Marcia Quakenbush. Yes Press, 1983.

Losing Uncle Tim, by Mary Kate Jordan, illustrated by Judith Friedman. Albert Whitman: Morton Grove, IL, 1989.

A story about a child's reaction to the illness and death of his uncle from AIDS.

The Moonlight Hide-and-Seek Club in the Pollution Solution, by
Rosamund Elwin and Michele Paules, illustrated by Cheryl Henhawke.
Women's Press: Toronto, 1992.

Tiger Flowers, by Patricia Quinlan, illustrated by Janet Wilson. Dial
Books for Young Readers: New York, 1994.
Two young children deal with the loss of their gay uncle to AIDS.

Uncle What-is-it Is Coming to Visit!!, by Michael Willhoite. Alyson:
Boston, 1993.

Books for teenagers

Am I Blue? Coming Out from the Silence, edited by Marion Dane
Bauer. HarperCollins: New York, 1994.
Anthology of short stories about teenagers who are gay or lesbian or
who have a friend or relative who is gay or lesbian.

The Arizona Kid, by Ron Koertge. Avon: New York, 1988.
A story about a sixteen-year-old boy with a gay uncle.

Breaking Up, by Norma Klein. Random/Pantheon: New York, 1980.
A story about a teenage girl whose parents are divorced and whose
mother begins a lesbian relationship. The father threatens a custody
battle.

The Case of the Missing Mother, The Pride Pack #2, by R.J. Hamilton.
AlyCat Books, Alyson : Los Angeles, 1995.
An action-packed detective story where fifteen-year-old Rebecca and
her teenage friends from the Lesbian and Gay Centre rescue
Rebecca's lesbian mother from a violent gang of anti-gay morality
crusaders. Good portrayal of a teenager's ambivalence to her
mother's outspoken campaigning on lesbian and gay rights.

Coping When a Parent Is Gay, by Deborah A. Miller. The Rosen
Publishing Group: New York, 1993.
Written for teenagers struggling to come to terms with having a
lesbian or gay parent, the book explores myths about
homosexuality, and examines the impact of the parent's sexuality on
family relationships, pointing out that many of the problems are
similar to those faced in heterosexual families. It stresses that

homosexuality is not inherited and that having a gay parent does not mean the child will be gay. The author tries to persuade readers that it should not matter what sexuality the parent is as long as the parent is a good parent. Contains a good reading list of books for teenagers about gay and lesbian teenage relationships. The title and context are unfortunate, as it is in the same series as coping with drug abuse, family violence and sexual abuse.

House Like a Lotus, by Madeleine L'Engle. Farrar, Straus & Giroux: New York, 1984.
A story about a teenage girl who develops a special relationship with a lesbian couple who live nearby.

'*Jack*', by A. M. Homes. Macmillan: New York, 1989.
A story about a fifteen-year-old boy who discovers that his dad is gay and at first finds it hard to accept.

Living in Secret, by Cristina Salat. Bantam: New York, 1993.
Amelia's mother helps her run away from her father, who has custody, and establish a new home and identity in California with her mother's girlfriend.

Now That I Know, by Norma Klein. Alfred A. Knopf: New York, 1987.
A story about a teenage girl who learns that her father is gay and that she must share him with his new lover.

Out of the Winter Gardens, by David Rees. Olive Branch Press: New York, 1984.
A story about the relationship between a sixteen-year-old boy and his gay father who have not seen each other for many years.

S. P. Likes A. D., by Catherine Brett. The Women's Press: New York, 1989.
An attraction between two teenage girls worries one of them until she finds a lesbian couple who give her a role model for love.

Stir-fry, by Emma Donoghue. HarperCollins: New York, 1994.
About a seventeen-year-old girl who lives with a lesbian couple in her first flat away from home.

Unlived Affections, by George Shannon. Harper: New York, 1989.
  A story about a boy who gets acquainted with the gay father he
  never knew after discovering letters his father wrote to his mother, in
  which the father explains how he came to terms with his sexuality at
  the cost of his marriage.

Who Framed Lorenzo Garcia?, The Pride Pack #1, by R.J. Hamilton.
Alycat Books, Alyson: Los Angeles, 1995.
  Ramon Garcia is a Mexican-American teenager living rough on the
  street because he's been kicked out by his parents for being gay. He
  is delighted when his gay foster father, a Puerto Rican policeman,
  offers to adopt him. But then the policeman is arrested and the
  adoption is in jeopardy. Ramon and his teenage friends from the
  Lesbian and Gay Centre are convinced that Lorenzo has been
  framed and set out to prove him innocent and make sure that
  Ramon has a gay father.

Sources for this compilation

Annotated reading list from *Coping When a Parent Is Gay* by Deborah
A. Miller.

Books for Children of Lesbian and Gay Parents, publication of Gay
and Lesbian Parents Coalition International (GLPCI), spring 1993.
Available from PO Box 50360, Washington, DC, 20091, USA.

Children's Books about the Gay and Lesbian Experience, Lambda
Rising Bookstores (see below for availability).

Just for Us newsletter, COLAGE: San Francisco. Fall 1995.

The Family Next Door magazine, **2** (2), Oakland, CA, 1994.

Ordering books

If not available from a UK bookshop, most gay and lesbian books in
print can be ordered from

Lambda Rising Bookstores,
1625 Connecticut Avenue NW,
Washington, DC, 20009-1013.

International orders by credit card.

**Tel. (001) 202–462–6969, fax (001) 202–462–7257,
e-mail lambdarising@his.com**

Include the following information in your order: title and author of book, your full name, your mailing address, your e-mail address, your credit card type, number and expiry date (MasterCard, VISA, American Express). For customers outside the USA, postage/shipping ranges from about 10 per cent to 25 per cent of the total cost of the order.

Index